Praise for Jeffery Smith's

WHERE THE ROOTS REACH FOR WATER

"A subtle, personal, and powerful book about the geography and experience of melancholia: its originality is striking and its language wonderful." —Kay Redfield Jamison, author of *Night Falls Fast* and *An Unquiet Mind*

"[An] idiosyncratic [work] of literature organized along the lines of 'The Anatomy of Melancholy,' written in the early 17th century by Robert Burton . . . Like Burton, [Smith] is productively unchoosy about where his instruction comes from, though beauty matters a lot to him; and he is good company while he meanders." —Diane Middlebrook, *San Francisco Chronicle*

"A beautiful, compelling, and haunting book. Jeffery Smith's capacious embrace of natural and cultural history makes this a unique memoir, one that illuminates the dark corners of melancholia in our human history." —Annie Dillard

"Not only a searing account of one man's battle against chronic depression, this deftly crafted memoir is also an intriguing cultural history of melancholy . . . [Smith's] conviction that depression has a spiritual dimension gives his graceful memoir wide-ranging appeal." —*Publishers Weekly* (STARRED REVIEW)

"Is it possible for a writer to convey the texture and contour of depression to readers who have never experienced it? It may be that depression is a foreign country, a place you can try to imagine but can never really know until you've been there. To someone who has more than once pitched her tent in that rough terrain, Smith's account is authentic." —Diane White, *The Boston Globe*

"[Smith's] narrative is vivid, it is insightful, and it has an unmistakable ring of authenticity . . . Through the use of an effective, elegant prose, maneuvered with such deftness as leads us to expect much from this writer in the future, he unveils for us a complexity that goes far beyond the realm of biological disease."
—F. González-Crussi, *Commonweal*

"What lingers in my mind from reading Jeffery Smith's book is his poetry of landscape and insights into life. What remains is respect for his courage to survive through writing."
—Chris Offutt, author of *The Same River Twice*

"*Where the Roots Reach for Water* differs, even radically, from all the rest of them [depression memoirs] . . . Smith found that he had to stop fighting, stop medicating and experience the condition fully: in other words, to let himself sink. This runs so counter to all of our cultural shoulds, our need to fight and resist and conquer, that it is almost shocking in its implications . . . A profound, life-changing search for the possible deeper meaning of the condition . . . Inspirational in a subversive, unconventional way."
—Margaret Gunning, *January Magazine*

"Provides a rich harvest of insights about the personal and cultural landscape of chronic depression and its potential to become a spiritual teacher to those in its embrace."
—Frederic and Mary Ann Brussat, *Spirituality & Health*

"Absorbing . . . Smith has not squandered his sorrows; he has described without sanctifying them or his struggle against them."
—Richard Stern, *Chicago Tribune*

GASPER TRINGALE

JEFFERY SMITH

WHERE THE ROOTS REACH FOR WATER

JEFFERY SMITH lives with his wife in the Appalachian foothills of Coshocton County, Ohio. He is at work on *Albums: Coming of Age in the 1970s—A Personal Documentary*.

WHERE THE ROOTS
REACH FOR WATER

JEFFERY SMITH

WHERE THE ROOTS REACH FOR WATER

A PERSONAL & NATURAL HISTORY OF MELANCHOLIA

NORTH POINT PRESS

A DIVISION OF FARRAR, STRAUS AND GIROUX

NEW YORK

North Point Press
A division of Farrar, Straus and Giroux
19 Union Square West, New York 10003

Copyright © 1999 by Jeffery Smith
All rights reserved
Distributed in Canada by Douglas & McIntyre Ltd.
Printed in the United States of America
Published in 1999 by North Point Press
First paperback edition, 2001

Library of Congress Cataloging-in-Publication Data
Smith, Jeffery, 1961–
    Where the roots reach for water : a personal & natural history
of melancholia / Jeffery Smith.
        p.   cm.
    ISBN 0-86547-592-x (pbk.)
    1. Melancholy.   2. Depression, Mental.   3. Melancholy—History.
    4. Adjustment (Psychology).   I. Smith, Jeffery, 1961–   .
    II. Title.
    BF575.M44S55   1999
    616.85'27—DC21   98-50420

Designed by Jonathan D. Lippincott

Grateful acknowledgment is made for permission to reprint the following:
    Excerpt from "Apologia Pro Vita Sua" from *Black Zodiac* by Charles Wright. Copyright © 1997 by Charles Wright. Reprinted by permission of Farrar, Straus and Giroux, Inc.
    Excerpt from *Divine Comedy* by Dante, the Carlyle-Wicksteed translation. Copyright © 1944 by Random House, Inc. Reprinted by permission of Random House, Inc.
    Excerpt from "Depression Before the Solstice" from *Country Music* by Charles Wright. Copyright © 1982. Reprinted by permission of Wesleyan University Press.
    Excerpt from "The Mound Builders," copyright © 1971 by Stanley Kunitz, from *Passing Through: The Later Poems New and Selected by Stanley Kunitz*. Reprinted by permission of W. W. Norton & Company, Inc.
    Lyric excerpt from *Old Cross Road is Waitin'*, by Bill Monroe, © (Renewed) Unichappel Music Inc. (BMI). All rights reserved. Used by permission of Warner Bros. Publications U.S. Inc., Miami, FL 33014.

Some passages in this book have previously appeared, often in significantly different form, in the following periodicals: *High Country News*, *Left Bank*, and *The Ohio Review*. Thanks to the editors of these publications for their permission to reprint those passages.

To protect their privacy, some of the places, friends, and colleagues—and all the clients—mentioned in this book appear under names not their own.

For Lisa

There is forgetfulness in me which makes me descend
Into a great ignorance,
And makes me to walk in mud, though what I remember remains.

Some of the things I have forgotten:
Who the Illuminator is, and what he illuminates;
Who will have pity on what needs have pity on it.

What I remember redeems me,
                              strips me and brings me to rest,
An end to what has begun,
A beginning to what is about to be ended.

—CHARLES WRIGHT, from "Apologia Pro Vita Sua"

BOOK I

SEEDTIME

I AM WALKING HOME, I kept telling myself. I live on East Third Street, in Missoula, Montana, and I am walking home, and by the time I get there this will be gone.

Or so I kept telling myself. I walked past the convenience store at the corner of Main, and in the light traffic of a Sunday noon, without waiting for the signal to change I crossed to the other side of Orange Street. Truth be told, I didn't believe a word of my little recitation. I wanted to; but by then I knew my enemy—as I called it then—too well to think I could just walk away from it. Earlier that day, to celebrate the coming of summer I'd been to a Sunday gathering with some friends on the west side of town. There in Barbara's yard we sat outside in the sun beneath a large maple tree. All about us the yard was festive with wildflowers: columbine, evening primrose, blue flax. Behind us her raised-bed garden was rich already with herbs and lettuce and greens. Over my shoulder with the breeze came the intimate smell of damp earth, a smell that could usually root any silliness right out of me.

But on that day I was unmoved. It was as if all these sights and smells had gone off into some murky distance where none of them would reach me. It was strange, but all too familiar, the way I could see these things but register none of the feeling they typically occasioned. I knew what this meant: it was back. For days before that brunch, there had been little hints and signs, but I'd brushed them off. And that was my inclination yet: it's just a passing mood, I told myself. I breathed in deep, to try to settle my mind. I wanted to believe if I would only focus more intently on the landscape, the gnawing clutter that was moving into my mind would disappear. So I leaned my head back and took in the horizon. Sapphire sky vaulted overhead. All around us the snow-peaked mountain ranges that frame Missoula—the Missions to the east, the Bitterroots to the west. But still I was unmoved.

I leaned forward again, returning to this circle of friends. Barbara and I were lovers, and we worked together as case managers at the community mental health center. Rita was also a mental health worker, and with her husband, Chris, I shared an Appalachian boyhood and a love of books. Tommy and Beth and their sons Evan and Campbell had previously lived in Asheville, North Carolina, and so had I. In Asheville I had scarcely known them, but in Missoula we had become close friends. The talk touched on baseball, music, wildlife, gardening, books, life in the southern mountains, religion—things I typically enjoyed talking about, or listening to smart and thoughtful people such as these talk about—and I could not speak; and I could not listen.

At one point Tommy turned in my direction. He seemed to be talking to me. Tommy was a kind, perceptive man, and it occurred to me that he must have noticed my trouble, and was trying to draw me into the conversation. I saw his lips moving, but his words were lost on me. I nodded my head, shrugged my shoulders, and turned away. Some other voice held my ear, and my mind was a tangle, a welter of confusion and overwhelm. I could only sit there dumbly. Beth picked her fiddle up off her lap and plucked and bowed it. I didn't care. I couldn't hear her either.

So my familiar was stalking me again. I felt its breath on my neck hairs. I could smell it. The spoor was everywhere around me. It was back, and it was nearly the longest day of the year; at our northern latitude the light would blanch the sky until past ten that evening.

The idea of abiding that light for ten more hours exhausted me. Maybe, I thought, maybe my familiar won't follow me home; maybe I can stand up and walk away from it. So I quietly took my leave and shanked my way homeward.

I continued walking south on Orange Street and crossed the bridge, keeping my eyes on the pavement at my feet. I am walking home, I reminded myself, and once safely across the bridge I ducked under the handrail and sidestepped down the bank to walk along the Clark Fork River. By then I was halfway home. There on the floodplain I tried to sole my feet to the earth's roundness, tried to keep my hold on this quarter of its curve. Instead I felt leaden and fit only to plummet. I leaned back against a cottonwood tree on the riverbank. Shining clear light fell in sheets down the sky. In the breeze the lime-colored cottonwood leaves were all atremble; they shimmered the light in every direction, like some radiant version of glory revealed. I noticed, but I did not see: in my eyes all that sparkle and sinew had gone to blunt and shear, a blare of light.

There was no mistaking it now. I knew well enough: it is arrived. I scuffed the toe of my boot into the dirt. I dropped my head to study on the ground, jammed my fists into my pockets, and once again started for home. No external event of weather or circumstance could account for its coming. All I knew was that it came that day rising, as it always did, not falling as if from elsewhere but rising as if it came from within, as inexorable as it was unbidden. I slogged on home and in my dark and damp basement room I crawled into bed.

Like light it rises: light so unyielding it will suck all shadow from the earth and wick all moisture clean out of you. However it happens it seems your vital fluid has seeped out some invisible rent in your flesh. Then you become a vassal: the curb-chain clasps about your ankle; the weight gathers you, the thin membrane holding you aloft gives way. You cinch your shawl about your shoulders, and let fall.

You let fall, or you prevail upon pills to arrest your falling. I knew what was ahead of me—for most of the previous eighteen months I'd been mired in one depressive episode or another—and I didn't want any part of it. Along the way I had acquired the diagnosis "Severe Depression, Recurrent." Eventually that was amended with the phrase "treatment-resistant," since in that time I had been tried on six different antidepressants. Some of them had not worked at all; others had worked fast and bright, yanking me up almost immediately, and then a week or a month later each one stopped working altogether, and no increased dosages would restore their magic. It was exactly as if I had gone immune to them.

But the November before that gathering at Barbara's, my psychiatrist had prescribed Zoloft, one of the "selective serotonin reuptake inhibitors." It began working within a week, I had a glorious reprieve, and my state of mind held for two months, then four and then five and then six. Before the Zoloft began working I was struggling to keep up with a full load of graduate-level courses at the University of Montana, and I was involved, for maybe ten hours a week, with the editing of two literary magazines. Then in December, after the Zoloft kicked in, I accepted a full-time job doing case management at the community mental health center. Behind the Zoloft I had no qualms about adding a job to my workload. I was busier than I'd ever been, but somehow I kept up with it all: got my schoolwork done on time and my magazine work done on deadline; at my new job, I put in my quota of billable hours and then some. I became hale and jocose, outgoing, endlessly social. I scarcely ever sat home of an evening and read. In April I started into the relationship with Barbara, my first attempt at intimacy in two years.

For those seven months the Zoloft delivered just what I wanted: I was, I thought, fixed. Normal. But now it too seemed to be failing. I must be some fool, I thought, ever to believe that my familiar was gone for good. Now it seemed he'd been waiting patiently all along, knowing his time would come around again. I wanted that son of a bitch out of my life, and for good. On Monday I called my psychiatrist, who instructed me to double my Zoloft dosage.

This was how it always happened: the dreams went first, then sleep itself. It might have been ten days later, or two weeks—I think we were into July, anyhow, and once again I was awake every morning at four, after finally falling asleep just a couple hours before. I was unable to return to sleep, but neither could I will myself out of bed. I couldn't summon the concentration to read, so I would lie abed for three more hours, staring at the ceiling until it was time to go to work. I was exhausted; but I could not get the sleep to remedy it. When it was time to ready myself for work the stairway to the kitchen and bathroom seemed too steep to climb, and then my arms felt too heavy to lift and wash myself in the shower. So I just stood in there under the water.

The higher dose of Zoloft had done no good. I ought to have known: all those pretty little sky-blue pills wouldn't ward this off once and for all. It was too good; I had been too happy. It seems remarkable, when the antidepressants reverse these seemingly inevitable and unrelenting episodes; it's common, in fact, for depressives to refer to their effects as a "miracle." Well, it seemed I'd had my miracle, and now it was gone. And now each day passed as if turned on some noisome crank, something slow and tortuous, to be endured but not engaged. Come what may and I did not care. Every moment of it was just one more thing I had to withstand before I could retire to my dim, damp basement apartment and crawl into bed.

Outside, the coordinates were all askew. On the Fourth of July I got three blocks away from the house and could not for the life of me figure how to get to the grocery store. Down the street I saw my neighbor approaching on the sidewalk, made like I didn't, and crossed the street. How could I explain that I was lost, in my own neighborhood? I had to check the street signs to discover where I was and direct myself to the store.

"Eat well and get some exercise," my friends would tell me. Sensible advice, but there were some problems: first, any such enterprise requires at least a modicum of hope. To pull on sweatpants and sneakers and get out the door you first have to believe that your circumstance might be improved; and I could not convince myself of that. The pills had failed, so why would anything else work? Then, second, there was finding the energy to exercise, when I could hardly get myself up and down the stairs.

Third, it was never a good idea to leave the house. In the world without I was a liability, blighted and incompetent. Depression is a state of utter *being*: I could do nothing. Life had to be reduced to its most basic level: for example, precooked food was essential. When I finally made it home from the store, I opened a can of soup and poured it into a saucepan. Pueblo, the gray tabby who had moved off the street and into my room the summer before, sat on her chair there in the kitchen and watched. I dropped a pat of butter into the cast-iron skillet. I cut some cheddar cheese for a sandwich. When the butter melted I put the sandwich in the skillet to grill. Then I couldn't remember whether or not I'd added any water to the soup. I stood there hovering over the stove and still I could not recall. The looks of the slop in the saucepan told me nothing. I dragged a spoon through it and a taste of it didn't help much either. Finally I walked over to the sink, filled a coffee mug with water, and poured it into the soup. And then acrid clouds of smoke billowed up from the skillet. The smoke alarm started bleating. Pueblo leapt off her chair and scrambled down the basement steps to our rooms. I climbed onto her chair and undid the battery in the smoke alarm. By then the soup was boiling over. So I cut off the burners, and sat down to my dinner: watery lentil soup and a blackened cheese sandwich.

Mid-July, and once again it looked as if John would run out of money before his August disability check came. So I went to his apartment to help balance his checkbook, and to try to persuade him to accept a budget plan. I had deep misgivings about the whole project.

This was the job I'd started the previous December, right after the Zoloft began working. In the mid-1980s, to finance my graduate work in Ann Arbor, I worked in a group home for the chronically mentally ill. There, I provided on-site "case management" to those afflicted with manic depression, clinical depression, and schizophrenia. I had no training or prior experience in the field, but I enjoyed the work, so when I moved from Ann Arbor to North Carolina in 1988, I got a similar job at the community mental health agency in Asheville. Eventually I left that agency to do case work with the mentally ill men and women who stayed in Asheville's largest homeless shelter.

Now in Missoula I was working once again for a community mental health agency. Such agencies aim to keep their often indigent chronic clients "in the community"—that is to say, out of state-funded psychiatric hospitals. This was the broad directive issued to community mental health agencies when "deinstitutionalization" of the mentally ill began in the mid-1960s, and large numbers of long-hospitalized men and women had to learn to negotiate the unstructured world of everyday independent living. We case managers were there to help our clients learn these practical skills and adapt to mainstream society: we tried to assure that they stayed up-to-date with their bills, we helped those so inclined find jobs, and so on. We were "mental health professionals," but our relationships with our clients were very informal. We dressed as casually as we wanted, and clients were never asked to pay directly for our services. And we rarely met with clients in our offices—instead we would visit their homes, or accompany them out into the community, to help them shop for clothes and groceries, or take them to the doctor's office, or we'd go with them to a restaurant for a piece of pie and a cup of coffee.

As I sat there with John I'd been doing this work for eight years. It was the only career I'd ever had, and mostly I felt competent at it. I had a good rapport with my clients, and the job suited me well: I liked the informality and the useful nature of our work. I enjoyed spending most of my working hours away from an office, moving about in the community. When we showed up in the morning, our calendars might be half filled with long-standing appointments—but we also had to be ready to respond to the inevitable large and small crises that our clients encountered. So each day was a mix of the planned and the spontaneous, which I liked. The autonomy of the job—our day-to-day work in the field was almost entirely unsupervised—offered plenty of freedom from administrative oversight.

Too, I enjoyed being an advocate for my clients, putting whatever diplomatic skills I possessed—and, when necessary, my cranky righteousness—to work for them.

But this was my first on-the-job episode, and it seemed all I could do just to get myself to the office in the morning. Whatever residency I might have in the land of "normals" seemed a product of medicine more than character. At the office every phone call, every home visit, every bit of documentation felt like drudgery. I was a month behind on my paperwork. At home I'd toss my mail, the bills along with the letters, into the corner, unopened. I hadn't balanced my own checkbook for a month. A pile of overdue library books sat on my kitchen table. I drove past the public library at least once a day, but it seemed more than I could manage to call to mind the necessary foresight, and lift the books off the table, and then carry them to my car, and then drop them off at the library. Any one of those steps was a challenge; accomplishing them consecutively was well-nigh impossible.

John and I got through our budgeting session all right, but I could barely look him in the eye. Overwhelmed myself by the practical details of everyday life, how could I in good faith counsel anybody else about them? How could I pretend to help "manage" anybody else's life?

Well, I'd been doing these things for years now, so I could function out of habit and knowledge, on a kind of automatic pilot, rather than from engagement and conviction. This felt hollow to me, a pretense, and it was exhausting to maintain. I'd begun to establish a pattern: first thing every morning I would attend to the essential tasks and the emergencies. Soon as I'd accomplished these—and some days that was by noon, some days by two or three—I would retreat to my basement room.

On July 23, I bought a novel, gift wrapped it, and mailed it together with a birthday card to my mother in West Virginia. Throughout my depressive episodes, she had filled my mailbox with reassuring cards and notes, and she called a couple times each week to check in. I knew some peace when I talked with her, and with the friends who phoned regularly to offer support and tell me jokes. Otherwise in my head some peer sat in judgment. To hear him better I would press my hand to my ear. Then I could make him out plain, right in there, playing and replaying a ceaseless inventory of my shortcomings.

I had given him—that voice, I mean—a name: Mr. Shoulder, I called him, because when I first made his acquaintance it seemed he was perched on my shoulder, watching and whispering into my ear. He wanted undivided attention: it was him with possession of my ear at Barbara's gathering, forcing me to block out the other voices so as to hear him better. But "Mr. Shoulder" was a misnomer—always, he moved quickly off my shoulder and wormed his way right there inside my head. Then I could hear nothing else. It was on account of Mr. Shoulder that I went all dumbfounded in company, could find nothing to say to anybody. By now he was with me loud and clear, shrill of voice, sharp of tongue, and painfully all-seeing. He would tell me who I was, and his judgment was lacerating, merciless. On the face of it he seemed to be no friend. But there was this: he knew my past, every moment of it and in particular detail, as no stranger could, and nothing was too trivial to escape his notice. He gathered all this intimate data into the great sweeping arguments he used to forecast my future: at every enterprise I would fail. There was no debating him. Over and over again he told me: You are haunted. You are hollow. You are beyond forgiveness and beyond hope. There is no point vowing to change.

At work and everywhere else, I heard his voice or some simulacrum. I was convinced that every group that gathered did so only to talk about me and laugh at me. They never looked at me—which I believed was their way of pretending they were laughing at something else. I believed that people had nothing better to do than pinpoint my shortcomings; that they had nothing more interesting than my faults to discuss. It was a curious sort of narcissism, one that reversed the indolent, languid pleasures of ordinary and occasional self-absorption. It very quickly turned any social occasion into torture.

Ordinarily, even in full health and in congenial circumstances I was lacking in the social graces; but now I could not force laughter, could not follow conversation, could not pretend any interest. There was no talking with anybody. I would walk past friends on the street and avert my head, hoping they wouldn't recognize me. There was no doubt in my mind: whoever should see me knew at a glance all my fester, all my rot, all my dull emptiness. I wanted nothing to do with your pity, or your comfort. What I wanted was to retreat from the world. But even in my basement rooms I could not get away from Mr. Shoulder. All I knew of myself was what his ongoing, undeniable inventory would reveal. This voice knew me, and I could not recognize myself. So I listened. This is what I believed: Mr. Shoulder saw true.

"Barbara," I was saying before we were out of Missoula County, "I am taking all my pills, talking with the doctor every couple of days, trying to take care of myself. I don't know what more I could be doing. Believe me, if I knew I would do it."

It was the last Thursday of July, nearly five weeks into this episode, and we were making the ten-hour drive from Missoula to the Oregon coast in hopes that a long weekend might somehow displace my depression and restore our relationship, which had started back in April with a headlong rush. Barbara was enthusiastic and witty, openhearted, and frank about her feelings. She was a native Montanan who had borne her two children young—she had an eighteen-year-old daughter and a nine-year-old son—and had worked for fifteen years loading trucks at Missoula's UPS depot. Her husband had been addicted to drugs and gambling, and one day five years before, Barbara had thrown him out of the house, and the same month enrolled herself in the university's social work program. She had kept her job at UPS to finance her education; when she graduated, the May before we met, she landed the case management job right out of school.

Barbara loved to read and around her cubicle at work she had pinned up poems by Mary Oliver and Wendell Berry. She cooked interesting meals, and could engage herself with you in a single-minded way that I had rarely seen. In the early days of our affair, I'd been

Zoloft-happy, full of an energy and hope I had never known, and I turned it on Barbara full beam. Her green eyes danced and sparkled, and her laugh fell forth free and sensual.

Or once upon a time it had; in the past month I had given her little to laugh about. It is one thing to work all day with people who are mentally ill; altogether different to try to have an intimate affair with one. For weeks Barbara had been telling me that she felt distant from me, that I didn't seem "present" to her, and that I didn't seem to enjoy her company on the increasingly rare occasions when we got together away from the office. I tried to explain that it had nothing to do with her, that it was just my depression—that I wasn't "present" even to myself, and that my life felt distant even to me.

When Barbara proposed this trip I couldn't help but agree; I thought a road trip might indeed help my situation. I had always welcomed the chance to get on the open highway for a long drive with a friend or a lover, with good music on the tape deck and ever-changing landscapes out the window. But by the time Barbara and I were an hour from town, I was feeling awkward and ungainly.

First she wanted me to tell her a story, as I'd done many times in the first weeks of our affair. But now I could not for my life recall any, so I started to invent one. Before I'd gone past the preliminaries it seemed to evaporate. I paused to try to recover it and couldn't even recall the names I'd given to the characters.

I quit talking and looked out the window at the mountains. I remember wishing I were out there, walking alone in the forest.

"That's okay, Jeff," Barbara said, "if you lost track of it." She looked over at me and laid her hand on my leg. "Want to just talk?"

I was more than willing to start in to some gossiping, to apply some judgment somewhere without. Cruel as it sounds, it was a welcome relief to me then, to inventory somebody else's shortcomings. It would silence Mr. Shoulder for a while. So I went at it with great gusto, and for a time the bitchery dissipated our tension with one another. But after a bit, embarrassed to be carrying on so, we stopped. Shortly the silence between us started to loom once again.

"Haven't we heard enough of this?" Barbara tilted her head toward the car's tape deck. At her invitation, on our way out of Missoula I had selected the first tape. Certain that my frayed nerves couldn't withstand anything livelier, I'd put on a Brahms string quartet.

She turned her face toward me and she grinned amiably. "If I'm going to drive I need to hear something more energetic and upbeat, and I'll bet it just might cheer you up too, to hear something a little more lively."

I gritted my teeth and clenched my jaw. She was wrong. I knew exactly what "upbeat" music would do—she'd tried it on me before. But I didn't mention it. Now, I'm well aware that somber Brahms is not everybody's idea of happy motoring on a bright summer morning; but right then "upbeat" seemed utterly false to me. All the same, I had promised Barbara that I would try to be a happier person, so I ejected the tape and offered to find her another.

She wanted to hear some world music, all percussive rhythm and no melody. It was upbeat, all right: within moments I felt bludgeoned by good cheer, and the bouncing, loping, and clanging rhythm rode on me as if it would possess my last nerve.

Over there on her side of the car Barbara smiled and swayed her shoulders and drummed her palms on the steering wheel. I was grateful that the song was in some foreign language; elsewise she'd have been singing along, too.

"Thanks," she said. "Now I'm feeling better."

I stretched my lips across my teeth into the shape of a grin. I fetched a book from my knapsack and opened it on my lap. After a time, I drew it nearer to my face, feigning absorbed interest. In reality I couldn't follow it from one paragraph to the next.

After ten or fifteen minutes Barbara stopped swaying and turned down the music. Out the corner of my eye I saw her look over at me. She was about to ask me for something. I moved the book closer to my face.

"Why don't you read to me?" she asked.

I acted as if I hadn't heard her. She kept looking over at me, though. Finally I lifted my head. "Huh?"

"What are you reading there?"

It was a novel. I showed her the cover.

"Why don't you read it to me?"

I couldn't imagine reading aloud, didn't think I could bear the sound of my own voice. Mostly, though, I didn't want my shell of privacy invaded. It was that simple.

"I don't know," I said. "I guess not. It's not the sort of thing I like to read out loud."

She grinned and shrugged her shoulders. Whatever. She turned the tape up again and resumed her dancing. I don't recall much about the rest of the trip. I remember getting to the Pacific coast; I remember walking along the beach. I didn't notice much of anything else. I didn't feel curious enough at Three Arches to look through Barbara's binoculars at the sea lions; nor did I care to climb into the lighthouse at Cape Meares.

Barbara thought I was avoiding her. It didn't help that in the last month we hadn't slept together even once. In our first weeks, I was experiencing one of Zoloft's side effects: in the words of the *Physicians' Desk Reference*, it can cause "ejaculatory failure, primarily ejaculatory delay." This did not decrease my desire in the least, and we had prolonged hours of lovemaking, and I'd been happy to please someone so much. Now, every time she drew near I'd plant a perfunctory kiss on her lips and pull away. But on our last morning at the shore we were calm and gentle, nearly loving, with one another: we didn't make love, but we were talking and laughing as we hadn't in weeks. After breakfast we walked to the beach.

She lifted her foot onto my thigh, hooked her hair behind her ear, and turned her grinning face to me.

"Still like my feet?"

Back in May I'd told her that I found her feet erotic. Now I stifled an impulse to quickly lift her foot off my leg. "Of course," I mumbled.

She moved nearer. Without thinking I moved away. Barbara yanked her foot back onto her lap and clutched it with her hands.

She looked out to sea and pursed her lips. "You don't want me, do you? Not at all anymore. Not ever. This is how some men get after a while. I know that."

"Barbara, please." I was frustrated, and ready to be back home in my dark room, alone and a little chilly. In my view the problem had little to do with gender and everything to do with depression. I swallowed and tried to soften my voice. "It's not you. I don't have it in me to want anything right now. Except to feel better, and I'm not sure anything could make that happen."

"And if it doesn't you'll just sit at home alone in your cave and keep people away," she said. I knew she was nearly out of patience with me, and now she spelled out her reasons. They were good ones: At first, she told me, I had seemed to her a respectful, gentle man. Now, in the past month, she went on to say, I'd been critical of her outgoing nature. Without good cause I had accused her of infidelity. I seemed to resent any attention she gave to anyone else, but was halfhearted when she attended to me exclusively. When our relationship started I had been warm to her children: I made tapes for Cleo, who was just starting to enjoy Bob Dylan, the Band, and the Byrds, who were some of my own favorite musicians. I told her son Andy bedtime stories, watched baseball on television with him, and went to watch his own ball games. Now I couldn't bear Andy's ceaseless energy, and I answered Cleo's questions with monosyllables.

I could deny none of it. I myself no longer knew the man she'd known in the spring. She was right—I had been an impostor. It wasn't willful, I wasn't trying to deceive her: I just didn't believe my depression would ever return. I thought the pills would go on working and go on working—although they never had before—and that the person they fashioned would henceforth be me. Now, as we sat there on the beach, I felt as if anything I might offer Barbara would be fraudulent and thoroughly contrived; there was nothing in me to give or offer.

But I wanted the ease we'd had a little while before to return. If the most I could offer was hope, then I would offer it. So I said to her, "You know, Barbara, this is all just temporary. It will go away."

"And who will you be then, when you come back?"

"Damned if I know," I mumbled at the sand. I raised my head and sought her eyes. "Honestly, Barbara. I do not know." I wanted to give her hope, but that's all the answer I had. This man she'd once known had shared a name with me; at one time his shape must have filled my features. But I had no hope that he'd return. I could be honest about that. I hadn't known him for very long myself.

After lunch we left the coast and drove inland for a couple of hours. In the motel room that night I fell asleep on a separate bed, with a remote control device in my hand. I had crawled over there knowing that my only other option was to lie awake staring at the ceiling while Barbara slept. So I flicked on the set, and at once I had an epiphany: Television, I said under my breath, television, come here and embrace me. You, my dear, you are tailor-made for depressives: I don't have to do a single thing, not even think, to enjoy you. I hadn't watched much television since I was a child, and I didn't have one in my apartment back in Missoula; now I thought, hey, why don't I take my next paycheck to the Salvation Army, and pick up a nice secondhand model?

Next morning Barbara was up early. She rolled me over to retrieve the remote control from beneath my stomach. With her thumb she punched at buttons until she made the chattering box over on the dresser swallow into its vortex the opening credits of *Green Acres*.

Then she turned to face me. I was sitting up in bed now, with my back against the wall. I patted the bed, wanting her to come and sit beside me. "Oh, *now* you want me there. That figures. Forget it. I can't go on like this, Jeff. You were watching television all night? I was waiting for you over there in that other bed. Remember me? I thought this would be a romantic time. I have children to support, you know, and I've spent good money and two vacation days on this trip. All of it gone to waste. No more. This is it. For you and me it is over. You plus your depression makes three and there's no room for anybody else in there."

She was right, of course. Long as I was in that condition, she was wasting her time. In the eight hours we spent driving back to Missoula, we spoke scarcely a dozen words to one another.

On a hot Sunday afternoon in early August, I stood outside the Green Hanger Laundromat in Missoula. Two weeks before, when I returned from Oregon, my psychiatrist had prescribed for me another happy pill, Elavil. Since I'd once briefly responded well to this particular antidepressant, he figured it was worth another try. He also increased my Zoloft dosage again. So far I'd noticed no improvements. On this day I had three weeks' worth of clothes in the dryers; depression doesn't get overworried about such niceties as clean clothes.

There in the parking lot I was standing at attention. I was being made to move; there was nothing for it but to move. My legs snapped out stiffly, one by one, in sidelong kicks. A client lived in an apartment above the laundromat; I hoped he wouldn't see my car in the parking lot and come down for a visit. My arms traced long stiff arcs through the sky; my elbows dropped woodenly into my ribs.

Then, apparently, it was time for some choreography. My arms and legs began to move together, then alternately. I must have resembled some short-circuited windshield wiper, or some marionette gone awry. But who—where—was the puppeteer? Who was in control of this body? People looked, looked away quickly, and then turned back slowly, but not unkindly, trying to puzzle out what this man was about. I couldn't enlighten them; nor could I make this exhibition stop.

Finally whatever was willing my dance just ceased. I went back inside, got my clothes out of the dryers, folded them into my laundry baskets, and drove home. I set the clothes down on the floor and rested on my couch. Now both mind *and* body seemed beyond my ken. And I despaired. I remember thinking: For months and months now I have fought this and fought it. And I have failed. I cannot lift myself out of it. All my old reliable escapes are gone—for weeks I've not gone to the library or into a bookstore. In the car I scarcely listen to the radio, and I haven't browsed my CD shelf in weeks. My walking boots are in the closet, absolutely clean and oiled; they haven't been on my feet since June. I haven't shown for my last several volunteer shifts at the animal shelter. I have lost Barbara. All savor is gone, all pleasure in experience and thought and imagination usurped. I am unable to see my way out of it, and I cannot reason it away. It is impervious to my plans and wishes, and unaffected by external events. All those pills—far as I knew the best thing humankind had ever devised for my malady—had failed. I could neither counter nor escape my depression. It has taken over my life, I thought: it is my life. And if this was to be my life, it seemed death would be preferable.

It wasn't the first time I'd had this idea. For several months of the previous twenty I would not cross any of Missoula's numerous bridges afoot: the water beneath beckoned that strongly. But now it was August and I felt alien—to other people, to creation, to my own body and mind—and I found no compelling reason why I should be restored. So maybe it was time to rethink my vow about the bridges.

The idea had common sense on its side. I had already considered my options: I could overdose on just about any of the several antidepressants that I had in the medicine cabinet (odd, isn't it, that most of the medicines prescribed for depression—the leading cause of suicide—can be used to achieve that very end?). Or I could lie in a tub of warm water and slice my wrists, watching the water go burgundy as my life ebbed into it.

Even if it was suicide, though, it was my own death, and I did not want to die by chemical poisoning. That left out the pills. And I had no bathtub. Some believe that men succeed at suicide more frequently than women because they typically choose more lethal means to carry it out: rather than the pills women most often use, men will use bullets or carbon monoxide. But my mechanical skills were nil. I had no idea how to hook up the necessary hose to my car's exhaust. I was fairly sure there was no instruction manual for this procedure, and whom could I ask for directions?

I could also forget about the gun. For starters, I didn't own one, but in Missoula that was no obstacle: I could walk into any pawnshop and choose from a veritable arsenal, and get a bargain too. That wasn't the problem. Problem was, somehow I had reached my thirties without having once fired a handgun, rifle, or shotgun. So I didn't know the first thing about buying bullets, or loading them. My own family back in the hill country of West Virginia and Ohio was full of men and women who routinely shot squirrels, groundhogs, raccoons, rabbits, and deer, but I had no stomach for it myself. On a gray spring afternoon when I was eight years old, for no particular reason I fired a BB gun into a cloud of birds at our backyard bird feeder. I watched from the back porch as one of the robins feeding there fell to the ground. I set out in a dead sprint, but by the time

I got there the robin was dead, and in the years since I'd never felt the urge to kill any creature.

Until now, that is, and this time I aimed to do it right. On account of my lack of manly skills I had to keep it simple. I also wanted my death to be useful, to accomplish some good. I considered taping high-powered explosives to my body and lowering myself down the face of the Glen Canyon Dam, so that my death would put an end to that mistake as well. But I had no clue where I might obtain the required explosives.

Hence my plan to drown myself; all other methods were out. Besides, I had always been drawn to free-flowing water, and a river seemed like a fitting place for me to die. Only thing was, I'd have to make sure my body would be left alone to rot in peace. The cells that compose me, I'd come to believe, would do better in some other combination. Freeing up those cells to join with some fitter, healthier structure seemed like the most lasting good I would accomplish in this life, the most useful death I could manage.

I wanted to put myself into the food chain, and I thought I knew just the place: I would follow Highway 200 along the Clark Fork River north and west out of Missoula. Twenty-five miles past Thompson Falls there was a remote section of river. There I would park my car, the pockets of my old corduroy overcoat lined with stones, and I would walk into the river and, like Virginia Woolf, I would surrender my weight to the current. Then my body would wash ashore, or so I hoped, and feed trees and wildflowers on the riverbank; and down from the nearby Cabinet Mountains, I hoped would come mountain lions and red-tailed hawks and coyotes, and perhaps the occasional wolf, to feed on my remains.

I liked this plan. That Sunday, I left my clean clothes on the floor in their baskets and carried my empty knapsack down to the Clark Fork. There on the bank, I selected enough large stones to fill the roomy pockets of my overcoat. I put them into the knapsack and walked back to my apartment, where I piled the stones on the closet floor with my coat tossed atop them.

That way I was always ready. I knew from my years of mental health work that an abstract inclination to suicide is one thing: worrisome, yet vague. If that inclination progresses to a particular plan—drowning oneself, say—and then progresses further—to where one chooses a site and obtains a pile of stones—then it's time for immediate intervention. So I knew enough to keep my plan to myself. If such fantasies of self-destruction have escaped you, gentle reader, they must be hard to imagine. The body I happened to inhabit had once been reliable enough in its yearnings for good food, music, books, talk, walks outdoors, the stars at night, the warm scent of skin. What had happened? It is hard to imagine—how can any living, thinking being crave its own demise?—when our bodies seem endlessly driven to cling to life, even amidst considerable pain and misery.

All this might sound like melodramatic attention-seeking, but it felt absolutely genuine. The arguments in favor of my demise had an alarming, nearly mathematical precision, and unequivocal conviction. To those who haven't experienced it, it is hard to explain clinical depression. This malady is explicable only on its own terms. Depression obliterates the tangible. It removes us to its own landscape, remote as the Yukon from the quotidian world where the great majority—including depressives in remission—live and love and work and plan. Those concepts—live, love, work, plan—scarcely apply here. Depression robs whatever present-day pleasure we're accustomed to deriving from them, and the future, to the depressed person, looks like nothing other than an endless loop of now. Nothing will help. Just drawing breath after odious, laborious, stale breath begins to seem pointless.

Some nebulous force has moved you into this chambered and unearthly landscape, its origins obscure, its meridians unmapped. It is a state unto itself. It is the Author—it was in my bones then, in a way no other Divinity had ever been. He had a logical narrative, a concrete plan, and a specific destination to take care of my problems in a way no wise Jesus Christ, no serene Vishnu, no omnipotent Allah, no smug smiling Buddha could: that was, the End.

Mostly I was inclined to oblige it, but not just yet. I still had a smidgen of faith in the pills. My psychiatrist was a kindly, compassionate man with a reputation for helping treatment-resistant depressives, and I trusted him. So on August 15, when he suggested adding another antidepressant, trazadone, to my regimen, I agreed.

I observed no immediate change in my mood, but I didn't really expect to. It's a great mystery to neuroscience, but it can take some time—weeks, even—for an antidepressant to have any effect. Three days after starting the trazadone I arose from bed—it had been another night with no real sleep—and could scarcely walk. I made ten or twelve tentative steps, from my bedroom to the foot of the stairs, before I crumpled. Next morning, my right side just rubbered out from beneath me as I walked away from the bed. On both those mornings normal navigating returned in an hour or so, and on both of them I just went on with my day.

But the following morning I awoke unable to hoist or roll my body off the bed. I was supposed to meet a friend for breakfast, and when I didn't show he came and carried me to his car. He slid me onto the back seat and we rode to the emergency room. The aides came out to the car, lifted me into a wheelchair, and rolled me inside. The doctors ruled out hypoglycemia, they ruled out aneurysm, they ruled out stroke and traumatic head injury. I lay on a gurney for six hours until the paralysis finally passed. In the late afternoon the doctors came and told me they had no idea what had caused it. They watched me perform some range-of-motion tests and walk about the ER, seemed satisfied that I was out of danger, and turned me out of the hospital.

By then I had a notion of my own. On my way home I stopped by the downtown pharmacy, and when I got to my apartment I called my psychiatrist.

"I've never heard of any such thing," he told me. "I don't see how the pills could be causing that. The *PDR* doesn't mention it."

That much I already knew. At the pharmacy I'd looked up all my antidepressants in the *Physicians' Desk Reference*, which is every doctor's standard guide to prescription medications. But I'd also talked to the pharmacist. She told me that if this particular side effect weren't common to any of those pills when taken singly, the *PDR* wouldn't be likely to mention it. It was the combination that made things hard to figure.

"It's your central nervous system they're monkeying with," Gwen said. "A very complicated operation to be throwing high dosages of three separate pills at, like so many darts. Who can say what might happen? I see it all the time: they give people five or six psychoactive pills, then act surprised when something like this happens." She shuddered. "I despise polypsychopharmacology," she said. "I even despise the word."

I didn't repeat any of this to my psychiatrist. I only told him that I was hesitant to add any more pills to my regimen just yet. Okay, he said. Sure. He paused for a few moments. "Well then," he said, "would you consider ECT?"

Electroshock therapy, in other words. I drew a breath and heaved a sigh. I held my silence.

Finally he quit waiting for an answer. "Or, if you think you can hold steady for a couple of months," he said, "there's a new antidepressant coming onto the market. The literature indicates it might work in a case like yours."

"I'll think about it," I said. Then I replaced the phone in its cradle and I lay back on the couch. Something wanted me stilled and slowed. This illness robbed my essence. My "me" was gone, and I wanted it back. For many months it had seemed imperative that I distance my depression—"it"—from "me." I was determined not to let "it" still "me"; I had too much to do.

But now it seemed there was no escaping "it." It wasn't going anywhere; and neither was I. We were either at a standoff, or we were inseparable: was "it" me, or was I "it"? Before that August day I'd never thought to ask myself such questions; I'd simply counted on the medicine to settle them. But I could ignore them no longer. Whatever this was, it had no interest in cooperating with my self-improvement schemes. It seemed time to square up with it.

Later on that evening I moved to the porch and stood there watching as the light lingered and softened the mountains around Missoula. The clouds pinked, the sky turned turquoise. I stepped off the porch, walked to the Clark Fork, and leaned against the same cottonwood trunk where I'd rested on my way home from Barbara's brunch two months before. Ravens wheeled from the trees into the

sky. Ash motes swirled from the wildfires that burned all that summer north and west of town. I turned my gaze to the ground. I
counted on my fingers: of the past twenty months, I'd been depressed
for nearly a full twelve.

At my feet a spiderweb hung between two fallen twigs and shimmered in some breeze even my moist forefinger could not detect. I
was thinking about the way that spider would gather unto herself
whatever suitable thing the unknowable breeze blew off the river. I
wanted this shadow to walk away from me; I wanted this voice in
my ear to cease. But I had no choice: not only had the antidepressants proven ineffective for me, I was now downright frightened of
them.

So over the next few days, I decided, I would taper off of them. I
knew how to do this: I could safely stop the trazadone now. With the
others, because my body was longer habituated to them, I would
titrate the doses: that is, I would reduce the dose by half night after
night, cutting the pills into smaller and smaller pieces until there was
nothing left on my fingertips but powders and grains. Without antidepressants to vanquish it, could a person have a life with depression?

I didn't know, but something within me shifted that day; some
husk split, and showed its seed. And I stood there that August
evening by the Clark Fork some new creature: I stood on the shore
of that river, as if it would show me what shape to take next; I stood
there and I wrote notes into the palm of my hand; I stood there by
that river waiting for my next skin; I stood by that west-flowing river
breathing deep and full, waiting to be changed.

BOOK II

STILL LIFE

It is some systematized exhibition of the whale in his broad genera, that I would now fain put before you. Yet it is no easy task. The classification of the constituent of a chaos . . .

To grope down into the bottom of the sea after them; to have one's hands among the unspeakable foundations, ribs, and very pelvis of the world; this is a fearful thing. What am I that I should essay to hook the nose of this leviathan! The awful tauntings of Job might well appal me. "Will he [the leviathan] make a covenant with thee? Behold the hope of him is vain!" But I have swum through libraries and sailed through oceans; I have had to do with whales with these visible hands; I am in earnest; and I will try.

—from "Cetology," chapter 32 of
Moby-Dick, by Herman Melville

CHAPTER ONE

I WAS BORN LUCKY, thirty-seven years ago, in the Ohio River valley town of New Martinsville, West Virginia. Just across the river in the Appalachian foothills of southeastern Ohio, both my mother's family and my father's family had settled generations before, and—this was my great good fortune—all those years later we were still planted there. My mother had been born and raised up Stillhouse Hollow—"Holler," in the local parlance—outside the village of Clarington, and among my first memories is a June evening in that hollow. It would have been 1965, since my mother was pregnant with my brother Jim. I was in the root cellar with my Grandma Thomas, helping her shelve the jam she'd canned earlier that afternoon, when Grandpa called down the stairs: "Let's get you outside and run the stink off your bones before it gets dark."

Even in the summer, in that hollow ringed by hills we lost the sun early, so we ran out into the yard and went straight for the pasture field. The coonhounds followed us, down the pathway that led from the porch stoop out past the garden and the barn, and then beyond to the cornfield, the potato patch, and the chicken coop. Finally we were in the pasture. There we angled right, toward Stillhouse Run, and I ambled along its bank from one sycamore to another, careening in broad semicircles out away from them into the broad green expanse of the pasture, the coonhounds baying and barking as they ran. We circled the pasture, then retraced our path back to the house. Spent, I lay down in the cool, dew-washed grass before the porch. The dogs circled me. Their tongues on my face tickled me into peals of laughter. I sat up to attend to them one by one, as Grandpa had taught me, calling them to me by name. They were lanky and long-eared, firm-bodied and clear-eyed. Their hindquarters swayed with their wagging tails, and I stroked their ears, soft as velvet with the veins tracing down like rivulets of rain.

My grandfather could incite them to howl—their treeing voice, he called it—but try as I might, I couldn't hit the right note to bring this on. I rose to my feet, high-stepped through the rhubarb patch, and leaned against the damp stone foundation of the brooder house. My grandfather stood in a circle of gleaming beagles, blueticks, and black and tans, his profile and theirs silhouetted against the orange and lavender skies of twilight as those plaintive harmonies echoed and shivered up the hollow. Fireflies twinkled as if they would foreshadow the stars.

Now we moved to the porch. I sat there between my mom and her father on a small rocking chair, listening to the mourning doves out in the woods. I loved their haunted low drone. I breathed in deep. I loved the rich damp smell of this place: the air mixing together the pure amphibian smell of the Run with the smell of all the plants along its banks and in the forest that grew up the hillsides. Grandma, done finally with her work, sat beside Grandpa reading. I stood and climbed onto Grandpa's lap, lifted his hat off his head, and put it on my own. The Thomases were mostly Welsh—"Black Irish," as they were locally known—and what little hair Grandpa had left was the same coal-black, almost blue, color as my mother's. They also shared the same olive-tinted skin, and vivid, nearly opaque brown eyes.

On that June evening Mom was twenty-one, and I was three: I was a "shotgun baby," born six months after she and my father graduated from high school. We lived a few miles down the Ohio, in the village of Hannibal, along the state highway in a house trailer that was perched on cinder blocks; in high winds the roof had a tendency to come loose. Mom was raised in this house, and we came up here a couple of times during the week, and always on Sunday.

As a child I traipsed without tiring in the woods up Stillhouse Hollow—named after the moonshining operation that Jed Fankhauser used to run two miles upstream from my grandparents' place—with that grandfather who seemed to know every tree in those woods, every animal track, and more stories than the Bible. I liked it here: up that hollow there wasn't any traffic to speak of, and things were quiet. I would pass hours wading in the Run, turning over rocks and trying to catch in my hands the salamanders and crawdads I'd find beneath them.

"Oh, am I hot," I heard my mother say, and I knew what that meant: she was going to walk down to the Run and stand in the water. She pushed herself up off her chair and held out her arm. I clasped her hand and we moved off the porch. As she stood in the water I lay out on that creek's bank, a dreaming and distracted child; and as I lay there the creek became a river, the river itself became sea, and the boy sprawled facefirst there on the bank became salamander, became mourning dove, became sycamore.

Then I came back to myself, another creature of this place. I rolled to my feet, walked a couple feet up the bank, and leaned back against that sycamore. My mother standing in the cool water. I looked up to the hills that sheltered the hollow as they shone in the dusk. I looked down the Run to where it met up with the broad, slow-moving Ohio. I lifted my head and breathed in long and deep, trying to plant the smell of that place into my lungs.

Surely I couldn't imagine then that I'd ever want to live out of reach of those hills, in some place where I couldn't hear the Ohio sing down out of the hills and wash the valleys clean even while we slept. And I did leave that place, but in the small of my back I can feel that sycamore. That smell is in my lungs still. I hope as I lay dying its vapor will rise off my cooling blood and those hills, those trees, those creatures fill the room.

I AM NATIVE to another landscape too: I was born under the sign of Saturn. After leaving off the pills, I had to learn some way to co-exist with depression; with such motivation, it seemed the concentration I needed for reading was restored to me. The idea of an inborn "temperament," which I came across before the end of August, was new to me, but I was soon enough convinced: my other birthplace had shaped me just as much as the forests and hollows of the Allegheny foothills.

These days the Saturnine landscape is difficult to describe. I say I belong there, but not simply because of my astrological chart, and not merely because I am on occasion clinically depressed. It's nothing so simple. For many centuries, saying that a person was "born under the sign of Saturn" was a shorthand way to indicate both individual character and a predisposition to clinical depression, or melancholia, as they more likely would have called it. To give you some sense of what that shorthand implied, I will have to condense centuries of history and speculation into a few paragraphs: To the early Romans, Saturn, their God of Agriculture, was a more or less unambiguous deity. Around the second century B.C., however, when later Romans incorporated Greek mythology into their own, they grafted onto Saturn's profile and biography most of the legends and traits associated with the Greek God of Agriculture, Kronos.

Kronos once was also the chief God in the Greek pantheon. According to Hesiod's *Theogony*, after hearing a prophecy that he would be usurped, Kronos lived in a state of perpetual jealousy and fear; he became so suspicious that he devoured all five of his children the moment they were born, to prevent any threat to his position. When his wife, Rhea, neared her sixth term, she decided to do all she could to save this infant. When she came due, she hid herself in a cave. There she gave birth to Zeus. The Earth Goddess Gaia, Rhea's co-conspirator, hid the infant away "in the depths of the holy earth," and swaddled a large stone in an infant's blankets. Gaia then carried this bundle to Kronos. Thoroughly deceived, he swallowed the stone at once.

When Zeus came to maturity, the story goes, Gaia beguiled Kronos into bringing up all that he had swallowed, first the stone (which was displayed in Delphi for centuries) and then the other five children. With his disgorged and resurrected brothers and sisters as allies, divinities all—Hestia, Demeter, Hera, Hades, and Poseidon—Zeus proceeded to wage war against his father, and eventually dethroned him. For his treachery Kronos was exiled from Olympus to the Underworld. There he retreated into contemplation and seclusion. Eventually he became associated with the chaos, misery, and darkness of that realm—and with the creative regenerating that began there. Hence his role as the Greek God of Agriculture. He also became known as the Father of Time—patient and enduring, if rather cold, distant, and weighted with worry.

Not long after the Romans passed these qualities to their god Saturn, they also mythologized the sky, endowing the planets and constellations with the qualities they ascribed to their divinities. To the planet they knew as the most distant, the planet whose orbit was slowest, the planet whose distance from sun and earth meant it must also be the coldest and the driest, they gave Saturn's name.

In the fifth century B.C.—two or three centuries before the Romans named the planets—Hippocrates wrote of a mysterious illness, long observed already and distinguished by its "aversion to food, despondency, sleeplessness, irritability, restlessness . . . fear or depression that is prolonged means 'melancholia'." This is the first known use of that term for the illness, though it is the Latin transliteration for a much older Greek word meaning, roughly, "bilious." Already by Hippocrates' time, physicians were inclined to attribute character and illness to the body's balance of "humors"; thus, after the Latin term for black bile, the humor believed responsible for the illness, Hippocrates named it "melancholia."

In the second century A.D. the Roman physician Galen of Pergamon formulated a comprehensive humoral theory, postulating that
there were four essential humors—blood, yellow bile, phlegm, and
black bile—which could combine into nine temperaments, with
many further combinations also possible. Galen held that each person possessed some share of each essential humor in a very delicate
balance; if that balance was lost, illness would result. Within that
balance, in most people one of the humors was thought rather more
prevalent than the others, establishing a sort of tonic note to their
character. A "sanguine" person, kept evenly warm by her extra portion of blood, was outgoing and generally satisfied with things. By
virtue of that surplus of yellow bile, the choleric was graceful, a per-
sonification of the prime of life, self-assured sometimes all the way to
being rather irascible. The calm, somewhat plump, phlegmatic.

There is a curious fact pertaining to black bile. Phlegm, blood,
yellow bile—the ancients had observed all these. But black bile—far
as we know, in all of creation there is no such fluid. Early on, it was
thought to be a toxic corruption of one of the other humors; by
Galen's time, its influence seemed so widespread and profound that
black bile was thought instead to be one of creation's original shap-
ing forces. Yet none had seen it. It was a wholly imaginary entity:
ideas about it were extrapolated from witnessing what were taken to
be its effects. "Black bile darkens the seat of reason," Galen wrote;
and so it was thought to be earthy and viscous, capable of slowing
body and mind alike. Then there was the odd, mixed character it
fashioned: loyal but misanthropic, largely solitary and withdrawn,
frequently irritable.

The atrabilious complexion and the melancholic illness seemed to
exist on a continuum, the symptoms of the illness looking very much
like acute versions of the temperament's distinguishing features. So
both were ascribed to black bile; in time the temperament was also
named after the humor, and both medical and common wisdom held
that while any other temperament might fall into the illness, being
born to the "melancholy" temperament would predispose—but not
necessarily condemn—one to "melancholia."

And it wasn't long before melancholics were linked with the

planet of Saturn. Belief in planetary influence over human behavior can be traced at least to the first century A.D., and it appears that already by then Saturn's influence was believed malign. Since both the melancholic illness and the temperament resembled the qualities traditionally ascribed to the mythological Saturn, it seemed to many that being born under the planet's influence would confer this disposition, and incline one to the illness. This astrological explanation was neatly fitted to humoral theory: Saturn was said to endow his children with an abundance of black bile, and hence with the ambivalences and antitheses of his character.

The seemingly endless modern appetite for books and stories about depression is nothing new—from Hippocrates on, melancholia and its very near kin, the atrabilious temperament, inspired volume after volume of medical theory, poetry, theology, and philosophy. That fall I came across two splendid, thorough histories of depression and the saturnine temperament, and much of what I say about them here is derived from them: Stanley Jackson's *Melancholia and Depression*, published in 1986, and *Saturn and Melancholy*, a rich synthesis of medicine, philosophy, iconography, and art history written by Raymond Klibansky, Erwin Panofsky, and Fritz Saxl and translated from the German in 1964; it is long since out of print. From these books I learned that there was an ongoing debate (still unresolved in some quarters) about whether or not melancholia was in fact an "illness," when it seemed very near to the everyday condition of those born to the temperament. The two were thought to be on a continuum, after all, and none were too precisely sure where on that continuum the temperament crossed over into a clinical condition. So, reading through those volumes today, it is sometimes hard to know whether a given writer is referring to the temperament or to the illness. To further confuse matters, in time the noun "melancholy" was used to refer both to the temperament and to the illness—Robert Burton's *Anatomy of Melancholy*, first published in 1621 and one of the classics of English prose, referred almost entirely to the illness—and then, by the Romantic Age, "melancholy" could also describe a mere mood.

(To clarify my own usages from the start: Like many, I dislike the term, but I use "depression" and "clinical depression," as well as "melancholia," to refer to the illness. When I use the term "melancholic," where it isn't clear from the context I will indicate whether I am referring to the temperament or to the illness. I'm also aware that "melancholia," as the term was used for twenty-five centuries, is generally synonymous with our "clinical depression"—but not always. Hard-and-fast clinical boundaries are new to mental illness, and are still somewhat less than hard-and-fast. At times, I saw in my reading, the old category of "melancholia" might include not only clinical depression but also the closely related syndromes we now call "bipolar disorder" and "obsessive-compulsive disorder." When drawn to cite these older works, I have weighed contextual evidence and tried to limit my citations to those plainly correspondent with "clinical depression.")

In any event, Saturn was implicated in both temperament and illness. While he might confer a handful of redemptive qualities (none of them much use in everyday human affairs), Saturn's influence was held to be mostly malevolent: he was believed to be the "Star of Nemesis" to humankind, and "Saturn's children" were widely considered the unhappiest of mortals. According to Klibansky, Saxl, and Panofsky, "Even when well the melancholic type is not normal."

Even after astrological determinism waned, because Saturn's attributes described in such an uncanny way the symptoms of the illness and the qualities of the temperament, in the popular imagination his synonymous association with them persisted for centuries. Some portion of this is with us still: we describe a somber taciturn disposition as "saturnine."

Meanwhile, humoral theory so satisfactorily explained human personality and illness that it held sway in the medical community for thousands of years, all over the world, until the beginnings of modern medicine in the seventeenth century. And now it's with us again. For most of this century, we've found the whole idea of "temperament" fairly offensive, since (taken to its literal ends) it seems to reek of biological determinism and racism and any number of other unfashionable *isms*. Our belief has mostly been for "nurture" as the chief molder of personality, self-esteem, intelligence, et cetera. But we're starting to wonder. Psychologist Thomas Bouchard's extensive and much-discussed Minnesota Twin Study—where identical twins separated at birth are reunited years later and find that they prefer the same brand of toothpaste and cigarettes, have the same hobbies, the same personality profile, the same phobias and mental illnesses, are married to women who look and act rather similar, and so on—surely argues for some inborn predisposition having formative power over and above the home environment. And many prominent researchers and physicians are now reconsidering humoral theory, or some version of it anyway. These "neo-humoralists," well aware that their position is at odds with our political sentiments, insist that they are talking about general categories and broad tendencies, not specific predetermined fates, and they point to recent biochemical research and longitudinal studies showing that a child who fits a certain behavioral and biochemical profile at age one, and even before, is likely to mature into that same certain kind of adult.

It isn't Saturn or black bile we call responsible today, but a certain profile of neurotransmitters and biochemistry—much of it resembling the profile we see in adult depressives—that leads modern-day humoralists to attribute to a child the "risk-averse" or "introverted" or "timid" or "inhibited" or "dysphoric" temperament. (Perhaps it's time to resurrect "atrabilious," or the full-bodied old "saturnine," if only to simplify the terminology.) Their labels tell us enough about the behavior they observe in such children; their research also reveals that many of these children suffer from hay fever, asthma, and allergies. As a child I sneezed and sniffled every year from March into November; still do. Sixty percent of the timid, at least in North America, are "blue-eyed and pale-complected"—that would describe me also. They are generally thin, which I was; and tall, which I was not. Longitudinal studies of twenty and thirty years' duration are showing us that these "tense, timid, and restrained" children—and about 15 percent of all children fit this temperament, while about 25 percent seem to be born sanguine—are more likely to suffer from clinical depression when they reach adulthood.

This high-tech and scientifically verified modern notion of temperament clearly fit me to the dysphoric type. You can say it that way, or this: at the moment of my birth no fewer than five planets were in Saturn's house. I don't rule out the influence of later events, nor do the modern humoralists—but if you buy these ideas, in large part the way I wound up on this melancholic landscape is simple: I was born here.

IT IS MAY 1967, almost two years since you saw this boy in a reverie on the banks of Stillhouse Run. Now he stands before a window in his family's new house in Schupbach Addition in Hannibal, leaning to rest his forehead against the coolness of the windowpane, resting his elbows on the sill and his head in his hands. This split-level ranch style is only a half mile from the trailer lot where he lived his first five and a half years, but to him it seems a world away. Every day this month, through all the packing and hauling and unpacking, it has rained: and every day, in his dreamy-boy melancholy way, he has come to this window, to watch the rain.

I was sure all that rain had something to do with our moving. Out that window I could see cranes and earthmoving vehicles on the floodplain: in recent months the Army Corps of Engineers, citing the necessity of flood control and the possibility of increased river traffic, had begun to construct a dam on the Ohio. Back at the trailer my mother and I had sat on the porch watching as these great earth-moving machines went to work: they felled the great sycamores that cast the shadows of their ancient crowns out over the river; they dis-mantled the fishing docks our neighbors kept on the river; they lev-eled the cornfields on the floodplain and scraped down the rich river bottom soil. Layer after layer of dust settled on our homes, our cars, our lawns. Then the pile drivers began, setting in place temporary coffer dams, and their constant noise—KA-chunk, KA-chunk, KA-chunk—kept us awake nights.

I can still hear it in my mind's ear: KA-chunk, and then a pause of perhaps twenty seconds, a pause just long enough so that you'd start to relax, and then KA-chunk. It went on around the clock, for a couple years even after our move, and this noise is there in my mind as a sort of soundtrack to this portion of my childhood. Things had changed, and that pile driver was a constant reminder. I rather liked a flood, myself. I remember staring out that rain-streaked window and wishing for the rain to fall and fall and fall until the river would rise up out of its banks again—as it had the spring before—vengeful and brown with great bat-winged waves roiling, and wash this dam and every idea of it all the way to New Orleans.

In truth the dam was just the latest development in the industrialization of Monroe County; it had been going on for nearly ten years even as I lay out on the banks of Stillhouse Run the summer of 1965. You couldn't see it or hear it from there, that was all. The upper Ohio was long since industrialized; but we were some thirty-five river miles to the south of Wheeling, a hundred and twenty downstream from Pittsburgh, and gifted with an agricultural plenty, so prior to the mid-1950s, our county altogether lacked modern industry. Then, riding the crest of the postwar boom, heavy metal plants had moved into the river bottom between Clarington and Hannibal, bringing with them a railroad spur; across the river in West Virginia two chemical plants were built in Wetzel County. My great-grandfather Elmer Thomas, who, like his father and grandfather and great-grandfather, spent his life building riverboats, was adamantly opposed to all this. "They'll be the death of this place," my mother remembers him saying. "I call that sort of thing not construction but destruction."

Elmer was in the majority. You might think those plants would appear to the locals more reliable and less risky than river work or mining or farming; still and all, the proposed industrial developments in Monroe County spurred a heated debate, and polls of county residents, conducted by the U.S. Department of Agriculture, showed "most of the respondents . . . very well satisfied with their present residence in spite of the lack of economic opportunity, lack of conveniences, and the apparent isolation of Monroe County."

The whole Monroe County riverfront in those years was a place where everybody knew everybody all the way back to Adam, it seemed, those small communities strung like pearls along the riverfront, each with a distinct identity of its own, and most of the residents descendant from the earliest white settlers. But the American industrial juggernaut thought it high time twentieth-century America found its way to Monroe County, never mind that the locals were already happy with what they had.

"Lack of economic opportunity . . . lack of conveniences . . . apparent isolation": by the 1950s, like phrases had been used for a century and more to describe life in the Appalachians. The Wisconsinan glacier that skimmed down from the Arctic millions of years ago and turned much of Ohio into a flatland had ceased some miles north of Monroe County; the terminal moraine makes of Ohio two separate states in all but name. Set in southeastern Ohio, hemmed in by hills and hollows, we had more in common—diet, music, landscape, dialect, politics, religion—with our across-the-river neighbors in West Virginia and Kentucky than with the other Ohioans who lived to our north in the industrial midwestern cities of Toledo and Columbus and Cleveland. When cultural geographers map out the "Northern extent of Southern influence" it generally follows right along that terminal moraine.

There are many Appalachias, and the same river that drew these industries to us had long meant we were never so isolated as some in those highlands that extend from northern Alabama to Maine. Monroe County was settled, like most counties in the Appalachians, by an admixture of Scots-Irish and German pioneers—as elsewhere, the Germans mostly in the valleys, the Scots-Irish more in the backcountry—who called this hilly (but never alpine) area the "Switzerland of Ohio." Early in the twentieth century much of its available farmland was under cultivation, and in the market towns the river joined us to—Wheeling and Pittsburgh to our north, Parkersburg and Louisville to the south—Monroe County's tobacco and cheeses and butter were much sought after.

According to family history, my mother's people, the Thomases, had settled in Clarington in 1798, having floated down the Allegheny from New York State to Pittsburgh then down the Ohio to Clarington. Mom's father, Jim, married Martha Dally—whose forebears had years before settled in the town of Sardis, thirteen miles south of Clarington, and established themselves on a seventy-acre plot of riverfront land as some of the finest farmers in the county. In addition to his farming, Martha's father was a Methodist circuit rider. Reverend Dally's ancestors had settled in the Shenandoah Valley of Virginia in the 1780s. Some of the Dallys stayed there, and others migrated up the Allegheny Mountains into western Pennsylvania. From there some Dally made his way down the Ohio to Sardis. His identity and the exact date remain unknown to us, but it seems to have been in the 1840s.

My father's people were relative newcomers to Monroe County, but they had a long history in the area, being among the first whites to arrive in Marietta, fifty miles downriver from Hannibal and according to some the first settlement along the Ohio after the opening of the Northwest Territory in 1789. By the 1820s, they had made their way from Marietta to Athens County, to our west a couple of counties, still in the Appalachian region of Ohio, where they were farmers, coal miners, and fiddlers. My grandfather Philip Smith married Joanna Cook, an orphan from Iowa who moved to Hocking County with her adoptive mother. My father was born in Nelsonville, in Athens County, and came with his parents to Monroe County in 1944, when his father took a job in a local mine. The Smiths lived then in Buckhill Bottom, a riverfront community between Hannibal and Clarington.

Mom was born in the family home in Clarington, with her Grandma Olive Thomas and the local midwife and herb doctor in attendance. During her childhood up Stillhouse Hollow, my grandparents raised poultry and hogs and cows, slaughtered and butchered and cured them at home, then sold the cuts at the Thomas Meat Market in downtown Clarington. Grandpa also worked construction, traveling off every week to work on crews in Chillicothe and later in Coshocton. Dad and Mom went to grade school together in Clarington, and were more or less involved from the seventh grade on.

In 1958, the Smiths were forced to leave Buckhill Bottom, to make room for the aluminum plants. They moved into the former Methodist parsonage in Hannibal, and when I was born in the last days of 1961, my parents brought me home to our trailer a quarter mile from the Smith house.

There I spent my childhood among extended family: both sets of grandparents were minutes away, and I regularly saw my aunts and uncles, my great-grandparents, great-uncles, and great-aunts. Before the dam came along, it was a wonderful place to grow up: an unincorporated village of five hundred people, the river before us and thickly forested hills behind. From our porch, from all of Hannibal, the new factories—we called them "chemical plants" and "aluminum plants"—were out of sight and earshot. We were about the only county in Ohio crossed by neither Interstate nor National Highway. After my mother's voice the first music I remember: rain on the trailer's tin roof. Before us what scenery: we were on the last bluff of the hills as they sloped down to the river's floodplain. Our trailer looked out over the floodplain, across the broad and ever-changing river, and onto the floodplain on the West Virginia side. Over there was New Martinsville, with its restaurants and music store and the Sears Catalog Store and Ruttenberg's Dry Goods. The bridge across the Ohio from Hannibal to New Martinsville was visible from our front yard, a half mile to the south, and had been completed just months before my birth; prior to that riverfront people in Monroe County caught ferries to get to West Virginia, where most of us did our shopping; all the way up the Ohio from Huntington to Wheeling, in terms of worldly conveniences the West Virginia side of the river was better-appointed than we were.

But that made no never mind to me. All day the boats chugged up and down the river, the barges piled with great glistening heaps of coal. On occasion the old paddle-wheel steamboats would come through, and we would hear their calliopes for miles before they showed. My father put a sandbox out in the front yard for me to play in, and my mother tells me that by the time I was nine months old I would sit there for hours, needing little in the way of company or outside stimulus. Already I was a watcher, and from that spot I could watch the traffic on State Route 7, I could watch the river, and I could see the trains going down the tracks on the West Virginia side. A couple of times a day the plant traffic came and went; but that was about all. Otherwise it was quiet.

In those years my father worked as a gas jockey and mechanic at Ed's Esso, the only filling station in town, just a couple hundred yards from our trailer on Ohio Route 7. Mom and I would walk over to visit him, and then walk another eighth of a mile to Schupbach's General Store, just across Main Street from Grandma Smith's, where Mom would buy our bread and milk and the occasional Popsicle, and in later years the Golden Books and Big Little Books that I would read and reread. There wasn't much in Hannibal, and most of it was on Main Street: the post office, voting booth, baseball field, the old cemetery. Here were its oldest and grandest homes, and the deep well of the Stalders', who would let you approach any time, drop the bucket, crank it up, and have yourself a cold drink of water.

The Methodist church, the center around which the town's social life revolved, was on Main Street too. Hannibal was founded in 1814 by Jacob Tisher, a German Methodist circuit rider. The church, built in 1871 after a fire destroyed the original erected by Tisher in 1817, with its brick building and white steeple looked like any other old country church. Baptists are the predominant mainline Protestant denomination further south in the Appalachians, but in West Virginia and southern Ohio, Methodists were and are in the majority. We were Methodist too: My Great-grandpa Dally had ridden the church's circuits all along the riverfront and back into the West Virginia hollows; several of my great-uncles and great-aunts served as ministers and choir directors and Sunday school teachers. My Grandma Smith was much involved with the Methodist women's group in Hannibal, and my Grandpa Smith donated his carpentry skills when the church added a wing in the late 1950s.

There was no other church in Hannibal. There wasn't much in

the way of cultural diversity. The opening of the plants did bring in some Catholic families, but there were no Jews, no African Americans, no Hispanics, and no Native Americans in the whole county. In my childhood, though, there were a lot of newcomers, people who'd recently moved in from Alabama and Houston and Pittsburgh and other similarly exotic places to take jobs as supervisors and administrators in the factories. All the riverfront towns grew "Additions" of ranch-style Lincoln Houses to house these newcomers.

For their part, my parents were all in favor of the coming of the plants. My mother, endlessly curious, welcomed the newcomers and their firsthand stories of life in other places—she had hardly traveled out of Monroe County. My father welcomed the factories for the opportunities they offered. He was ambitious, and willing to work hard: while still in high school he had piloted the Duffy ferry boat across the river, walking the three miles to the ferry after school, and back home again at midnight. He was also smart—graduated eighth in his class of ninety-four—and a gifted athlete, a fine enough quarterback to be named third team all-state. My mother, who was three months pregnant on graduation night, finished third in the class. Both were offered college scholarships, but the conventions of that time and place held sway: they were married right after they graduated, and moved into that trailer in Hannibal.

Dad was a mechanic, not a miner, a man who kept his car well tuned always. He could have made more money working in the mines, like his father and grandfather and great-grandfather before him, but he chose instead to work at Ed's. There he won honor after honor for his courtesy and his outstanding work as a mechanic and body-detail man. He wanted to pass this along to me, and on his days off we would wash the car together. It was a gorgeous car, a tan '64 Chevy Impala (I would weep when we traded it, in 1969, still looking as it had years before under that maple outside our trailer). He would take me fishing, sometimes to the river and more often to a small stream or run; often his father would join us too, and sometimes one or another of Dad's five brothers. I liked plenty to fish, but I wasn't as attentive as I ought to have been: I preferred staring at the current, slipping into that sort of trance where I couldn't tell if it was the water or the steam bank that was moving.

In 1965 the Mobay Chemical Corporation, on the West Virginia side, announced plans for expansion and Dad applied for a job there; my mother was pregnant and his pay at Ed's was not going to support us now. Dad got a job as a laborer. Within two years he was made a foreman, and that was when he bought that new suburban-style house in Schupbach Addition.

It was my mother's eyes that showed me the shifting hues of the world. In the sun they gathered off the horizon a topaz glow, and when she was angry they went the orange of the fire in the grate; when she laughed they danced and the irises sparkled with yellow; when she crouched alongside our dogs and gathered them into her embrace her eyes softened to the shade of damp earth. She was young and people admired her: all kinds of people. Old people, young people, men, women, children. She could talk with anybody. It was always a little amazing to me that her circle included me.

My mother was also a great reader, from a family of readers, and she read to me from the start. I was insatiable for books and stories, and finally she had to establish a three-story-a-day limit. To this day she maintains that I responded to that limit by teaching myself to read, so as to increase my daily intake. Whatever the case, she endowed me with a love of books. We had no public library in town, and were too poor to afford to buy many books even if there had been a bookstore within fifty miles, but the Southeastern Ohio Bookmobile stopped off in Hannibal for ninety minutes every other Monday, and Mom and I anticipated these visits like nothing else. She was an avid reader of mysteries and modern novels, and the bookmobile librarian took us both under her wing, so that every other Monday we each had a little pile of books personally picked for us by Peg, and the whole bookmobile to choose from on top of that. I became a book-drunk child, the proverbial flashlight hidden beside my bed to shine after I'd been put to bed.

In the trailer we picked up one television station, and in a very snowy way; but I never felt deprived. I loved music, and we always had that. We had a console stereo in the trailer, one of those faux-walnut jobs with a turntable and a radio, and it got a lot of use.

Mom had Johnny Mathis and Righteous Brothers albums, and Dad had Johnny Cash and Hank Williams and Buck Owens; both of them liked Patsy Cline, and of course I did too. I liked all of these, liked anything I could sing along with, would sing along with the M-I-C-K-E-Y farewell song on television (the only show I remember watching with any regularity while we lived in the trailer), sing along with all those silly Mitch Miller records, sing along with the state song of West Virginia every evening at six when WETZ Radio in New Martinsville went off the air. (This was several years before John Denver recorded "Country Roads, Take Me Home," which is now the official state song.) I sang with little awareness of pitch or tune, my mother tells me, but I sang with feeling; in fact, it seems I couldn't sing along with the Mouseketeers, or with the state song, without crying a little.

Mom and I would take walks too, and on our walks she taught me how to gently catch lizards and turtles and insects, and we would put them in terrariums when we returned home. I'd watch them for hours. I liked to watch the praying mantises: I loved their felid-shaped heads, and the way they would gather into their angled and supplicant limbs any cricket or fly I would release into their vicinity, and raise that bounty slowly into their mouths. Throughout my childhood she helped me nurse injured birds back to health, she let me bring in tadpoles to watch them become frogs and toads, she stopped when she saw a box turtle crossing the highway—to keep it from being run over, and also to pick up and bring home with us. For some reason I was taken with turtles, and Mom would let me feed it bugs and raw hamburger, and then after a few days we would walk it to the woods and let it go.

Four months after we moved to Schupbach Addition, I started school. Roughly half the kids in my class were "town kids" and the other half "hill kids," from back in the hills and hollows away from the now more modern riverfront. Some of their fathers labored now in the plants, having swapped the farms and the mines for a more steady income; most, though, lived the way white people there have for generations: mining or farming. The hill kids every morning endured hour-long bus rides to school, and many wore hand-medowns, and some of them brought into the classroom the rich scent of the barnyard.

From the start I preferred the company of the hill kids, and went to their farms when I could, to spend weekends and overnights. In those farmhouses I would awaken at the crack of dawn, go out with my classmates to gather the eggs and help with the milking, then come back inside to eat breakfast, the old smell of the houses all about us. As the sun began showing over the eastern hills we would eat the freshly gathered eggs with bacon or ham from the hogs everybody raised, the radio inevitably tuned to WWVA out of Wheeling, which broadcast its blend of bluegrass, old-time country, and newer traditional country all over the central Appalachians and up into the Northeast as far as New England and eastern Canada. WWVA's early morning broadcasts were aimed at their large farming audience: in those hours they favored the old-time string band music and bluegrass, and the farm families I stayed with would set into foot-tapping and occasionally whistling along with those tunes, then fall utterly silent when the farm market reports came over the airwaves. My own relatively citified feet could not resist that music, and I would wait out the market reports quietly impatient for it to resume. Sometimes on Saturday nights I would join my hill kid classmates at their barn dances. Everybody whose church didn't forbid dancing showed up—we passed our partners around and around, little boys like me and my classmates easily sharing a dance with our parents and grandparents while the local old-time string band played square dances and cakewalks.

Such remnants of our past were mostly getting away from us, though. As my Great-grandpa Thomas had foreseen, within a half generation life in Monroe County was thoroughly transformed. In those same years the Appalachian Regional Commission began to take an interest in us. Founded in 1964, this Great Society agency was charged with the task of raising our "deprived" lives to the American standard; it seems their idea of bettering life in the region was to train us to live elsewhere. The biggest part of the agency's budget went toward building roads that spidered us out of our hills toward Columbus and Charlotte and Detroit and Baltimore.

Having left the farm and rejected the mine, believing—accurately, as it turned out—that there was no future in either, my dad had no meaningful work to teach me. How do you mentor a son for factory work? Our world was changing, and it was left to my mother to show me how to fend in it. What she taught me to love is what I most love still. So this is what I did as a child, while the world outside changed its shape and tenor: I read; I plunged into creeks and overturned rocks on the banks, looking for lizards and crawdads; I walked in the woods, and I studied on the creatures of the ground. I leaned against trees. And I read some more.

According to Jerome Kagan, the foremost contemporary humoralist, an "inhibited" or "risk-averse" child is likely to display "a natural tendency to move away from the world to thought, imagery, and reflection." An "avoidant" personality, Kagan calls this. I was avoidant, yes, but I cannot say that I was "dysphoric": my "natural tendency to move away from the world" gave me reverie, and that, I liked. This is exactly why I so hated that pile driver: it ruined my reverie. But in time I got accustomed to it, or it ceased, and I went on with my old ways. I lived my childhood in a daydream—that is, when I didn't live in some story or some song that would cast the same spell, travel me into some other dimension, just as studying the other creatures or watching the river could.

To some my habits were worrisome. There was a small stream running through the schoolyard, where I would crouch at recess to look for salamanders and tadpoles. My third-grade teacher called Mom shortly after the start of the school year with a concerned observation: "Jeff spends all his time at recess staring down at the ground, playing with insects and reptiles." Mom defended my right to do as I pleased with my recess time, as long as I wasn't bothering anybody else. She explained my solitary inclinations by telling teachers and neighbors that I'd been "born with an old soul."

I turned eighteen two days before 1979 became 1980; I was by then pretty much a true child of the Me Decade, sensitive and raised up on the national media. In the Schupbach Addition house our television reception improved, with a roof antenna that would pull in the Wheeling station, and the Steubenville station, which gave us NBC and CBS—and on a good clear evening we could get the ABC affiliate from Pittsburgh. Then we got cable, and had five new stations, including an independent Pittsburgh station and PBS from both West Virginia and Ohio universities. So, I grew up watching *My Three Sons* and *The Brady Bunch* and *The Johnny Cash Show* and *Love, American Style* and *Mary Tyler Moore* and *Rhoda* and *Sanford and Son* and *The Waltons* and *Mary Hartman Mary Hartman*—but I lost track of television entirely in 1976, when my parents did some remodeling and moved the set to the new "family room" in our basement.

Many things changed in 1976. The dam was completed, and it occupied your entire field of vision anytime you looked toward the river. The community swimming pool opened, with tennis courts attached. But with me little really changed; the woods, my books, and my music: that was more or less my life. For my tenth birthday my mother had given me a table radio, and I listened to country and pop and any oddball stuff I could find on the AM dial. We could receive nothing on the FM dial until our cable signal was boosted in 1975, and then I could listen to WDVE out of Pittsburgh, all kinds of rock and roll in the last days of great free-form radio. Given my nature, it's perhaps predictable I formed a great liking for the introspective singer-songwriters then so popular: Carole King, James Taylor, Joni Mitchell, Paul Simon, Jackson Browne, Elton John, and eventually Bob Dylan. (For all my love of music, though, I could not learn to play the guitar and still could not carry a tune.)

Then—this was in May 1976, the same month my parents moved the TV to the basement—one Saturday morning, on my weekly walk across the Ohio River bridge and then to the public library in downtown New Martinsville, for some reason I pulled from the shelf a volume of F. Scott Fitzgerald's short stories. I can still see that book, with the bands of orange and gray around the cover. That day I hauled the book down to the riverbank and read it right through. I had always loved a story, but this, I see now, was the first time that a writer's voice—as opposed to a story—spoke straight into me. After that day I cared little about sports or television. And I moved my evenings into my bedroom, with my books and my music. Finding that voice was such a singular experience that straightaway I read all of Fitzgerald's work, and then moved on to Willa Cather, and then Hemingway; before I left high school I also found my way to Joan Didion and Tom Wolfe and Norman Mailer and John Cheever.

I was unmistakably my mother's child, and my brother was Dad's. By the time I was in high school our home was like two separate households. There would be Dad and Jim, at our round kitchen table with the black Naugahyde chairs, angled at one another throughout the meal, talking about pistons and compression cycles and torque wrenches and God knows what all.

Straight across the circle similar angles would incline my mother and myself, usually with the dogs on the floor beneath us waiting for the occasional scrap of meat. We might be talking about a book, or about yoga—on the PBS station out of Athens, Mom had discovered an instructional yoga program, which she watched every day, practicing right along with the teacher, and within a couple of years she was teaching yoga herself, at West Virginia Northern Community College in New Martinsville and in Wheeling too, trading out her pay for psychology classes. We might be talking about running, which Mom did faithfully, years before it was popular. We might be talking about a song we'd heard on the radio that morning before I went off to school. We might be talking about Jimmy Carter—Mom liked him, but I think I liked him more: I'd volunteered to pass out leaflets for his 1976 campaign, welcomed having a fan of rock and roll and literature in the White House, an idealist—and someone who disliked dams too.

Mom and I would still be talking, when Dad and Jim would slip away into the garage, one thin wall separating us, to start up the bikes. The noise drowns out our talking. It is an evening ritual. They ride when Dad comes home from work. They come back to the house minutes before Mom puts dinner on the table. They take off their biking gear in the basement, change into jeans, and come to the table, the rich oil-gas mix the bikes burn for fuel all over them. Then after dinner they retire to the garage again for further tinkering.

On Sundays we went to Dad's races. He rode motocross, which was, as the name implies, a cross-country through-the-forests style. I despised going to the races, always took a sack of books and hiked into the woods as far as I could go—the noise of those races was mind-warping, literally the same as fifteen or twenty chain saws going all at once—not to return until all was silent. My brother, even as a child, served in Dad's pit crew and had his own minibike before he was eight. I wasn't sure which end of a screwdriver to grasp. Dad had found his place, and he was driven to better it. He rode and rode and he worked on bikes, honed and honed his engines. And he won, and won, and won; attracted the attention of some corporate sponsors, got bigger and better gear, kept on winning. And at work he was the same way: no high school graduate ranked so high on the company ladder. He was up at four-thirty and off to work until five or six every night, always available for their calls, doing his utmost for the company.

I didn't understand his devotion to machines, or to the company, or to chemicals. By the time I finished high school I knew I was not made for filling any of my native area's available roles for a man— schoolteacher and coach or miner or plant worker, boss man or hourly. I wanted to be a journalist, so I went to Ohio University in Athens, the first in my immediate family to attend a four-year college. Before my first year was out I had gleefully abandoned anything so practical as journalism and changed my major to English. I had decided that I would gladly become a professor if it meant I could live out my life in towns like Athens. The place really agreed with me. I was still in Appalachian Ohio, so my native landscape was still all about me, and there were hundreds of people who cared for books and music as I did; it was not a difficult adjustment for me to make. After my first year of college, Mom and Dad were divorced. Even after twenty years of marriage, nobody seemed surprised— they'd been so different from one another, from the start, that the bigger surprise was they'd lasted for so long. By his choice my brother, sixteen when they split, remained with my dad. My mother was remarried two years after the divorce, and my father waited fours years before remarrying. I was happy for the both of them; and now that my boyhood home was broken, it seems I planted myself even more firmly in Athens. I stayed in town during the summers, delivering pizza, availing myself of the university library and the free outdoor concerts and theater. My world kept getting bigger all the time, bigger than I'd ever imagined it could be as a boy in Monroe County. There was so much music!—and at the university's music library I tried to teach myself how to listen to classical and jazz; there were so many books, and there were so many people from so many different places.

It seemed all this high-falutedness might alienate me from my homeplace—but in my senior year I learned that one of the finest modern American poets, James Wright, was born and raised thirty-five miles north of Hannibal, on the Ohio in Martins Ferry. One of Wright's best-known poems mentioned his hometown's Shreve High Football Stadium. I shivered when I saw those words; I had played a couple of junior high football games in that stadium, run the quarter mile on its track several times. It was odd, to see local place-names and landscapes in anything like a poem, let alone poems that won Pulitzer Prizes. I read another splendid contemporary poet, Stanley Plumly, himself a graduate of Ohio University, who was born and raised in Barnesville, Ohio, in the same county as Wright, and I saw described in his work another town where I'd played football and attended harvest festivals. It had never occurred to me that literature might occur virtually in my own backyard, hewn from the very sights and smells and sounds so familiar to me. I studied and studied Wright's work, was inspired to try my own hand at poems, and eventually wrote my senior honors thesis about Wright. (I would later learn that Wright was manic-depressive, and had one of his worst breakdowns in Missoula, while visiting with his dear friend and fellow poet Richard Hugo.)

Place mattered, and mattered deeply; I had known it in my bones, but this was the first time I'd ever been able to relate it to my reading. After I finished college, I was certain that I didn't want to become a professor of literature, but uncertain about what I did want to teach and research. Feeling that I didn't want to leave Athens County just yet, I deferred my graduate school plans, rented a farmhouse thirty miles from town, bartering work on the place for rent, and spent a year mostly in retreat. Eventually I realized that I wanted a broader approach to questions of landscape and culture and art, and I decided to pursue a doctorate in American Studies at the University of Michigan.

When I left Athens—single, of course, having had two fairly serious relationships in college but unready or unable, when it came down to it, to commit to anything lasting—I moved up the "hillbilly highway," U.S. 23 North, the route of out-migration for millions of Appalachian natives before me who'd fled the poverty of southern Ohio, eastern Kentucky, and West Virginia for the industrial jobs to be had in the Detroit area. It was the first time I'd been outside of Appalachia for more than a week. There in southeastern Michigan I moved through a fevered scape of concrete, steel, and glass, but at first that scarcely bothered me; I was on my way to becoming a college professor and I couldn't let something so mundane as an oppressive landscape get in my way.

Of course, I did not pursue the Ph.D. in Ann Arbor, but I did learn some valuable lessons: for starters, I learned that I was not, not, cut out for life as an academic. Looking for some way to maintain contact with the everyday world I had found my way into mental health work, which became my career. I learned about homesickness, and how much I loved the traditional country music I'd heard as a child, how linked it seemed to my native landscape. I traveled to Monroe County a couple of times a month, and to the Smokies or to the forests of southern West Virginia anytime there was a long weekend from school. As my first year in Ann Arbor came to a close, my Grandpa Thomas had a stroke, and I moved back home and spent the summer up Stillhouse Run helping my grandma care for him. I found it nearly impossible to go back to Ann Arbor when that summer ended, but I was duty-bound and obeyed that, rather than the small still voice within telling me to stay.

I am sorry that I did. After that school year ended, Grandpa died, and I decided to leave Ann Arbor. Instead I went looking in the Appalachians for jobs in the mental health field, learned that Asheville, North Carolina, had a slew of them—and a beautiful setting, close to all sorts of wilderness—and moved there. I settled my-self into an isolated cove some miles out of Asheville, living in a log cabin built in the 1830s that lacked central heat, telephone service, and indoor plumbing. The cabin, raised all those years before with logs as stout as horse flanks, was at the base of Cold Mountain; right behind it the Smokies started to stair-step north and west, into the sky toward Tennessee; off the front porch you could see Mount Pis-gah and the whole Balsam Range as it receded toward South Car-olina. The East Fork of the Pigeon River sparkled and danced in the front yard. I would wade knee-deep into the river's chill and watch the brook trout seek shadows.

I believed I'd made my own home in the world. I'd seclude myself there for days and days and walk ceaselessly in the forests. Alongside my cabin I put in a large organic garden. In the fall I cut and split my firewood. I petitioned and marched and carried signboards, and did a few other things too, trying to help save the native forests and fauna of that area; I did some writing and media work with the grassroots environmental groups whose causes I shared, and I did some editing and wrote features for *Katuah*, the bioregional journal of the southern Appalachians. I did volunteer work at a homeless shelter in Asheville, then took a full-time job there; I became in-volved with advocacy groups for the homeless, and took part in various local and national movements intended to better their lot.

Looking back from that August in Missoula, it was a little stun-ning that I'd ever had such an appetite for human company. There in the shelter we would have eighty guests on an average night, and twenty or thirty church volunteers; plenty of interaction was called for on every shift. But we also had a wonderful working schedule—in essence we worked three twelve-hour shifts per week, leaving plenty of time for my solitary walking, writing, and reading.

It was a good life. But after four years of it I'd come to feel stag-nant and restless; looming just ahead of me I could see "burnout," the bane of any mental health worker, coming my way. And I had no other trade. I didn't know what to do next. One evening in January 1992 I set up camp on the mountaintop behind my cabin. The moonless sky was that night beswirled, animate with stars; it was hard to believe it held any blackness. I studied on the stars overhead. I blurred my eyes to make the shapes of the constellations come plain, and under my breath named the animals I could see. She-bears and scorpions and swans, I reminded myself, hold up the heavens.

I took no note of Saturn's position in the sky that evening; I knew nothing about him then. As I sat by the fire I decided that I would move to Missoula and enroll in the University of Montana's environmental studies program. I had no idea what sort of meaningful and supporting work I'd pursue if I obtained that degree, but that wasn't really the point: the point was I wanted to give myself over to reading and writing entirely—which was also honoring a saturnine proclivity, for solitary study. Of course once in Missoula I wasn't faithful to that proclivity for long, threw myself back into mental health work first chance I got—but that might have been my saturnine indecisiveness, or missing my work, or the Zoloft, or my poverty, or some combination of these.

Whatever. What I need to say for now is, the impulse that came over me that night under a January sky in the Carolina mountains was mostly saturnine. I wanted to pull back from the world some too, another wish very saturnine. As I looked back from Missoula that August, knowing then what I did about Saturn's influences, it seemed his shadow was on my brow every place I'd been, at every age. At any rate, that night under the North Carolina sky I loosed myself into the stars, and from that night forth I hung a little unhinged; I am a little unhinged still.

I SPENT THAT SPRING AND SUMMER saying my goodbyes; I sold or gave away everything but some clothes and a few books, and bought a beat-up twenty-year-old Ford Econoline. In mid-August, with all my worldly goods packed into that van, I left the Appalachians for Montana.

It would be my first trip west of the Mississippi, and apart from my years in Ann Arbor the first time I'd been away from the Appalachians for long. But I didn't worry: I was going to make a whole new life, and if that required a whole new landscape, so be it. Four days after leaving the Carolina mountains I parked the van at a primitive campground in the Badlands of South Dakota. It was early morning, and I loaded my backpack and set out into the Sage Creek Basin Wilderness.

There seemed to be no other humans in that silent and sere grassland. I climbed a butte for a vista and the view stole my breath: I'd never seen any such expanse as this. Out there on the plain, bison and pronghorn antelope roamed and cavorted. Here and there I could see prairie dog towns.

I made my camp atop another butte, in the center of the prairie. When the sun set, in a riot of reds and golds and grays—I never saw sunsets like this at home, unless I were atop a mountain—it dropped finally out of sight as if it had rolled off the corner of a table. I faced my sleeping bag directly east so that the first light would awaken me. I lay down beneath a great dome of stars; I'd never guessed there was so much sky. The moon rose and choruses of coyotes quivered the still night air.

Next morning I arose exhilarated. The air was dry, and the breeze carried the brisk smell of sage; it fell lightly into my lungs, nothing like the oppressively humid August air back home. I decided to do some exploring. I thought I'd make a quick hike to the sandstone cliffs, pinnacles, and cathedral-like formations to the south of my butte. By eye I gauged it to be a half-hour walk, and I thought a quick little jaunt would get my blood going. It looked so straightforward I didn't even bother to check my topographical map. So I left my campsite empty-handed, with no maps, no water, and no food. I was experienced enough at finding my way around in the forested backcountry of the Appalachians; in this plain and open country I thought it would be no trick to just walk to those formations and turn back around.

I walked in a southeasterly direction for about thirty minutes, then another quarter hour, then another. And those formations looked no nearer. In this dry air, I guessed, maybe it was a little tricky to judge distances. I turned to look for the long butte where I'd spent the night and saw three dozen of them, all looking more or less alike. There were no landmarks, nothing but what seemed an eternal sameness. The ground was packed so hard it hadn't registered my footfalls, so I couldn't retrace my steps back to my campsite. Worse, there was a score of crisscrossing bison trails; there was no telling which one I'd followed to this spot.

The sun pelted me. The direct unsullied light of the West was nothing like the muted light of the humid Appalachians, and in the absence of that humidity I had misjudged not only the distance but also the heat; my shirt was drenched with sweat. I later learned that the temperature that morning was right around one hundred degrees. Mostly I was thirsty. I aimed myself for a high butte to my west, hoping the vantage point would allow me to see my campsite. I got there but could make out nothing familiar.

The sun was mounting in the sky. I decided to head back in the direction I thought I'd come, hoping that by dumb luck I would stumble back onto my campsite. I'd walked about a half mile when my stomach clenched and my heart began racing. Heat stroke. I knew I had to get some water. There was some in my pack, of course—but it was back at camp. I couldn't figure whether I should expend whatever energy I had left in trying to find my way back or just try to find some water hereabouts. Likely there was none about. This was the driest place I had ever seen, far drier than the Appalachians ever got, even in a drought. Despite the name, there was no "Sage Creek" here. That was a drainage, yes, but it looked as if it hadn't seen a flow of water in years.

It was getting hard to think clearly. I was panicked. I'd never been so lost in any wilderness. I spotted a cluster of cottonwoods further south and decided to set out for them; they were the only deciduous trees around, and perhaps they indicated the presence of water. I made my way there, stopping now and again to rest; and beneath those trees there was indeed some variety of pooled moisture. So I sprawled on my stomach to slurp from a mucus-colored seep. Within minutes I retched that viscous liquid back onto the sand. I rolled onto my back and lay there feeling feverish.

In the cinder-black eye of the vulture who was by that time trail-

ing me from above I thought I saw myself reflected: lying still, pros-
trate and fetal. Prey. A chill ran down my bones. I wobbled to my
feet. If I pointed myself north I might sooner or later find my way to
the road or to the van, where I had stored several gallon jars of water. So I walked as I could, a couple hundred yards at a time, stopping often to let my heart slow; and then I began to crawl. I could
hear the blood coursing through me trying to flush the heat out of
my system. Finally I went altogether dry and fatigued. I lay down. I
figured I would either arise in the late afternoon when it was cooler,
and try then to find my way to the van; or I would die there on the
open plain and feed this persistent vulture.

What happened next sounds so unlikely I hesitate to tell it: as I
lay down my head, I heard coming from beneath the earth the sound
of water on rock. An underground spring, and it sounded as if it
were close to the surface. I found a hole that dropped straight down
to it. I reached my arm down the hole up to my biceps and wriggled
my fingers in the water. I stood up, yanked off my shirt, extended my
arm back down the hole, let the water soak my shirt, and pulled it
up to my mouth. Over and again, I did this, squeezing water from
the shirt into my mouth, over my head, down my chest. I later
learned this underground spring was the only fresh water in that
wilderness. Call it happenstance that led me to this water, or call it
good fortune—it sure as hell wasn't wisdom, or intelligence, or common sense.

Could be, I thought as I reoriented myself and started toward the
campground where my van was parked, that I will learn in this region the art of paying attention. I sure to God needed to learn it, and
the place seemed to demand it. I wanted to be cleansed and sloughed
and spawned anew by the western light.

My first months in Missoula, I thought I had indeed been transformed. I was going at life in a headlong way. I taught writing to college freshmen and I enjoyed that work; I began writing in earnest
myself; with some fellow graduate students I helped to start a literary journal devoted to environmental writing and visual art. The
community seemed preoccupied with books and landscapes, just as I
was. It was a heady autumn and it passed buoyantly; I believed that
I had myself a new life, just that easy, just that quick.

At Christmas I caught a ride home with another Appalachian emigrant, and despite my new life and my pleasure at being back, something vague shadowed me that whole journey. There were inexplicable bouts of irritation. I'd grow weepy for no particular reason. Back in Missoula that January it continued, and worsened. I'd worked in mental health long enough to guess what the matter was. It was hard to figure. I saw no reason why depression should strike me then, when life seemed to be going so well; but I also knew it didn't always bear any relationship with the events of one's life. For a time I thought it was just the weather: like many valley towns, Missoula is prone to winter inversions. From mid-January into March we scarcely saw the sun. We lived instead under a low-lying ceiling of clouds and we breathed the noxious sulfurous gases they trapped and held in the valley: emissions from auto exhaust and from the paper mills just outside of town. Half the people I saw on the street looked on the verge of tears; the other half appeared likely to reveal and employ a concealed weapon. There was a lot of talk about "SAD"—the "Seasonal Affective Disorder" brought on by the short and dim winter light in northern latitudes—and I hoped that this was enough to account for my state of mind.

But when the inversion lifted, whatever was pressing in on me did not relent. I wanted to avoid seeing a physician, wanted my condition to be simple enough to treat with a dose of right living. So I began exercising vigorously, I took all the vitamins and supplements alleged to tweak brain chemistry, I ate scads of fish, bananas by the bunch, brewer's yeast by the handful. Still it kept right on. By then— late March—I was hardly sleeping; I roamed the Missoula streets night after night, reciting to myself every tract or proverb or poem I'd ever set to memory. I had not even an anthropological interest in the propositions put to me by the hustlers and streetwalkers. The sermonizing of Brother Red, Missoula's hellfire-and-brimstone street-corner evangelist, raised the small hairs on my neck. So I avoided him too. All I wanted was to keep up my litany, meaning to wall out the obsessive and repetitive ruminations that circled a rut into my mind, and to keep walking, trying to exhaust myself toward sleep.

Those efforts failed too. One morning early in April I ended my nightly peregrinations at the university infirmary. I trudged into the doctor's office weeping; within the hour she had diagnosed me with "Major Depression," and prescribed Elavil, generically known as amitriptyline. That night I slept long, peaceful, and sound. Within a couple days I felt altogether fresh and hopeful; in all, it was as if I had been reinhabited. My little spell seemed just a glitch, fixed by nothing more taxing or complicated than swallowing my pills every evening, and I went about resuming my life. Which lasted for two months. In June, when I cycled into another depressive episode, the Elavil did nothing against it.

You know already about the year that followed. When the Elavil stopped working, I found myself a psychiatrist. In the following months he tried me on five further antidepressants, singly and in various combinations, to little lasting effect. That episode dragged on through the summer and continued into the fall. Finally, in November he prescribed Zoloft, and I had my seven months' reprieve, the one that ended on that June morning as I sat with my friends alongside Barbara's garden.

WHO KNOWS WHERE THIS—or any—landscape begins?

To biological psychiatry, the landscape of human clinical depression is mostly contained within the three pounds of sponge-like gray matter that we call the brain. The brain has its own geology—its different strata came into being as we evolved—and the portion of the brain where melancholia strikes is very near to its molten core: the limbic system—the "reptile brain" common to all vertebrates—which includes the amygdala, the hypothalamus, and the hippocampus. This ancient region of the brain is responsible for many of our primal emotions, especially rage and fright, and it regulates many essential functions: thirst, hunger, sexual drive, body temperature, heart rate.

Its presence in such a primitive area of the brain leads some to speculate that in evolutionary history melancholia might even precede our incarnation as *Homo sapiens*. Its persistence suggests that it's passed from generation to generation; and back to Hippocrates, medical writers have observed that it runs in families. So in recent years genetic researchers have tried mightily to isolate the particular genes responsible for clinical depression. They have had absolutely no success. Their best guess is that the predisposition to melancholia involves a large number of different genes, each making a small, virtually undetectable contribution. Biological psychiatry, for all its apparent success treating its effects, has had little success finding its origins: "Those of us teasing out the neurobiology of depression," a prominent American researcher wrote in 1998, "somewhat resemble blind searchers feeling different parts of a large, mysterious creature and trying to figure out how their deductions fit together."

We do know a few things: the success of the selective serotonin reuptake inhibitors, as well as magnetic resonance imaging and blood serum levels, suggests that depression can sometimes be linked to decreased activity of one or another neurotransmitter—serotonin, norepinephrine, acetylcholine, dopamine, and gamma-aminobutyric acid have thus far been clearly implicated—or to the functioning of their particular receptors on the other side of the synapse. We also know that the overactivity of various hormones might cause depression. Blood tests reveal that many depressives have markedly decreased levels of certain fatty acids, carbohydrates, and amino acids, many of them known to affect neurochemistry.

This much we know, and somewhat more too; but none of it offers any trail back to its origins. So, trying to simulate the way human depression might begin, we have subjected chimpanzees and bonnet monkeys and gorillas and golden retrievers and beagles and house cats and rodents to a barrage of experiments: we have separated them from parents and siblings; we have administered to them repeated jolts of high-voltage electricity; we have intentionally depleted them of essential hormones. We've done all this intending to render in these animals a "learned helplessness," which is thought to resemble human clinical depression.

The etiology of this learned helplessness suggests that in defense-less young animals, repeated traumas will induce chronic activation of the hypothalmic-pituitary-adrenal (HPA) axis—the system that directs the body's response to stress. Thus activated, even when there is no apparent risk the body remains prepared to "fight or flee," so the animal can scarcely attend to activities that might distract from that imperative. It lives, in other words, as if it were always under threat. Appetites for food, sex, and play appear to be suppressed. The animal hardly sleeps, and mostly remains isolated from its peers. Some researchers believe that this chronic activation of the HPA axis has long-term ramifications, that very early on it establishes essential neurological pathways for melancholia, which may not emerge in its full-blown form for many years after the original traumas.

These findings may have some application to human depression: cerebrospinal fluid, urine, and blood levels of many depressives evince dramatically elevated counts of cortisol—the hormone released by the adrenal gland to prepare the body for the "fight or flee" response—which indicates they suffer from "chronic HPA axis hyperactivity." This might explain the curious, immobilized yet restless sensation reported by many depressives: the body frozen in a state of stress, ever-prepared for flight or fleeing—but it suggests only a partial explanation for how those who endure traumatic childhoods might become depressed in later life. And none can say with any certainty what "chronic HPA axis hyperactivity" might have to do with the neurotransmitter problems seen in many depressives. Nor does this clarify why some who are abused as children do not develop clinical depression in later life.

Nor does it tell us why so many who were not abused wind up with this "chronic HPA axis hyperactivity." Like any ancient landscape, this one is unspeakably complex: many researchers are now inclined to believe that just about every portion of our individual lives—our genetics, our culture, our family upbringing, our personal history past and present, and even, some now argue, exposure to certain "depressogenic" toxins; or excessive levels of electromagnetic radiation; or unknown fungal, viral, or bacterial agents—might play some role in the origin and eventual expression of melancholia. So perhaps we will never find a single model for the genesis, development, and unfolding of melancholia: perhaps it is as singular in its history and expression as its host.

All we can say with any certainty is that no matter its divergent origins and pathways, the eventual expression of melancholia results from biochemical changes in the brain. Those pathways turn out to be remarkably durable: a single melancholic episode can last a year or more. Fully 50 percent of those who experience one episode will relapse within eighteen months; 70 percent of those who have a second episode will have a third; and of those who suffer three episodes, 90 percent will thereafter experience repeated relapses; some of those will segue into a never-ceasing depression.

Those hard-worn pathways will deliver you onto one broad thoroughfare, the encompassing experience we call clinical depression. On the brain there is some new map, and you there in your chair are about to go for a ride. But you're unlikely to travel straight across the horizon; perhaps we should call this pathway a chasm, this journey a free fall. At any rate it has arrived and this is how it will start: In the amygdala, the neural systems available for attending to externalities slow nearly to a halt. Those responsible for attending to subjective information hit their peak level, and stay there.

This is how it feels: It remakes the world. It begins, and the familiar world without is seen as if through isinglass: recognizable in its outlines, but dimly. It loses substance: sight and sound and scent alike are gone unaccountably bland. Your vision has gone within; you are enwrapped by inner experience, none of it pleasurable. You are resident now in some parallel universe, a place inclined to resist the concrete nouns, verbs, and adjectives we use to describe other landscapes. For all its visible pain, insistent reality, and worldly effects, the true melancholic landscape exists, finally, only in the imagination—because that is where melancholia mostly expresses itself. So for centuries we have resorted to the language of analogy, trying to summon it by comparison, trying to fit to the imagined melancholic landscape the flora and fauna it might spawn, the creatures we imagine particularly adapted to it. My intent is not to be "anthropomorphic," projecting human qualities onto other creatures; to get some sense of this place we must contemplate those creatures imagination wants there. Of course, the facts and data we consider "objective" are useful too; in trying to represent this region every parcel helps.

Think of what follows, then, as a kind of field guide to the melancholic landscape.

HEAVEN: Even though Saturn lives in the farthest reaches of the firmament—or maybe because he does—there is none.

SOLAR SYSTEM: Of course, this melancholic landscape is his anyhow, so here Saturn is utterly dominant. There is absolutely no evidence to support the idea that a full moon will exacerbate this particular mental illness.

SKY: It would seem as if the darkness is where melancholia lives, or at least where it chases us; it has been endlessly likened to the dark. To the alchemists, melancholia was "the garment of darkness." "Avoids the light" is listed as symptomatic of melancholia in physician's manuals back to the ancients.

When the four temperaments were assigned a characteristic quarter of day, the third quarter (3 p.m. to 9 p.m.) was assigned to the melancholic type: think of the slanting vespertine light of late afternoon, the aching regret that comes to us sometimes at dusk as the light of another day declines. Today, we know that in melancholics, daytime peak hours do tend to occur in those late afternoon hours—several hours later than the peak hours of most. The diurnal rhythm of melancholia is all around more nocturnal—the body temperature tends to warm at night, rather than cool down for rest—and temperament and illness both are thought to tend to the "night owl" type.

WEATHER & SEASONS: "Depth psychologists" speak of melancholia as a "wet" time, as if it were full of tears and release, as if it were some sort of springtime.

Perhaps it seems so as it relents, but those in the midst of an episode are more likely to refer to its sterile aridity. Spring is to many depressives an utter mockery of their inner reality: T. S. Eliot wrote "April is the cruellest month" while recovering from a nervous breakdown. After a springtime walk in 1896, the melancholic Austrian composer Hugo Wolf wrote: "Only I, although like the humblest grass of the fields one of God's creatures, may not take part in this festival of resurrection, except as a spectator with grief and envy." And this, the season of rebirth elsewhere, is the time when Saturn/Kronos is most inclined to devour his children: among depressives suicide rates are highest in May and June.

Humoral theory and traditional Chinese medicine seem to acknowledge this: both liken the melancholic temperament as well as the illness to the season of autumn and its dry chill. Saturn is said to rule the constellations of late autumn and early winter, and seasonal studies of melancholic artists reveal that for many, autumn is their most focused and productive season.

There is an undeniable link between the cycle of seasons and melancholia: some depressives seem prone to summer episodes, and others to winter; over time, I've observed that my own episodes tend to begin within ten days of the solstices, usually within a week of June 21 and within a couple weeks of December 21, and relent as the equinoxes near, in September and in March.

Of the four winds, the melancholic temperament was associated invariably with Boreas, the cold winter wind from the north. Of the four stages of life, it was likened to the decline of old age.

EARTH: Of fire, water, sky, and earth, both humoral theory and traditional Chinese medicine linked the melancholic temperament to the earth. Black bile was invariably compared to the soil, and often to shit. Kronos and Saturn served their respective cultures as Gods of Agriculture.

Of earthly landscapes, the melancholic disposition was often associated with mountains: their vertical arrangements could represent the melancholic's fluctuant emotional state, and mountain regions offered caves and nooks and crannies aplenty, where this reclusive type might seek isolation.

SUBTERRANEAN: We'll get there sooner or later.

FLORA: In the ninth century A.D. the Arabic astrologer Alcabitis wrote of Saturn: "To him belong the oak, gallnuts, the bark of wood, pepper, olives, lentils, myrobalan, barley . . ."

I wish I knew what all this meant. Unfortunately, far as I've been able to determine Alcabitis did not further elaborate, or explain his choices; perhaps his contemporaries understood such associations implicitly. Some make good sense: gallnuts seem fitting, being a sort of parasitic or fungal growth—much as melancholia can seem—that forms into goiters ("nuts") on plant tissue; the "bark of wood" might allude to the rather stiff, crotchety nature, the perennially furrowed brow thought to be particularly saturnine; myrobalan, a dried fruit long used in the East for its astringent properties, might suggest Saturn's austere drying effect. Lentils, and other legumes—as well as potatoes and mushrooms and truffles, long as we're on the subject— were often associated with the saturnine temperament and illness, largely, it would seem, for their underground funk.

In ancient literature the association of oak trees with the melancholic complexion is almost canonical. The oak will retain its browned leaves even through the winter, releasing them only when new buds are imminent in the spring. Just so, melancholics were believed parsimonious, retentive, and inherently resistant to change. That old oak will cast a broad and jealous shadow, making it difficult for nearby seedlings to garner any light, and it was said that the gloomy shadow melancholics throw blunts the pleasures and peace of their intimates.

The seemingly congestive effects of black bile inclined physicians to try to purge it, so herbs with that effect were used to treat melancholia for centuries: white hellebore, colocynth, and wormwood among them. In sixteenth-century Europe, melancholics were advised to place naturally damp herbs—such as the streamside plants common watercress and water parsley—on the brow, like a plaster, to counteract their earthen dryness.

According to Cesare Ripa's 1593 *Iconologia*, the illness is best represented by "a barren tree," since "melancholy produces the same effect on men as winter does on vegetation." True enough. On the other hand, Caspar David Friedrich's 1801 drawing "Melancholy" shows an impassable wilderness of flowerless, tangled limbs and harsh thistles. This also looks right.

FAUNA:

Insects & Arachnids: The haunted, self-destructive tendencies of melancholia cause the Navajos to speak of it as "moth craziness." Nigerian melancholics are wont to complain of "ants creeping in the brain."

Amphibians & Reptiles: In their exceedingly metaphoric view of nature—they were, after all, trying to transmute all matter into spirit—the alchemists associated with melancholia the salamander, the cold-blooded creature they attributed with the ability to survive the flame.

Avian: The common raven, native to nearly every continent, was most commonly linked to the melancholic temperament and illness. It is an intelligent bird, and the melancholic type was thought by some to be gifted that way. But more prevalent was its darkness and its rapacious affinity with death and rot. Too, in folklore the raven is often the prophet of doom, the bearer of bad news, the crier of end times—and its prophecies seldom go unfulfilled. Likewise the melancholic has been thought an apocalyptic sort; and Aristotle thought the melancholic offered, like the raven of legend and song, "true prophecy."

A sixteenth-century German shepherd's calendar shows an owl perched alongside a clearly melancholic man; in traditional iconography the owl represented the night, misfortune, and loneliness.

Because of its observed loyalty and seemingly sad demeanor, Virgil Solis in the sixteenth century thought the swan was the bird most representative of the melancholic temperament.

•   •   •

Mammals: Solis held also that the "gloomy elk" bore kinship to melancholics.

Ramler's *Shorter Mythology*, published in 1820, named the bat "the animal always symbolic of melancholia." Like the bat, melancholics tend to be nocturnal creatures inclined to seek out enclosed, darkened places.

The Wheel of Life, a French illuminated manuscript of the fifteenth century, illustrates the melancholic temperament with a boar hog—contentious, earthbound, snuffling, inclined to root about or even wallow in the vilest muck, a pure force of nature, always difficult to domesticate.

The twelfth-century theologian William of Conches, and many others before and after, believed the ox and the ass—stubborn, intractable, firm of foot, slow-moving, but reliable and steady in their labors—to be the animals most constituted like a melancholic.

An Italian medical manual from the seventeenth century likened those of the melancholic temperament to the hedgehog, the ancient symbol of hesitation. *Saturn and Melancholy* offers a translation of that text: "The melancholic is subject to such strong inhibition that he can only achieve his labors, if at all, at the cost of great agony— in the same way as the female hedgehog delays giving birth to her young for fear of its prickles, thereby making the birth yet more painful."

Numerous illustrations show that familiar human figure in the chair, head in hands, with a cat curled up somewhere in her room. They seem to us ceaselessly curious, aloof, solitary, rather self-absorbed, contrary, easily spooked, mostly misanthropic but fiercely loyal to a select company, ambivalent, like the boar quick to go feral—is there any other nonhuman animal to whom we attribute such a stereotypically saturnine nature?

Jungian therapists and theorists, borrowing from aboriginals the world over and drawing on their own clinical observations, maintain that the particular animals who come to us in dreams are summoned "collective unconscious" (which some think embedded in our DNA), to teach lessons fitted to our present emotional circumstance. According to James Hillman, we can regard those animals as "carriers of soul, perhaps the totem carrier of our own free soul or death soul, there to help us see in the dark." That August I came across this sentence in the work of Jung's disciple, Marie Louise von Franz: "Frequently, depressed people dream of voracious lions or other devouring animals." Mountain lions—also known as panthers or pumas or catamounts—had been regularly in my dreams since I lived in North Carolina.

Into the daylight world of observable, quantifiable data. "In nature there is nothing melancholy," wrote the poet Samuel Taylor Coleridge in "The Nightingale"; but in fact, besides humans, many other animals are known to suffer indigenous melancholia. Even outside our laboratories and zoos, where incarceration alone can be blamed, field biologists and veterinarians have observed it in dolphins—who are believed on occasion to commit suicide—in all the primates, in felines small and large, in birds and dogs and horses, and in bears. We have attempted to treat it in nearly all these species. Curiously enough, our neurochemical treatments appear to work best for other animals whose social arrangements and inclinations most resemble ours. For example, they are quite effective with dogs—terrestrial animals who tend to organize themselves into somewhat hierarchical packs—while for solitary animals such as cats, antidepressants have proven themselves virtually worthless.

The Dictionary of Psychological Medicine, edited by D. Hack Tuke and published in 1892, was the standard diagnostic reference manual of its time. Under "melancholia," it mentions the standard set of symptoms observed by Hippocrates and consistently noted in melancholics since. Those who complained of these symptoms would be diagnosed with melancholia; but often there were other symptoms to be observed about the melancholic—certain bodily maladies, recurrent dreams, particular behavior patterns. For thousands of years, physicians attended closely to these, and also to the patient's gender, social status, occupation, and religious beliefs. Over the centuries these "peripheral" symptoms and personal factors were classified into what we might call "subdiagnoses" or "variants" of melancholia; coming at the end of a long tradition, Tuke's *Dictionary* provided physicians with a handy list of fifty-four of these, to help them pinpoint the specific manifestations of this ever-variable illness and plan treatment accordingly.

Should your own descent lead you to your local psychiatrist, he or she is likely to pull down from the bookshelf the most recent edition of the *Diagnostic and Statistical Manual of Mental Disorders* (*DSM*), the bible of modern psychiatry and our therapeutic culture, and ask you these nine questions:

- Do you feel sad, empty, irritable, tearful?
- Have you lost interest in your normal activities?
- Have you lost or gained any weight in the past month?
- Are you sleeping less or more than usual?
- Do you feel restless, or slowed down, physically speaking?
- Is your energy level low?
- Do you feel guilty or worthless?
- Are you having trouble concentrating or making decisions?
- Are you thinking about suicide?

If you answer "yes" to any five of these questions, the *DSM* will tell your physician, you qualify for a diagnosis of "Depressive Disorder." If you are among the 10 percent of men and women who experience these symptoms in alternation with periods when you have a markedly decreased need for sleep, accompanied by rapid speech; extravagant buying, traveling, or sexual behavior; and delusions of grandeur, you will be diagnosed with "Bipolar Disorder." Either of these diagnoses can be modified with just a few adjectives: "Mild," "Moderate," "Severe," "Chronic," "Recurrent," "With Psychotic Features," "With Catatonic Features," "With Postpartum Onset."

As for those old saturnine terms: in the *DSM* the rich suggestiveness of "melancholia" survives only as a seldom-used label for those who suffer a particular variety of chronic depression.

The diagnosis of "dysthymia" does perhaps give a nod to the old notion of the melancholy temperament: "a persistent subacute state of diminished pleasure and irritability." The "cyclothymic" experiences chronic mood swings, like the bipolar, but not to such extremes. Both seem rather ghosted and insubstantial alongside that old saturnine character.

A persistent canard holds that certain earthly landscapes tend to nurture human melancholia: the fourth-century Egyptian monk Cassian, one of the "Desert Fathers," believed that "dwellers in the desert" were especially prone to it. According to Burton, the ancient Greeks and Romans thought themselves particularly susceptible to it, since among their people "not less than one in a thousand" suffered it. In the Elizabethan era, the British Isles were thought especially hospitable to it; for years, those on the Continent considered the British a "splenetic" people (the spleen being the organ thought responsible for the presence of black bile): their wet, foggy climate, their apparent tendency to melancholia. In a best-selling book of the 1880s, *American Nervousness*, George M. Beard wrote that our climate helped produce the then-rampant melancholic variant "neurasthenia," which he defined as "fear of society, fear of fear, fear of everything."

In reality, though, there's little evidence that melancholia favors one climate over any other. For centuries it has been known—on every continent and in nearly every culture, presenting itself in a whole array of physical and psychological and spiritual manifestations, attributed to widely varying causes, and attended with a whole host of rituals, chemicals, and sacred roots.

Some call contemporary America the Prozac Nation. "Depression is the ailment of our time," Peter Kramer wrote in 1996, "germane even for those who don't have it." Over a lifetime, one in four American women and one in ten men will seek treatment for an episode of "severe depression." (Many will not seek treatment: experts claim that at least half our depressives go undiagnosed and untreated.)

You will have noted the gender discrepancy. Feminists argue that our culture's unequal gender roles cause this difference; to them, it strains credibility to attribute such an enormous difference simply to biology. Some clinicians suspect that many men who suffer depression avoid clinical diagnosis by "masking" and "self-medicating" depression with alcohol or street drugs; these will be diagnosed instead as "substance abusers," or never diagnosed at all. Cross-culturally, the 2:1 gender proportion is more-or-less constant, which leads others to seek biological explanations: Some suspect the more cyclical rhythms of womanhood. A few neurobiologists think testosterone itself offers some protection against it.

There are also some age discrepancies among the American depressed. An American born around 1910 would have about a 1 percent lifetime chance of developing depression; if born around 1925, that likelihood increases to 5 percent, and if born around 1940 it jumps to 15 percent. Among the generation born around 1960, nearly 20 percent have already been diagnosed. And for thousands of years, there was yet another good reason to associate Saturn with melancholia: Saturn's orbit around the sun takes about twenty-nine and a half years, and it was almost stereotypic that the illness would first occur, as mine did, within a couple years of one's thirtieth birthday. But among those born since 1960, first onset happens more often around age twenty.

It's plain: This ancient illness is experiencing some great new age in contemporary America. This slow, contemplative, dilatory illness thrives in our busy time. This even with our unprecedented economic well-being and technological innovation. This even with our great medical sophistication, this in an age when we consider ourselves better equipped than ever to combat it.

As for the bodily landscape. Here it is nowhere particular, as we've seen—and it is also everywhere. It can descend on women right after childbirth, and even after a successful birth, postpartum depressions can be among the most serious, sometimes leading young mothers to infanticide and suicide. Depressives smoke at a rate three or four times that of the general population; in recent years some physicians have been prescribing antidepressants to those who can't seem to give up their cigarettes. Rates of high blood pressure, diabetes, and coronary disease are in the case of each roughly eight times higher among depressives. Depressives are known to suffer far more ulcers than other adults.

Those who suffer asthma and allergies are thought also inclined to depression. Most victims of closed head injuries and spinal traumas suffer it, as do many cancer patients. It would be hard to dispute that the discomfort and worry attendant to any of these conditions might bring on depression, or the medications administered for their symptoms, but mere correlation cannot imply causation. Sometimes the "somatic" illness comes first, sometimes the melancholia.

Its nature is protean, and dendritic. We almost invariably think of depression as a "psychological" problem, a "mental illness." But because "somatic" illnesses are often coincident with depression, in cultures where the self is not, as cultural anthropologists are wont to say, "interiorized," those who suffer the classic symptoms named by Hippocrates will instead refer to the illness by naming those "physical" symptoms—the ones we're inclined to consider utterly separate from depression. So a person of Latino or Mediterranean extraction whom we might consider "depressed" will fail to mention his moods but complain instead about his "headaches"; one of Chinese descent is likely to mention having a backache; a native of the Middle East could refer to "heart troubles" or persistent "stomach pain." The social scientists have manufactured yet another verb to describe this phenomenon: these cultures, they say, "somatize" depression. In other words, it is in the brain—but it's in the body too. In such fashion does melancholia confound the Cartesian mind-body split.

Depictions of the melancholic type dating back to the early Middle Ages generally show a balding man—and in fact, depressives are now known to be more likely to evince "male pattern baldness"; those who don't go bald often will go gray at an earlier age. If the melancholic were a woman, the hair was long, entangled, wispy, a little greasy-looking. Said character typically was shown with a lean build, to indicate the ectomorphic body type thought common to the

temperament, and also to indicate, in that age's ever-allegorical manner, that a person of this temperament had an eternal hunger and
would never be satisfied. In these illustrations the countenance of the
melancholic is nearly always cloaked and shadowed—this is one
who likes to block out the sun, likes to hide—or it is given a "mud-
colored" complexion, the tawny blush painted in the features by all
that atrabile. Typically the melancholic is leaning on a cane or a
crutch, to indicate the uncertain gait, the awkwardness visited upon
his limbs by his stiff, indecisive, all too often preoccupied nature, as
well as the stumblebum damage those qualities would incur in an
age when people's travels were mostly afoot. (Among those of the
saturnine disposition the sixth-century Greek physician Alexander of
Tralles also claimed to observe with some frequency—and I am not
making this up—a "morbid stiffening of the middle finger.")

"This leaden and poisonous mood," William Styron called his depression; Emily Dickinson wrote of the "Hour of Lead" when "the
Nerves sit Ceremonious, like Tombs." When the ancients wanted to
fit their divinities and constellations to the metals, the planet's slow
revolution and Saturn's sometimes poisonous influence (I'm speaking
chiefly of the melancholic temperament and illness; it's also worth
noting that the medical term for lead poisoning is "saturnism")
caused him to be regarded as the ruler of lead. Interestingly enough,
some believed that Saturn made it his business to sow leaden seeds in
the earth.

But all this lead is not merely imaginary: these metaphors grow
straight from the body. The melancholic's limbs feel weighted, blood
and bone and muscle alike gone viscid with some invisible burden.
Sixteenth-century English physician Thomas Elyot's *Castel of Helthe*
refers to melancholia as a "hevyness that exhausteth both natural
heate and moysture of the bodye, and dothe dulleth the wytte, op-
presseth memorye, and darkeneth the spirites." Its weight likely accounts for the backaches that plague so many depressives; that
weight presses us into the floor, and podiatrists have observed that a
long siege of melancholia can flatten the arches of the feet. And there

is also the almost stereotypical portrait of the melancholic with head in hands. We see it in van Gogh, and in medical manuals dating back at least to the fourth century. In picture after picture, here is the melancholic: seated at table or on the bed, disarray all about and work tools abandoned, of course—but that posture is all you really need to tell you who he is: shoulders bent forward in a slouch with the head cocooned between them, palms flush to the forehead.

It appears to weight the flesh. Eyeing myself in the mirror that August, I saw what earlier times called the "face of Saturn"; the "mask of depression," it's called in more modern books. I'm sure you've seen it: The face stiff and inexpressive, eyes a cipher, frown lines etched into the forehead. But the mouth is where your eyes linger, or where they fall, then bounce away. Lips curving down to collarbones like a half-moon. The whole mouth drooping its way right down the chin, as if it would in time fall to the floor. Drooping exactly as if it were weighted, in fact. What happens in depression— and this too is a mystery—is that the triangularis muscles at the sides of the mouth begin to lose their elasticity. Just as they would if they were weighted.

Make no mistake: *Gravitas* is its very name. And who can say why? Many claim that the slouching "body language" of a melancholic broadcasts a clear and unconscious signal: Stay Away. So perhaps the reshaped visage and carriage intend to maintain the melancholic's solitude. Or perhaps this *gravitas* is simply a gradual sloping toward the earth, a drifting into the ground. And perhaps this is just the point: in tandem with the mind the body will haul the depressive nearer to the Underworld. For if there is no heaven in the melancholic landscape, there is certainly a hell, and not only one— we have the belly of the whale; we have all manner of chasms and maws and tunnels and caves of despair; we have the pit of Acheron, the Hades of myth and poetry. Over and again, through all these years, melancholic writers locate themselves in a "sink," a "pit," a "slough." St. Thomas Aquinas referred to his melancholia as "the abyss that covers my face." So many hells are there in the melancholic canon that one begins to suspect the hand of Beelzebub himself in its cause and spread.

So many hells are there that the netherworld would seem melancholia's very homeplace. Kronos/Saturn was, after all, long resident there. And it is worth recollecting where Dante's *Divine Comedy* begins. According to his first biographer, Boccaccio, Dante suffered from both the melancholic temperament and the illness. Here he is, setting off unwittingly into the Inferno:

In the middle of the journey of our life I came to myself in a dark wood where the straight way was lost.

Ah! how hard a thing it is to tell what a wild, and rough, and stubborn wood this was, which in my thought renews the fear.

So bitter is it, that scarcely more is death.

"Scarcely more is death." To those who know melancholia, the phrase offers instant, brand-name-style recognition. Biological psychiatry refers to its mental processes as "vegetative": functioning just enough to maintain necessary bodily performance. "Scarcely more is death." The melancholic lives, but scarcely. Melancholia lives, but cheek by jowl with death.

This is its very essence, and it is also the paradox at its core, the antithesis of its sundry antitheses. Hell, Hades, so on and so forth: aren't these places generally populated by the dead? Their punishments and deprivations thought to befall us only after bodily life ceases? Yet by the score melancholics with pulses yet intact find themselves transported to such places, and count themselves kindred to the bodiless and damned souls therein. They draw breath—they must be living yet—but in every inhalation, the sulfur of that infernal region.

I'd had as much as I wanted of walking in this nether land. No more of this neither-here-nor-there living for me, I was thinking that August, as I was taking my survey of this landscape. This was nowhere. I recognized this hell, and far as I was concerned, there was no life about it.

What I wanted was my old life back. The one I'd had when the Zoloft was working. That was what I called "life" now, and I wasn't going to let it go so easily. That life, I could learn to inhabit. To anyone who might restore it, I would have begged like a man out of last chances: Okay, I'd say, maybe I did make a mess of it once or twice, but I'll do better this time. Promise. A few months of training was too short, that was all. I'm ready now, really ready. I wanted some express hydraulic to haul me back up to that place where death was death, and life was life, and the two were clearly distinct and altogether separate places. I'd had enough of this death-in-life. One couldn't keep a foot in both these worlds, surely. Anyway it was a straddle my awkward limbs couldn't manage. One didn't *live* there, not in that hell. I wanted out, never to return.

That being the case, I ought to have been more careful what I prayed for, and what I prayed to, when I stood by the Clark Fork River that evening and decided to quit the pills. For in the American West, a river—or a spring or a creek—might at any time just pour itself down some hole and it might stay subterranean for a mile, or two, or ten—and you can only guess where it will resurface, if it ever does. And without bearing this in mind I stood by the Clark Fork that August evening, praying to be changed, asking those waters to ferry me elsewhere; and it seems now that river listened, and did indeed take me to some other place—it went, as these western rivers will, underground.

The husk split, and showed its seed, and the seed fell into the earth. With it now the darkness would have its way.

CHAPTER TWO

IN MY EIGHT YEARS as a psychiatric case manager I'd never heard
of any treatment plan to guide a depressed client whose medications
wouldn't work. It's not that it didn't happen; when it did, the
psychiatrist would try a new medication, or admit the client to
the hospital for a long-term stay to try him on new pills, or as a last
resort start him on ECT. The success of the medical model was always implicit in our treatment plans. But I was less and less sure it
would do much for my own depression, so I decided to try something else.

My friend Don Hamilton had two years previously sold his traditional veterinary practice in Asheville to begin practicing homeopathy with animals. Over the telephone Don told me he'd had some
success treating depressed animals, and suggested that I try a homeopath.

I was skeptical. I didn't doubt the powers of homeopathy to treat
some conditions: a few years before, in Asheville, I had sustained a
cut on my cornea, an injury my ophthalmologist thought incurable.
Given the moisture of the eye, he told me, the depths of the cut
would likely never heal. Above those depths a curtain of tissue
would grow from one side of the wound to the other, and that was

the best we could hope for. "That curtain will be prone to falling," the ophthalmologist told me, "and when it does the unhealed depths of your wound will be exposed, and I'm afraid very painful. Our only option is to treat that when it happens." In fact it happened several times that year—all it took was for me to brush my hand across my face too energetically, or get swiped by a low-hanging branch in the woods, or for one of my cats to rub against my face, and there it went. At such times I had to patch my eye, take codeine for the pain, and stay home for a few days.

Not long after I met Don, it happened again. On his afternoon off he stopped by my house with a dropper bottle of a homeopathic remedy. "Just take a few drops," he told me. "Wait an hour and if it still hurts use a few more." He left, and I went into the bathroom and removed my eye patch. I squeezed the dropper full, leaned back my head, and pinched the bulb. When the fluid struck my eyeball the burning was profound; the remedy must have been 80 percent alcohol. I ran to the phone and called Don. He laughed. "Try it orally," he said. I did, and to this day have had no further trouble with my cornea.

But a lacerated cornea is very different from clinical depression. One is a tissue injury, a specific and acute condition with a clear etiology; the other (at least in my case) a deeply seated syndrome, intermittently reappearing for no known reason, with broad-ranging effects. I doubted that any "remedies" derived from minerals and plant parts could affect something so unyielding. Depression required strong medicine, I believed, the kind that is gussied up in a well-equipped research laboratory, medicine with well-documented benefits and formidable side effects too.

Now, though, I was desperate. A friend well versed in alternative medicine suggested I talk with Dr. Donald Beans, a homeopath who'd practiced in Missoula for some years before moving to Bigfork, a small town on the eastern shore of Flathead Lake. So I phoned and briefly told him my story. He was nonplussed. In an even, confident tone he told me, "I've treated dozens of cases of depression and many cases of schizophrenia and bipolar disorder too." We talked a while longer and he told me that he had years of professional experience with mental illness, having begun his medical career as a psychiatric nurse.

I didn't see how I could do any better. A few days later, on a gorgeous late August afternoon, ten days after I decided to quit the psychotropic medications, I drove two and a half hours north from Missoula, up through the Flathead Indian reservation and past the cherry orchards along the lake, to Bigfork. Dr. Beans was a short, slight man, dressed in a pair of cuffed tan poplin trousers and a short-sleeved sky-blue cotton shirt. He took a very long history from me, asking what seemed like a lot of irrelevant questions. At its end he offered me no diagnosis, no speculation about the particular causes of my case. And he knew my background well—it was some distant part of his own; he knew I was expecting something. Finally he grinned and said, "All right. If you need to, you can walk out of here today thinking that you now have an 'agitated depression.' Sorry, but I don't recall the *DSM* number for that one."

He stood up, started out of the consultation room, and gestured for me to follow him. "That's one way to look at it." We went into a room full of glass-fronted cabinets, all stocked with amber vials of pills. He slid a paper cup from a wall dispenser, and shook dozens of small white pellets from one of the vials into the cup.

"And here's another," he said. "I am going to give you a high-potency dose of Calc Phos." He handed me the cup. "Cheers. That's short for Calcarea Phosphorica. That is the 'constitutional'—he made quotation marks with his fingers—remedy indicated by what I can see of your personality, and by the particular constellation of symptoms you've described to me today." He handed me a cup of water; I upended the paper cup of pellets into my mouth and chased them with the water.

"Homeopathy is old," Dr. Beans went on. "In many respects it is older than allopathy, the kind of medicine you're familiar with. Homeopaths have been treating what allopaths call 'psychiatric illness' for a long, long time—since the days when allopaths were still chaining the mentally ill to the walls. One of the first modern mental hospitals—meaning a hospital that didn't use constraints and chains—in this country was opened by homeopaths." He went on to tell me that this "Calc Phos" would not necessarily suppress my symptoms.

"That's what ordinary modern medicine considers healing. And it has its usefulness. But that's not what classical homeopathy aims at. We hope," Dr. Beans said, "that we've found the right remedy. If we have, it will work with your constitution's native strengths and inclinations. Right now for some reason your system is out of balance. Healing can begin only by restoring that balance." He handed me two small amber vials. One, he told me, was the same high-potency Calc Phos he'd just administered, and the other was low-potency Calc Phos. "The low-potency," he explained, "you should take when you feel yourself slipping a little. The high-potency is for when you feel like you need a firm kick in the ass. You can call me anytime, but you'll learn pretty quickly which one you need and when." Then he gave me some instructions: I wasn't to drink coffee, since that might antidote this particular remedy. He told me that I might notice the remedy's effects in minutes, or that it might take days—it was hard to predict. He described a peculiar effect any constitutional remedy might have: "aggravation," he called it, wherein my symptoms might for a day or two become worse. Dr. Beans assured me this was the only "side effect" known to result from homeopathic remedies.

He went on: "In the long haul you might, as that balance returns, begin to feel some separation from your symptoms, and that might give you some insight into them. It might not be pleasant. As that balance begins to come back, it might be painful for you to go on as you've become accustomed to."

I raised my eyebrows and opened my mouth. I wanted to ask him: Exactly how do I reckon with *that*? Is there a remedy for that pain?

He lifted a hand and continued, answering my unspoken question along the way: "Sooner or later, I hope, this remedy, or maybe another one—it's pretty hard to tell at this point—will help you learn how to integrate your depression into a life that might feel more natural to you than the one you're living right now. One that makes better sense to your native constitution, to your temperament. At some point in this process, if my previous experience with depression means anything, you might want to seek out a good therapist."

I was already more or less convinced there was such a thing as a "temperament," a "native constitution," but Dr. Beans's offhand characterization of my life as "unnatural" made me somewhat defensive. This was the life Zoloft had given me, and it was the closest I'd ever felt to "normal." But I had taken an immediate liking to Dr. Beans—he was frank and witty, skeptical and urbane. I trusted him. And if there were no side effects, the only risk this medicine posed was to my allegedly "unnatural" life. It looked as if I had to make myself willing to take that chance.

Too, my first visit, which took nearly ninety minutes, cost only sixty-five dollars—including the two ampules of Calc Phos, which he estimated would last me for at least two months. I had been spending nearly two hundred dollars a month on antidepressant medications, and in a typical month another two hundred on quarter-hour visits to my psychiatrist; because of a "preexisting condition" rider placed on my policy, the mental health center's group insurance plan would cover none of these.

As I drove down Montana Highway 35, heading back to Missoula in the late afternoon, Flathead Lake was on my right, whitecaps bellying up as the sun fell off its surface and the wind started. Beyond the lake the sun dropping behind the Salish Mountains. On my left the Swan Mountain Range aglow with the vespertine late afternoon light.

I was noticing things. I was taking things in, finally. It was a great relief. Perhaps, I thought, this is just the power of suggestion, the hope we're all inclined to feel after consulting with a confident doctor. I pulled my Toyota onto the shoulder of the highway. I sat looking out over the lake, to the mountains and the sun starting its descent behind them. Something in me was loosed and it started without my knowing it: I felt wetness on my cheeks. It was the first time I had wept in months; surely this was not owing merely to suggestion. I sat there for a good little while. As dark came down I put a tape into the player and started the car back down the road. As I drove I sang along; it was the first time in many months that I'd felt like singing.

I was feeling somewhat restored to myself: a week or so later I phoned my veterinarian friend Don, who'd moved from North Carolina to New Mexico not long before, and talked him into a week of hiking in the red-rock and canyon country of southern Utah. I had some vacation time coming to me, and it had been a while since I'd felt capable of getting out of the house, let alone into the wilderness, and I wanted to move on it while the weather was good. So after work one Friday afternoon in mid-September I packed the Toyota and left Missoula.

Ordinarily I enjoy long drives alone, but this one—which ought to have taken about fourteen hours—turned into a miserable, sleepless, thirty-two-hour haul. In the car it seemed I had become some modern-day Jonah. Just outside of Missoula, as I was searching for a cassette, the dome light gave out. I pulled off the highway, used a flashlight to find the tape, and set out again. Within an hour, before I was out of Montana, the tape deck shorted out entirely. The radio wouldn't work either, and a fuse wouldn't fix it. Then, just across the Idaho border, my Toyota sedan began to shimmy left and right on the road. When I loosened my grip on the steering wheel it seemed I might careen right off the road. It was no surprise, really: shortly after arriving in Montana, I'd sold the Econoline and relied on my bicycle to get around. But when I took the case management job, a car became essential, and another case manager had offered me this one for just three hundred dollars. It was in good condition, and had a lot of character, but it was about fifteen years old, by virtue of age alone a little prone to such troubles.

My original plan had been to drive on to Salt Lake City, eight hours from Missoula, spend the night in a cheap motel, then leave for the Escalante River area, where we would spend the week. But on that Idaho highway I figured there was trouble with the CV joints, and I knew if they gave out the car was useless. I didn't want to break down in a remote area—which would describe just about all of Idaho and Utah—so I decided to stop in the nearest city and have the car attended to first thing Saturday. I spent that night in a Denny's Restaurant in Idaho Falls, drinking iced tea, eating from the salad bar, reading, and waiting for a garage to open. Next morning I learned that the problem was indeed the CV joints. It took the garage six hours to replace them, and I left Idaho Falls sometime after three in the afternoon, still nine or ten hours from Escalante.

It was a long, long drive. With only the whine of the tires to distract me, Mr. Shoulder had ample opportunity to speak his mind. And his voice worked at me like an itch I couldn't reach. Along the way I stopped again and again, at truck stops and gas stations and convenience stores and scenic overlooks, for soft drinks, for a cigarette, for junk food, for a view of the landscape, for small talk with the locals—trying everything to get him gone. And it seemed to work—I'd be talking about the weather, or sitting on a picnic bench looking out at the Wasatch Mountains, and that voice would recede. Then I'd get back into the car and find Mr. Shoulder still there, patient as ever. He had the compelling narrative, and he knew it, the one that fit my true shape: I was a fraud, insensitive, dull, and unimaginative. I was incompetent to operate in the world, and I spread my contagion even to inanimate objects, to tape players and CV joints.

For the past couple weeks I'd been feeling better, but maybe I'd gotten ahead of myself. Perhaps I wasn't ready for such a long trip, and with no music there was nothing to distract me; even the scenery was little help. Perhaps that was the problem: behind the wheel for all these hours I had too much time to think, and after a sleepless night I couldn't wrestle my mind to one spot and hold it there. The night before, driving hadn't been so bad—but then I'd had music, at least for the first couple hours. Then there were the CV joints to worry about—and I am a born worrier; give me something specific to worry about and my mind is occupied for hours. To that end, it was almost as good a focal point for mental occupation as music.

Now, though, there was nothing specific to worry about, and since I was in no condition to think, my old pal Mr. Shoulder, always there in my hour of need, was thinking for me. Briefly I considered pulling off the Interstate and buying a Walkman—after all, I had this box of tapes along, and still had before me the long drive back to Montana after our backpacking trip. The music might keep Mr. Shoulder at arm's length. I lightened: now I had a plan. Then reality descended. My emergency reserve of cash had all gone toward the repair of my CV joints. I avoid credit cards, and had just enough cash to get to the Escalante area and back to Missoula. So the Walkman was out.

I took another tack: against Mr. Shoulder's voice I began slowly repeating to myself some small list of consolations and reassurances, trying to defend myself against his droning harangue. But I couldn't convince myself. I had been feeling better, but still there was something amiss. This was the problem: something in me was loosed, all right, and it seemed I would soon lose shape altogether. For all the leaden nature of melancholia, I could not weight myself, could not feel substantial: I was restless and ghosted. It seemed I was all bloat and sallow, a candle guttered for good. I did not like to haul such freight into the wilderness, but I was hoping that this sojourn out of the world and into canyon country would chase some of this murk from me.

Don was asleep when I finally arrived at our rendezvous site, a state park close to the Escalante trailhead, in the small hours of the morning. We'd done a number of wilderness trips together, and we had a sort of unspoken routine, so preparing was easy. Within a few minutes after sunup we had readied our gear and divvied up our food.

But then I stood over the trunk of the Toyota for a long, long while. All my necessaries for the week were settled into my backpack. I had room in the top flap of the backpack for a couple of books and no more. Which would they be?

Now Don was pacing. Surely, hopefully, we wouldn't have much time for reading anyhow. He reminded me: In the southern Appalachians he and I had been rained into our tents several times, and on those trips we'd had ample time to read every word of the books we'd brought along, and then to swap them. But that hardly seemed likely in southern Utah; more rain had fallen on us in a single Carolina night than fell on this region in a typical year.

From a certain point of view, I knew he was right. But I did not share that point of view just then. I was in anguish. I could not narrow my choices to two books. Used to be, a single volume of poetry would outfit me for any trip into the woods. No longer, it seemed. When I hadn't been able to narrow my choices back in Missoula, I'd filled a small box with the likely candidates, and now I riffled through them. What would I want to be reading out there? Fiction, poetry, field guides, natural history, humor? The field guide was essential. How could I choose just one other? I had no idea what I would be in the mood for. So I decided to take a variety, but still within some limits: I allowed myself one novel, one volume of poetry, and one book of natural history. Plus the field guide made four. Forcibly I arranged and zippered them into that top flap. I set the pack down to let Don know that I was ready.

Then, as I settled the box back into the trunk, the cover of another book caught my eye. How could we live without Hunter Thompson? I picked it up and wedged it down into my pack, there between my sleeping bag and the food. Edward Abbey's *Desert Solitaire* was on top of the box now. Both of us knew that book well, but it was about this very part of the world. And how could I leave Cactus Ed here to swelter in the trunk? He'd be much happier in the canyon. Besides, it was a small mass-market paperback and wouldn't take up much room. Then there was Annie Dillard's *Holy the Firm*, a book I liked to travel with always. Cactus Ed's saturnine cussedness (misanthropy is a most saturnine quality; and a brief tour through his journals reveals the extent to which Abbey suffered recurrent and brutal episodes of melancholia, for all of his life) demanded her as an antidote. And it was a very slim volume too. So in it went. Now I spotted a volume by Charles Wright. I typically read one of his poems every evening. Why should I disregard my rituals?

Finally I got a brainstorm: my knapsack was in the back seat of the Toyota. I fetched it out of there, and with some very precise arranging I was able to fit into it the remainder of the box. Nine books in the knapsack, five in my backpack. Fourteen books, for a week in the wilderness. This was two per day. It seems ridiculous now, but that morning I didn't see how I could live on any less. We loaded our packs into our cars and drove off to the trailhead.

The Escalante, the last river in the continental United States to be discovered, flows across the Colorado Plateau through the northern reaches of Glen Canyon to meet the Colorado River some fifty miles from our trailhead. We planned to hike about ten miles upstream to a sheltered overhang along one of the river's feeder streams. There under the overhang we would set up camp. We parked our cars at the trailhead and hoisted our packs onto our backs. Then I held out my arms and Don held the knapsack while I thrust my arms into its shoulder straps. The lumpen sack of books rode on my chest like a papoose, only much less elegantly. Don stood back, looked me over, and bent over double with laughter. We walked to the trailhead. He signed us into the guest register: "Don and the Escalante Bookmobile. Come find us if you run out of books."

It was a pleasant day, sunny and in the seventies. We hadn't seen one another for months, so Don and I caught up as we hiked alongside the Escalante. All about us were cottonwoods and willows and oaks, a panoply of ferns, and above us red-rock arches in the canyon walls. The enclosure, the fresh wet smell, all the vegetation—it was a little like being in an Appalachian hollow. Our directions were to proceed about eight miles upriver, to the fifth creek coming into the river from the east, then up that creek another couple of miles to find the overhang.

We made slow progress. I had a fifty-pound pack on my back and maybe another dozen pounds of books on my chest, and I was not in the best physical condition, so I had to stop and rest fairly often. It was late in the afternoon by the time we turned up that fifth creek. Here our only trail was in the creek itself—there was no streambank to speak of. The red-rock canyon walls dropped down sheer into the creek. The water was warm enough, but the current was strong and the rocks on the river bottom were unstable. In places the creek was nearly too deep for walking and here we had to punch our way through, propping our walking sticks against the canyon wall to

keep our balance. But under my load and in that heat, it was re-
freshing to walk with my boots full of water.

Before we'd gone a mile up this stream, though, we came upon a
new navigational quandary. We stood side by side in the water and
looked it over. Thirty feet upstream the creek dropped over a rock
shelf. This wasn't the problem: the shelf was only a foot high, an
easy high step. The problem was right before us: after it dropped
down the shelf, the creek split into two pools. These pools were evidently much deeper than the water where we stood: there was a lot
more water flowing into them than there was flowing past us. Back
home we called such pools "Sinkholes."

Lucky for us, there was a way to proceed upstream: the shelf was
apparently the horizontal bar of a T-shaped rock formation, and the
vertical bar of that T made for a handy, if rather narrow, passageway
between those pools. We eyeballed the bridge: it was maybe four
inches across, just wide enough to support a single boot sole. Hell,
that was wider than a tightrope, and the drop wasn't too drastic, and
the pools would make for a nice soft landing, so I volunteered to go
first.

Now, I am an awkward man, even when unburdened on flat and
dry land. We'd already hiked about nine miles or so, and I was fatigued, which probably didn't do much to improve my coordination.
Added to that, my boots were heavy with water. You can see this
coming: I'd made, oh, maybe two steps on that passageway when I
began to totter and stumble. My load was not too precisely balanced, to say the least, and when I reached my walking stick toward
the canyon wall, trying to stop my fall, I lost my footing entirely. Beneath the load of books I dropped straight into the water, walking
stick in hand.

The pool was deep; and I was heavy with ballast. I recalled my
childhood swimming lessons and flattened my body into the floating
position. Don't ask me why, don't ask me what I was thinking. This
all happened in about the time it's taking you to read a couple of
these sentences, and I am at the best of times no good at thinking on
my feet. Of course, bearing all that weight—a backpack, a knapsack,
calf-high leather boots filled with water—no way was I going to

float. Hoping to find bottom and stop my descent, I shoved my walking stick down. It sunk right into the muck and I could not yank it out. Quicksand, and I was still sinking through the water. Sinking pretty quickly, as a matter of fact, what with all those books.

If I reached bottom I'd have to propel myself back toward the surface, which would involve trying to plant an arm or a leg in that quicksand. This was the sort of thought that could impel even me: do something, anything, and do it now. So I reached down and released the waist belt of my backpack. As the pack lifted off my back, its weight pulled me toward the surface.

For a second or two it did. Then I was heading down toward the quicksand again. Don't forget that knapsack laden with my walkabout library: it was clinging to my chest, and of course we'd rigged it backward, with the buckles back against my shoulder blades, and clean out of my reach. There wasn't a chance in hell that I was going to get out of it. It was like a straitjacket lined with books, or a concrete cummerbund. I seemed fresh out of options. So I did what you, or any other sensible person, would have done immediately upon landing in that pool: I swam. Against the weight of the books and the backpack and with those fifty-pound boots on my feet I kicked and stroked and thrashed and got myself to the surface and over to the edge of the pool.

Of course Don had crossed the passageway without incident and he stood atop the shelf with his hand outstretched. He bent from the waist; I clasped his forearm and he clasped mine. I wedged one boot against the shelf and the other against the passageway and as Don lifted I walked up the rock wall, stepped over the shelf, and stood in the stream, a little shaky but mostly okay.

"Hey," Don said as we stood there laughing, "you look just like a mule. It just hit me: with all those packs strapped on, you look just like a mule."

"Well," I said, "far as I'm concerned that is a compliment. You might have said I look like an ass."

"I've got a book for you to write," he said. "It's a kind of *Walden* in Reverse. Like that utopian novel E-r-e-h-w-o-n? You could call it *Nedlaw.* N-e-d-l-a-w. Got a nice ring to it, I think. Here's your story:

Somewhere in Walden, doesn't Thoreau count all the books he had with him at the pond?

"Didn't he have something like a hundred and fifteen books, and all but fifteen of them unsold copies of his first book? I'm sure I don't have the numbers right but that was the idea, wasn't it? Well, here's your story: You write about this trip, how you bravely hauled four-teen books into the Utah wilderness by the sweat of your own brow and by virtue of your ingenuity—I have to say, I don't think Thoreau himself could have thought up that rig you've got strapped to your-self. Then you print it up, sell it by mail order, on the Home Shop-ping Network, et cetera, et cetera, and next time you come back you can bring all the unsold copies plus your fourteen books, and then you write a sequel about that trip. Infinite possibilities, I'd say. You could keep writing sequels and keep coming back."

It sounded good, the way our laughter, from down deep in our guts, filled that canyon.

"Yep, I can see it now, it could be a whole series: one man's pas-sionate defense of his right to carry half his body weight in books anywhere he damn well pleases. 'Where I hiked and what I hiked for.' 'Where I drowned and what I drowned for'—"

"Hey—"

"Oh," Don said. All the comedy drained from his voice. "Sorry about that. Guess that was a little close." I'd told Don about my old suicide plan.

"Don't worry about it. Actually, I was just going to say— and please God don't strike me dead for this, I promise this is the first and last Virginia Woolf joke I'll tell, but I'll wager she never thought of that—strap on a boxload of books and walk into the water."

Now Don was laughing hard, and I wanted to spin it out a little more.

"That way, once you get there, wherever it is, you've got plenty to read. Should the afterlife present such opportunities. Like carrying a book everywhere just in case you have to wait in the bank or the doctor's office, you'd be well prepared. I personally think Dear Vir-ginia would have liked this idea. Not much reading material in a pocket full of stones."

• • •

All that week we walked about in the bowels of the earth; on the surface, far as we knew, things went on pretty much as they always had but we didn't care to know about it. We hauled in no radio, no means of hearing the news of the world. We'd gone seeking absolute isolation, and we had found it: all week long we neither saw nor heard signs of anyone else. For the rest of the week I managed some-how to suppress the gift for misadventure that led me into the Bad-lands wilderness with no maps and no water and into this wilderness with, yes, map and water aplenty but also with maybe a slight sur-plus of nonessential items. And speaking of those: by some miracle all fourteen of my books remained perfectly dry during my little freestyle workout.

Days we walked and walked, and—do I have to tell you this?—I read not a single one of those books. The walking was grand. It was the rhythm: my footfalls fell on my ears in perfect iambics, in line with breath and pulse. It was the rhythm, and it was the pace: walk-ing, I could attend to things at my own rate, and they did not over-whelm me.

Hundreds of feet above us, at the top of the canyon wall, junipers and pinyons hung on the saddle and every night we watched them silhouetted very briefly against the moon. One night from some-where above us in the desert we heard a loud throaty wailing, not unlike a train whistle or the cry of a baby. We both guessed it was the scream of a panther. If that's what it was, it was the first time either of us had heard this almost unearthly sound, and we were thrilled—and maybe a little spooked—by it. The moon receded, stars sprang forth, and we watched the constellations spin and drift in the narrow slot of sky that appeared above the canyon.

Late on our final afternoon there, I sat myself on a rock in the stream, out before our overhang. Don was off hiking up the canyon. The light spread, danced, shimmered, laced, and spun onto fish and flotsam. The next day I would drive back to Missoula, and the fol-lowing morning I would return to work. I was trying not to think about this. As I sat there in the late afternoon light, the sun shifted away from us. The cool of the river rose into the canyon. Up through her webbed purchase on the red-rock canyon wall I saw a desert lizard seeking equilibrium: looking for some place where breath and blood and heat and water and light would come into balance.

I adore the demeanor of any lizard: with their wattled, wizened skins even newborn lizards appear old. Like all of us, they are well adapted: those wattled skins are watertight, enabling them to retain moisture for long hours at a stretch. When the need arises they can shed body parts to survive, easily dropping a tail to escape a predator.

But they are also incapable of generating any body heat on their own. Their cold blood puts them at the mercy of the sun and a dozen other externals they cannot shape precisely to their liking. I watched closely as this lizard gave herself to the changing light and scuttled up the rock to whatever sun-washed spot held the balance her blood required. And I wished for courage: to likewise give myself over to the changing light, to surrender to whatever my blood needed for balance, to mark my foot sole flat to some place, and to let that place shape me precisely to its liking.

Thirty-odd hours later I was back in Missoula, knocking at Ron's door. It was 8 a.m.; I'd made it back to town four hours before. My legs were sore. The air here smelled like city. It was an ungodly hour to be at work.

Ron opened the door and squinted. It was an even ungodlier hour to be knocking at somebody's door.

"Hey, good morning to you, man." Ron raised his coffee cup. "Come in and have some java." His eyes settled on the brown sack clutched under my arm. "Oh, man. Great. You've got my smokes."

Ron liked to smoke, but he didn't much like going out in public to buy his cigarettes. So we case managers delivered them to him. We were Ron's "payee"—meaning that his monthly disability check came directly to our agency. We served as payee for most of our clients, depositing their checks into an agency account and then doling out the money in twice-weekly payments, following a budget drawn up by the client with his or her case manager. Monday and Thursday cigarette deliveries were figured into many budgets.

I handed the grocery bag to Ron. He gently lifted out the carton, worked a flap loose, and extracted a pack before sliding the carton into a kitchen cabinet above the sink. He folded the sack along its creasings and knelt to put it into a cabinet. I sat down at the kitchen table.

"Want one?" Ron stood over me, shaking loose the bundled cigarettes in the pack. Not today, I told him, thanks anyhow. "Sure," he said. "Grab one if you get the urge. Mind if I light up now?"

Years before, in Ann Arbor, when I'd just begun working in the field, a staff psychiatrist told me his three-question diagnostic test for schizophrenia: Do you smoke? Drink more than ten cups of coffee a day? Despise television? It was a crude joke, but subsequently I'd seen its truth: in those group homes you rarely saw any schizophrenics in the television room. And for reasons still unknown to the clinicians and neurologists, the great majority of schizophrenics will smoke cigarette after cigarette, lighting a fresh one off the end of the last, and drink a dozen to twenty cups of coffee a day. I have long wondered if these habits were observed prior to the psychotropic age, whether schizophrenics use the nicotine and caffeine to try to stimulate themselves over and above the lethargy antipsychotic medicines tend to instill.

Ron got his cigarette going and turned his chair to face me. "Here to make sure Ron is being a good boy, doing everything Pappa Mental Health Center tells him?" Ron was not on my caseload, but his own case manager was out of town, and I was the usual standby with him. For the third time in my nine months on the job, I'd been dispatched to check on his "med compliance." Ron tended to go off his pills regularly; he was no threat to the community when he did, but by the terms of our service contract with him, if he refused to take his meds as prescribed he would be dropped from our caseload.

From the top of his refrigerator I picked up all five of Ron's medication bottles: in addition to the antipsychotics typically prescribed for schizophrenia, there was an antidepressant; there was lithium for the manic-depressive symptoms Ron sometimes exhibited; there was an anticonvulsant for the slight seizures that might be epilepsy or might be caused by an antipsychotic taken in the past or present (and Ron had been on nearly every single one of them); and there was another pill meant to mitigate the side effects that all these rendered. This was the "polypsychopharmacology" Gwen had spoken of.

I owed every mental health job I'd ever had to those pills. "Deinstitutionalization" happened entirely because of advances in psychopharmacology: thanks to the antidepressant and antipsychotic medications that began appearing in the 1950s, illnesses like schizophrenia and manic-depression and chronic clinical depression became more manageable, and it became possible to contemplate what was then called "normalization." The current term when I was working in Missoula was "mainstreaming," but the work itself was about the same: we were trying to help these men and women move themselves, to whatever extent possible, into the American mainstream. So the pills were at the very center of our treatment plans, and medication compliance could be legally forced, by a procedure called "outpatient commitment." To be committed involuntarily to a psychiatric institution, usually a person must threaten physical violence to another or to oneself. With the outpatient commitment proviso attached to them, men and women like Ron were deemed certifiable and committable simply for refusing to take their medications. In some cases this was fully justified. Off their meds, some of our clients were truly a danger to the community.

Now I brought down off the refrigerator a clear plastic box, the size and shape of a small briefcase. The box was partitioned and labeled according to the days of the week and times of day: Morning, Lunch, Dinner, Bedtime. Our nurse filled these boxes every Monday, dose by dose, and one of the case managers delivered them to the clients that afternoon. Our clients typically had fairly bewildering medication regimens; with so many pills, with so many varying dosages, with so many different times of day to take the pills, those boxes were a great help.

I looked through the top of Ron's box. Last filled the previous Monday, it still held a week's worth of pills. Then I tapped a pile of antipsychotics from their plastic bottle onto the table and began counting them out two by two. For some of our clients, the psy-

chotropics rendered miracles. Folks once thought to require backward restriction unto death were, with the right medication, found
capable of living independently, of taking pleasure in games and
work, and even, in some cases, of finding useful work. We believed
this is what our clients wanted. Hence we were dogged about people
being "med-compliant." It often happened, though, that clients did
not share our priorities.

Ron was pacing and talking, lighting one cigarette after the other.
I went on trying to count out the pills, but the pattern by now was
plain: Ron hadn't been taking his meds for some time now. Some
clients courted disaster when they went off their meds. With Ron,
though, and with many others, it was never so clear. Ron seemed to
be doing well: his small apartment was fairly orderly, with just a
faint stale smell about it. The refrigerator was well stocked, and recently cleaned; his bedroom and bathroom were neat. The living
room had its usual piles of books and magazines, and the ordinary
clutter around the stereo where Ron kept his tapes and LPs. In all,
his apartment seemed better organized and more recently cleaned
than my own.

His personal hygiene was good too. His eyes were clear. He'd
shaved within the last couple of days. It appeared he'd washed his
hair just the night before. (In every job I'd had, we had to observe
personal hygiene closely, and make detailed notes about it in our
client charts: in the process of mainstreaming, personal hygiene was
taken to be an important indicator of mental health.)

I thought that all Ron's nervous energy might dissipate if we
talked about something besides mental health agency protocol. I'd
noticed that his guitar case was propped against the couch. I nodded
toward it. "Been playing some, have you?"

"Oh, man, have I been playing." He smiled broadly. "And I'll bet
you know what."

"Let me guess," I said. "Dylan. Gotta be Dylan."

He laughed. "You would say that. No way, man. Neil, Neil, Neil.
Neil Young." Ron and I had a running debate about the relative
merits of Bob Dylan and Neil Young. Each of us liked the both of
them in no particular order, so it was more discussion than debate; if

I was talking up Dylan, he tended to defend Neil Young. If he was talking up Dylan, I would take up for Neil Young. Ron was a passionate student of music, so I always learned something from our discussions.

"What songs are you working on?" I asked.

"Well, I played for about four hours, I guess. Worked on a few things, but mostly 'Powderfinger.' You know that one. Those great solos in there, that's what I was working on. They break my heart. So full of spunk, and so sad too, G, C, D, and the occasional timely seventh. What I want you to do is name me one Dylan solo on electric that comes close to the ones on 'Powderfinger.' "

"I'm afraid you got me there, Ron," I said. He was lighting another cigarette. He grinned and blew a plume of smoke toward the ceiling. I went on: "How about you name me a Neil Young lyric as good as 'Tom Thumb's Blues'? Or 'I Dreamed I Saw St. Augustine'?"

"I don't know, man, you know I can't. I mean, who can write a song like Dylan anyhow? Neil ain't half bad, and you know it yourself." He grinned again, and so did I.

I nodded at the guitar again. "What inspired you?"

"I picked it up because I can play again without embarrassing myself. The pills make my hands shake so damn bad I can't make a chord or hold on to a pick, let alone do both at the same time and hit the string I'm after."

It was good to hear Ron sounding so enthused about something. Life with depression is nothing next to life with schizophrenia, which typically allows no remissions whatever, and admits few pleasures at any time. Schizophrenia is not a "split personality," as is commonly thought; it is a disorder characterized by extremely disorganized thought processes, so that in a schizophrenic the logic and coherence and reality-based thinking we tend to prize are fairly sporadic, and sometimes nonexistent.

Because we understand so little about the etiology and neurochemistry of schizophrenia—far less than we understand about clinical depression—the antipsychotic medications we've applied to it are extremely nonspecific, meaning they tend to cause noxious, and sometimes irreversible, side effects. They stiffen the joints and set up a trembling that makes it difficult for those taking them even to hold on to a cigarette. In time this stiffness leads to a hunched and closely held posture, and to the stiff-legged gait that is sometimes called, after the first antipsychotic, the "Thorazine Shuffle." Subsequent antipsychotics have somewhat ameliorated these effects, but they are rarely without their own dire effects, making applied psychopharmacology for schizophrenics something like a rigged crapshoot. With such side effects it was easy to understand why so many of our clients—the majority of whom were diagnosed with schizophrenia—were inclined to refuse their medications.

Ron was talking again: "Can you believe that, man? I can play again. I am so excited." He lit another cigarette and exhaled the smoke forcibly. Word was, Ron had been a superb guitarist before his first schizophrenic break, which struck during his first year of college. He'd been studying physics here at the University in Missoula, nineteen years old, by all accounts a brilliant young man.

"Will you go back and write that in my progress notes? They write it in my goddamn treatment plan every time we fill out that form, under 'Recreation.' " With his free hand Ron gripped an imaginary pen. He scrawled in the air, and his voice took on an officious, bureaucratic tone: " 'Ron will play his guitar for ten hours a week.' Five minutes before, the dumb fuck just wrote, under 'Medical,' 'Ron will take his meds as prescribed.' I try and try to tell you people, Jeffery, can't have it both ways. Can't have the pills *and* the guitar. Not in this life. Oh well." He mashed out his cigarette. "Hey, do you know anybody I can jam with?"

I told him I would ask around. "Look, Ron . . ." I started and could not find the words to go on. I still had some work to do here, and I was uneasy with it. Med compliance was no small thing, and I was obliged to discuss it with him.

"Ron . . ." I tried again and got no further. This aspect of the job had always troubled me—the level of control we could exert over another life, the choices we could take away. And now I was not being med-complaint myself, and my position felt compromised.

"Jeff, I know," he said. "I could have saved you the work if you had just asked me: I haven't taken a pill for over a week. Today will be the eleventh day, if you want an exact number for my progress notes. I'm not going to try and hide it. But look at me. I'm okay. I'm playing my guitar."

What could I say? Ron had never threatened any other person, so the risk was mostly to himself, and right then it was a little hard to see just what that risk might be. But I had to do something. I decided to try reminding him that if he continued to refuse his meds he would wind up back in the state hospital at Deer Lodge.

"I don't care," Ron said. "I've been there before, and I like the people." He paused to light another cigarette. Even after eleven days off the meds his hands still shook so badly he could barely steady the lighter at the business end of his cigarette. "It ain't so bad there." This was common enough. Many of our clients told me they enjoyed their stays at Deer Lodge. Life in the "normal" community was hard work for them, twenty-four hours a day. Even with medication and clubhouses, and the attentions of case managers, nurses, occupational therapists, art therapists, recreational therapists, social workers, and psychiatrists, it was exceedingly difficult—nearly impossible, in fact—for many of our schizophrenic clients to feel integrated into "normal" society. For all the good the pills can do, they seldom eradicate entirely the symptoms of schizophrenia, and the side effects they cause clearly communicate some manner of handicap. In the state hospital many found a kindred community, a sense of belonging, and a chance to relax from our expectations that they fit themselves to the mainstream.

I suggested that Ron drop in at the "clubhouse." This was our day treatment center, and it was just down the street from his apartment building. I knew he'd heard all this before, but it was about all I could offer: there, I told him, he could shoot pool, draw, work, paint, or learn to use a computer, and find all sorts of clients and staff members to jam with.

He scowled. "That place is a ghetto," he said. "Just all them crazies and you sorry-ass bastards who can't find anything better to do with your working lives than chase after us wiping our butts. I'd rather be at Deer Lodge."

But, I remembered, the hospital had recently instituted a no-smoking policy. "On a good day you might get to smoke just six or seven cigarettes," I told Ron. "You'd be dependent entirely on the goodwill of whatever staff members you could find who'd be willing to escort you outdoors. And with winter coming on that might be hard to come by."

"I don't care," he repeated, more emphatically this time. "Might do me some good to cut back." I was shocked. Ron loved his smokes. He'd made his choice. I wasn't inclined to argue.

"I'll be back tomorrow morning to check in," I said. "Anything you want me to bring?"

"Nope," he said. "Don't need a thing. A visit will do me fine. I'll be looking forward to seeing you," he said.

I stepped out of Ron's apartment into the September morning. It was the first day of autumn. A breeze had cleared the air. In the equinoctial light the maples that overhung Third Street glowed brilliant yellow, and the sky hung deep blue behind them. The air smelled vaguely of cinnamon and drying leaves. We wrote "progress notes," as Ron knew, for every contact we had with an agency client, and "Subjective, Objective, Assessment, Plan" (or SOAP; our work was laden with such acronyms) was the required format for the progress notes. As I walked back to the office I mentally composed my note for Ron's chart. The "O" was the hard part—it appeared to me that without his meds Ron was entirely lucid and clear. This was unexpected according to the medical model. I was supposed to come down on the side of the therapeutic plan, and in this case I didn't see how I could.

Passing the front door of the Food Bank on Third Street, I looked across the street. Easy enough to walk over there, cut inside, and retreat into my basement rooms. But I had determined in Utah that once back in Missoula I would try to put in full workdays once again. I needed to keep this job, and as my time with Ron would indicate, working with schizophrenics was a good hedge against self-pity. So I walked another couple blocks up the street, to our office on the corner of Third and Higgins, and sat down in my cubicle looking out at the Clark Fork River. I set about readying my September paperwork: mileage forms and time sheets had to be submitted that afternoon or I would not be paid. I got them done, and then pulled out my appointment books going back to mid-July. The notes in my client charts were that far behind, but I was feeling optimistic that I'd get them caught up soon.

After an hour or so I was summoned to the waiting area. "It's Judith," the receptionist told me over the intercom, "and she does not want to come back there." Judith was on her way home from the Food Bank, where she worked mornings bagging groceries. She was a gentle woman, much beloved among our staff and other clients.

I looked at the clock on my desk. In ten minutes I had a lunchtime appointment with Donnie, another client. I phoned his house, got a machine, and left a message to let him know I'd be a little late. I knew this was going to take a while. Before going to Utah, I had made an appointment for Judith to see a cardiologist. She was into her sixties, and she'd had bypass surgery five years before. Our nurse thought Judith needed examining, and soon. She had a history of atrial fibrillation—her heart didn't always fully contract, which left blood pooled in the bottom of her heart, where it tended to form into clots. The occasional good strong contraction would flush those clots directly from her heart and into her bloodstream, and could cause strokes when they reached her brain. Our nurse thought this was happening to Judith: she seemed to be having trouble buttoning up her blouses. Such trouble with manual dexterity, the nurse had told me, was a good sign that Judith was having small strokes.

Thing was, Judith wanted nothing to do with any cardiologist. "Last time they tied me down to a table and run all these tubes and wires into me," she told me out in the waiting area. She drummed her palm against her thigh. "They passed these machines over top of my body. I ain't felt the same since. I consider those machines foreign beings. The aliens are inside my heart now, and that's what's the matter with it. And you want to take me back to the same person who put them there to start with. I don't think so. I don't want those machines messing around my insides."

I did my best to change her mind, presented her with every reason I knew for her to see the cardiologist, offered to accompany her into labs where the EKGs and MRIs would be performed.

"But you can't do anything about those machines, can you?" she asked.

No, I told her, if she went to the cardiologist I didn't think there'd be any getting around those tests.

"I don't think so, then." Judith looked at me evenly, with no malice, a woman whose mind was set and would not be swayed. "No, I don't think I'll be going to that heart doctor. I'm going to get along home now." I followed her out the door and told her goodbye. I leaned back against the building and watched her cross the Higgins Street bridge. She walked hunched and bent; her eyes never lifted from the sidewalk, not to look at the river, not to glance up at the mountains, not to greet a passerby.

I remembered: even when I was Zoloft-happy there had been days when my job overwhelmed me. I looked down the street toward my apartment building and contemplated a break: I could walk over to the bakery and get a cheese roll, maybe walk down by the river for a few minutes. But I had to get to Donnie's. I went back into the office.

It was nearly empty, as always. About the only time you would find a gathering of case managers there was first thing in the morning, when we congregated for brief staff meetings. As I walked to my cubicle, Peter, the only other case manager in the building, asked if I had a moment. He motioned for me to sit down at his desk. Peter was our "team leader," a fellow case manager who was also my direct supervisor; he had been at this work for many years and never seemed to be rattled by it.

"How's your first day back?" Peter asked. I told him about Ron, who was well known to him, and filled him in on Judith.

"My goodness," Peter said. "Some day you're having." He paused. "How are you doing?"

"I'm okay," I said. The month before, Peter had listened sympathetically to the news that I'd stopped taking the antidepressants. Since he was my immediate supervisor, and because my choice defied so many of our agency's operating principles, I was grateful for this.

"Thanks for asking." I looked at the clock and started to rise from the chair. "Talk with you later. I've got to go get up with Donnie."

Peter leaned back in his chair, then inclined toward me. "Jeff, Donnie called while you were with Judith." Peter paused and looked down at his desk. With his fingers he pulled a paper clip out of its bends. He looked up at me again. "He told me that he's firing you."

I fell back into the chair. In our office Donnie was considered a difficult client. He was a lonely and combative man in his mid-thirties who complained bitterly about his isolation, but refused to go to River House or seek friends elsewhere. Once we discovered a mutual enjoyment of campy movies and cornball jokes, Donnie and I managed to find common ground. He would call up sometimes just to tell me a joke, which was taken to be a good sign; evidently he'd never phoned his previous case managers for anything except to complain.

Donnie had a hard time of it. He had a bum leg, from a bicycle accident he'd had as a child, leaving him with a marked limp, and he had an ulcer too. That was no wonder, because Donnie also suffered from "paranoid delusions," as we called them, and he suffered them in spades. He believed that his father had hired the Missoula police department, and the community mental health center, to spy on him. He bragged to me from time to time that in retaliation for our meddling in his affairs he had put a bug on his previous case manager's home telephone. "I heard phone sex and everything else on there," he told me. "I really found out the truth about you guys. I'll bring the tape someday and we can listen to it in your car. I wish I'd asked James for her number. She was hot. Worth whatever he paid for her."

He also was convinced that television actresses and newscasters were watching him through the set, and speaking to him directly. And he believed that either the police department or the mental health center, or both, had outfitted the heating vents in his apartment with hidden cameras and microphones to keep moment-to-moment watch of him. (Because this last might sound plausible, I need to point out that while we did in fact work closely with him, we never would have intruded upon his privacy in such a way.) Donnie could get violent—the year before, on a downtown sidewalk, he'd assaulted a passerby whom he thought was reading his thoughts—so we tried diligently to discourage his speculations about being spied upon.

This was exceedingly difficult. To every schizophrenic I'd known, the ideas, suspicions, and convictions we called "delusions" were ineffably real; it was just about impossible to convince them otherwise. Donnie was tenacious about his "delusions"—he seemed sometimes to think about little else—and it was a real challenge to keep him from talking about them. That work, we called "redirecting" a client's thoughts—really a fancy-pants term for changing the subject—and sometimes I could tell Donnie a joke, or get him to talk about the last bad movie he'd seen, and that would refocus him.

This was the first time in my mental health career that a client had fired me. "You know how Donnie can be," Peter said. He rested his hand on my forearm. "Let me know if there's anything I can do. In reality I think this is a good thing. You need to cut back a little. Don't sweat it. This is the longest Donnie's ever stayed with the same case manager. It was just a matter of time. Don't take it personally."

It was hard not to. All year long Donnie and I had kept a standing weekly lunch appointment; every Monday at noon we went to the 4B's restaurant down on Brooks. We always had the same waitress. Invariably, Donnie ordered iced tea and french fries, and once she caught on to this the waitress would bring them to our table shortly after we were seated. He tipped her well. Above all else Donnie valued order and consistency, and in my early months on the job I'd done my best to maintain those. Recently I'd not been so reliable for him, had canceled a couple of our lunch dates and never got around to making them up. He had every right to fire me. It wasn't Donnie's crankiness that got me fired; I had let him down.

Back at my cubicle I filed away my progress notes, which were now updated only as far as the last week of July. I said goodbye to Peter, and got my coat off the rack. I turned in my completed mileage form and time sheet to the administrative assistant, and marked myself "Out" on the chalkboard. Under "Time to Return" I wrote "Tuesday 9 am." Four and a half hours into my first day back, and already my resolutions had gone out the window. Soon the month's end would come, and once again I would not reach the one hundred billable hours expected of us every month. My first months on the job, I had regularly exceeded that "shop standard"; the last couple months, though, I had just tossed the printed reports into the trash unopened, too ashamed to look.

I walked back down Third Street, climbed into the Toyota, and drove to the music store to look for a recording of Beethoven's late quartets. In those months chamber music and the ancient modal tunes of Appalachia were all the music I could bear. Mostly I wanted music without words, piercing and unsentimental, and I found New Age too vapid and superficial, while symphonies and concerti were too dense, too overwhelming. In the store's Classical section I found the Beethoven recordings and carried them to the checkout line. The woman who rang up my purchase wore gold round-rimmed spectacles over calm and deep blue eyes. Her eyes were really striking: there was a deep peace in them, as if she had stared down some chaos and held its gaze level with her own until it retreated. Her forehead was freckled and for all the calm in her eyes, there was nothing somber or resigned about her face; she looked ready to burst out laughing at the slightest provocation.

"Where did you get those glasses?" I asked her. Her eyeglasses had a twining, delicate filigree on the temples and bridge, such as you never see on modern frames. I heard myself say that I wanted to find a pair like them. On Zoloft I had bought myself four pairs of glasses, in seven months' time, trying to find a pair that fit my new personality. I didn't mention that to this woman. I seemed to be starting a conversation; I was too surprised to mention much of anything. As a rule I was rather bashful, always averse to making small talk, and lately I'd had enough trouble talking, even with my friends. What was I doing?

"They are, as you may have guessed, genuine antiques," she drawled. She paused, and I could sense her condensing a long story. "I lived in Alabama"—just what I'd have guessed from the accent— "and a friend of mine named Eve found them in an antique store and gave them to me." The drawl was suddenly gone and from her accent I guessed that she was actually a native of Montana, and a perfect mime too.

She tore my receipt off the spool and handed it to me with the discs. "Party music," she said, grinning at me.

She rested her hands on the counter before her. I didn't grin back. I was looking at her hands. They were without adornment of any kind: she wore no bracelets, no nail polish, no rings, but I couldn't take my eyes off them. They were small and capable and strong-looking, yet graceful; they were beautiful.

"Sorry about that," she said. I looked up. "I don't usually comment on people's purchases, for just that reason. People are really sensitive about their music tastes. You really have to watch with the used stuff they bring in to sell back, too. Don't joke, don't even imply a judgment. Whew. Makes me want to say: It's only music. It's just to enjoy. Why worry about it?"

That wasn't it, I wanted to say. That's not why I went silent. I'd started this conversation without thinking about it, but then it seemed my native reserve came back to me. For several long seconds I didn't say anything. In recent weeks a childhood speech difficulty, a stammer that had been entirely absent for twenty-five years, had returned, and it was making me hesitant to speak under the best of circumstances. The real problem, though, was that I could not get ahold of myself. Really, I had scant idea who I was—couldn't summon sufficient certainty about it to present even the simulacrum of a coherent being. So I didn't much trust the voice that came from my mouth to speak what I believed or thought or felt, if I ever knew what I believed or thought or felt. Consequently most of the time I chose not to speak at all.

But I needed to reassure this kindly woman that I wasn't upset with her joking. "That's okay," I finally managed to say, "no offense meant, and none taken." I stopped. "W-w-w-w-w . . ." I had no idea what I was going to say next, and the stammer effectively silenced me anyhow.

I looked at her again. She held out her hand. "I'm Lisa. Lisa Werner. Glad to know you." I leaned toward her and rested my elbows on the counter. Slowly her hand came down and rested briefly on my forearm. It was cool and comforting; there was commiseration in her eyes. She lifted her hand slowly upward and away; in the periphery of my vision her bare arm looked like a bird taking wing. "Go on home and make yourself some tea, and play your Beethoven," she said. "It'll help, I think."

She was right. I went home, thinking I was in for the day. I took a mug of tea to the basement, put one of my new CDs into the player, and lay back on the bed. Within minutes I was weeping, not the shallow tears of sentiment but the deeper, more sustained sobs of catharsis.

This was what I needed. When the disc was finished I rose from the bed and put on my shoes. I went up to the kitchen and fixed some lunch. I washed my dishes, and then I walked up the street to return to work.

IF I'D EVER HAD A COHESIVE NOTION of what depression was and what it meant, that autumn it collapsed.

It wasn't only my own experience with it, or what was happening at work, or what I had learned from Dr. Beans. I'd believed without question that our biological explanations for it meant the condition was invariable across time and cultures. Our way produced results, quickly, and fairly efficiently; so I assumed that we were onto it, on our way to having it under control. It had never occurred to me to consider cross-cultural approaches to depression. But in late September in *Depression and Culture*, a 1985 anthology of writings by cultural anthropologists, I came across this from Anthony Marsella: "Depression apparently assumes completely different meanings and consequences as a function of the culture in which it occurs." Marsella and the other anthropologists in this book claimed that our definition and understanding of depression was narrow and ethnocentric: "Depressive illness and dysphoria," wrote Arthur Kleinman in the book's introduction, "are . . . not only interpreted differently in non-Western societies and across cultures: they are constituted as fundamentally different forms of social reality."

Melancholia has a quartet of classic symptoms, observed since Hippocrates: depressed and fearful mood, diurnal mood variation, insomnia with early morning awakening, and a loss of interest in one's surroundings. Thus a modern American depressive will recognize the condition when reading Hippocrates, or Burton, or a monograph quoting contemporary melancholics in Saudi Arabia or Portugal or Chile or Iceland.

Beyond these symptoms, though, it seems almost infinitely variable. We're inclined to think of "suicidal ideation" as a clear symptom of melancholia—it's on the *DSM*'s diagnostic list and three-quarters of those North Americans diagnosed with depression mention it. But only one-quarter of the Japanese natives who evince these "classic" symptoms report thinking of suicide. We tend to think of "guilt" as an essential symptom of depression, and it too is prominent on the *DSM*'s list. But only one-third of those Iranians who suffer melancholia report feeling any guilt.

In fact, according to Byron Good, in Iran the "dysphoric affect" we consider part and parcel of clinical depression "is not equated with simple unhappiness"; instead, "it has profound religious and personal significance." In many cultures depression is not even defined as illness but as "a more or less 'natural' result of the vicissitudes of life" and approached, according to Sri Lancan anthropologist Gananath Obeyesekere, "as an existential issue." If it isn't conceived of as an "illness" in these cultures, in numerous others melancholia isn't even thought distinct from the self—"in many non-Western languages," according to Arthur Kleinman, "the linguistic equivalents of 'anxiety' and 'depression' simply do not exist." Of course, people everywhere know these emotions; in some cultures, apparently, they aren't deemed "Other" enough to be given a name. And according to Obeyesekere, in many cultures that approach it in these ways, depressives function effectively in society even when their condition is at its worst.

In other industrialized cultures, herbal remedies and other treatments we consider "alternative"—not truly "safe" or "effective" because the AMA has yet to approve them—are widely used. European psychiatrists are far less likely than their American colleagues to prescribe antidepressants; for many years, long before it became popular in the United States, German psychiatrists were more likely to suggest the herb St. John's-wort to melancholics. All over Europe and in Canada too, psychiatrists are inclined to offer the depressed patient the nutritional supplement L-Tryptophan, an amino acid with effects very similar to an SSRI antidepressant; this nutritional supplement was banned by our FDA just before Eli Lilly began to market Prozac. According to Great Britain's leading medical journal, *The Lancet,* physicians there are inclined to offer depressives homeopathic remedies, which they believe to be safer (no side effects) and just as effective as antidepressants.

Which raised some questions: Why are we on this side of the Atlantic so enthralled with our pills? And how did we go from "melancholia"—with the fifty-odd variants listed in Tuke's *Dictionary,* all recognizing the particular context and specific nature of a person's symptoms—to our "clinical depression," seldom modified to suit the individual case except in clinical terms: "Recurrent," or "Severe," or "With Psychotic Features"?

Tuke's volume was published in 1892. Less than a decade later, the American historian Henry Adams, visiting the Great Exposition of 1900 in Paris, stood in the Gallery of Machines. There, he wrote in *The Education of Henry Adams,* he felt his "historical neck broken by the sudden irruption of a force totally new." Adams "began to feel the forty-foot dynamos as a moral force, much as the early Christians felt the Cross." The automobile had been introduced in 1893, and according to Adams, "in these seven years, man had translated himself into a new universe which had no common scale of measurement with the old . . . the nearest approach to the revolution of 1900 was that of 310, when Constantinople set up the Cross."

There on the cusp of the twentieth century, Adams foresaw its contours. The United States was amply blessed with the natural resources required to build an industrial economy, and we already had in place an ethos that treasured untrammeled expansion, material progress, and limitless individual wealth more than natural grandeur or cultural diversity.

The business of America was and is business, and we were quick to discern that the machine could make possible expansion and wealth beyond anything previously imaginable, that it could fabricate an American Empire, and we embraced the Machine Age with a righteous vengeance. It is difficult now even to imagine the world Adams had known in his youth, a world comparatively free of machines. The silence. The slower pace. The smell of trees and animals on the breeze, rather than exhaust fumes. In the kitchen the chopping of knives, the smell of the wood-burning cookstove, the stews and soups long simmering. Not the tearing open of plastic packaging and the thin metallic ping of the microwave announcing another meal ready for the table. The very air an expanse of silence, with no television, no "you've got mail," no telephones let alone cell phones, no CDs, no radios, no beepers.

The machine has changed our everyday domestic lives just as much as our landscapes and our means of transport; our working lives just as much as our poetry and our music. How else did it happen that we suddenly became willing to forgo melody for the clamor of rhythmic dissonance—not so different from, say, the clanging of a train across the landscape—and the old prosody for the flat, often monotonous cadences of free verse? Don't get me wrong: I like free verse above formal poetry—probably because I am a child of my time, and unless joined to a melody, rhyme and meter sometimes sound artificial and stilted to me. In the twentieth century, the sound of the machine has become the sound of our lives; without its echo, music and language strike us as anachronistic—inapplicable, irrelevant luxuries. Too slow, too sonorous to suit our times.

The dynamo displaced the virgin, as Adams prophesied, and consequently we have convinced ourselves that the science and "rational thinking" that engineered the Machine Age would yield some singular, absolute truth unavailable to religion and the older, more interdependent ways. We have adopted the machine as a model: systematic, efficient, uniform, and perfectible. We have compared that model to human nature and to the nonhuman natural world, and we have found them wanting. And those same machines have given us unprecedented means to impose that model upon the natural world—including, of course, our own bodies—so that we can make them better conform to those mechanistic standards.

Those who accuse the medical model of "reductionism" claim it adheres to those mechanistic standards and fails to acknowledge the breadth and diversity of human ecology. Physicians began applying the medical model to mental illness around the turn of the century, and very quickly such time-honored particular diagnoses as "religious melancholy" and "love melancholy" and "neurasthenia" vanished altogether, to be lumped under the faceless rubric of "depression," with no reference to the quirky individuality each case of the illness presents. If the body is thought analogous to a machine, then it is believed to be an isolated and self-contained entity, and any problems it develops are thought to arise from malfunctions in one of its "systems," and not from without. Which would fairly describe the contemporary approach to clinical depression: psychiatry pays little attention to the patient's particular social and cultural background. As if these bear no relation to the illness—a rather impersonal way to approach a condition that feels very singular to each. And when we speak now of "depression," we speak exactly as if some engine has gone awry: we refer to "neurotransmitter deficits" and "biochemical malfunctions."

In some respects a reductionist approach to this illness is forgivable. Neither this chapter nor this volume is thick enough to provide a thoroughgoing history of our ideas about this illness, and it is all a long befuddlement anyhow. There is an old notion that Saturn will present innumerable obstacles to any work concerning him, and that seems to be proven out in the history of our researches into melancholia. Since Hippocrates, volumes upon volumes, whole libraries of clinical studies and poems and memoirs have been devoted to it, and still the illness remains elusive to us.

Consider, for example, a question we've been debating for thousands of years: Where is it? In this time and place, we believe depression a biological problem, centered in the anatomy of the brain. Over the years, many have claimed that it originates in the mind—

that it is chiefly a creature of the imagination—wherever that organ may be. As we've seen, others place its origin and its expression in the larger body. And some claim that melancholia arises from the soul.

And for all these centuries, here is what has mystified us most about melancholia: it proffers all these dramatic effects, spreads itself all over body and soul and mind, dumps on us all this weight, all this agony, even causes suicide—it brings us all of this and with, as Hippocrates wrote, "no apparent cause"? Its origins are unseen, its reasons unknowable. It appears to be the perfect revenge of an evil deity: served up cold and remote from whatever instigated it. This is not the way we want the world to work.

It is an enigma. So in our time we have mostly abandoned trying to puzzle out the "why" questions. Perhaps this is a respectful concession to its mystery: since they are different from one person to the next, trying to discover what scientists call the "ultimate" causes of melancholia would likely turn into an endless, fruitless task. We have limited ourselves to the "how" questions—finding the "proximate," observable biological causes: to investigating and treating those, we can apply our machines and medicines; and the apparent success of those medicines has, it would seem, pretty effectively convinced us that this is the best approach to depression. Having seen so many clients and friends benefit from antidepressants, and hearing so many in the larger culture extol their benefits, even after the pills ceased working for me I was inclined to agree.

Perhaps we regard the pills so highly because we fear depression, as well we should: in one of five cases it leads to suicide. It is potentially a fatal illness. But—and I want to say this without slighting anybody who has suffered the suicide of a loved one—it seems our disdain for this illness goes beyond that. We have declared war on it. Far more than one in five cases of coronary disease, cancer, and diabetes prove fatal—and American pharmaceutical companies spend great sums of money researching medicines to treat them, but they spend just as much trying to develop new antidepressants. And they earn back their money: in the 1990s one antidepressant drug or another was every year the second most frequently prescribed medication (the most frequently prescribed was an ulcer medication).

Little wonder that cultural observers call ours "The New Age of Depression." But in previous "Ages of Melancholy"—in Renaissance Europe, in Elizabethan England, and to the nineteenth-century Romantics in Germany and Great Britain—the illness was taken as a great gift; painful and trying, yes, but on the whole a worthwhile experience—desirable, even. Fops and wannabes who didn't suffer it learned how to pretend that they did.

But ours is the Age of Anti-Depression. For many reasons: depression (and to a somewhat lesser extent the melancholic temperament) derails the "efficiency" and "productivity" widely used to measure job performance in the modern workplace. It makes a tedious challenge of the relentless social demands—the "networking"—nearly any job places upon us these days. In our work we strive above all else for "success," and the depressions of countless "successful" people—actors, prominent attorneys, politicians, pop musicians, newscasters, writers, and so on—attest that depression cares little about such worldly measures of one's worth. Perhaps in bygone days, when far more people labored at home, the temperament and the illness could be accommodated: a melancholic could work in solitude, at a pace better suited to him or her, and often at physical tasks that might ameliorate its effects. But for most of us, those days are long gone. Measured by the work hours it costs corporate America, depression ranks with coronary disease and lower back injuries as one of the most costly maladies of our time.

Also, both the illness and the temperament utterly defy one of our time's cardinal requirements: that we maintain a rigorous, sunny optimism, and that we pretend toward it, or spend toward it ("the retail cure"), if we don't genuinely feel it. It's hard to know how this attitude came about. It's at least curious, possibly even indicative, that the word we've substituted for "melancholia" in this century has also become synonymous with our term for a drastic economic downturn. The economic marketplace has shaped our world nearly as much as the machine—that is, if one can neatly separate the two—and surely the marketplace has shaped the way we conceive illness, and dictates the sort of temperament we consider acceptable.

Corporate capitalism seems to require a certain amount of feel-good optimism, a Panglossian sense that these supermarkets and shopping malls full of an ever-increasing bounty of virtually indistinguishable consumer goods represent the best of all possible worlds, the very acme of human accomplishment. We all know in some subterranean way that owning these goods will not make us any happier over the long haul. But for some reason we remain vulnerable to such lures, and these days buying more than we can afford seems almost an act of patriotism.

This makes sadness and pessimism seem downright subversive, so we try to keep them from public view. Films and pop songs are test-marketed before national release, and sent back to the studio for redoing if the test sample finds them unduly sad. Cable radio enterprises beaming classical music out to the masses have taken to programming out movements in the minor keys. In October of that same year, barely two months since I had quit the pills, I drove from Missoula to Bozeman to hear the psychologist James Hillman deliver a lecture about depression. Hillman screened for us a British documentary entitled *Kind of Blue*. In this film, depressives frankly discussed both the gifts and the drawbacks of the illness and of antidepressants. There seemed to be no particular bias or agenda; the filmmakers seemed more interested in presenting the perspectives of intelligent, thoughtful depressives and letting the audience draw its own conclusions.

The soundtrack, I should mention, leaned rather heavily on some of those minor-key movements. According to Hillman this documentary received awards in Great Britain and at the Telluride Film Festival in Colorado; but it failed to attract any American distributors. Apparently because the prospect of corporate sponsorship was unlikely, our Public Broadcasting System took a pass on it. None of our myriad cable networks picked up on it, even for a middle-of-the-night airing. "They all said it was just too slow," Hillman told the audience in Bozeman that afternoon. "That it wasn't uplifting enough, not as optimistic as it needed to be for an American audience."

In spite of all available evidence, modern-day Americans keep trying to convince ourselves that happiness is the natural state of our species. Our kind was meant to conquer and work and laugh and spend, we believe; not to sit about head in hand. So our science explains not only the melancholic temperaments ("dysthymia" and "cyclothymia") and clinical depression, but also more explicable and transient states of sadness, such as mourning the loss of a loved one, not as age-old natural life experiences, painful but necessary, but as biochemical deficits to be readily vanquished with a pill.

I want to be fair about this: Biological psychiatry has restored millions of people to the life they desire, and there is no better way to measure a treatment model. Its relentless efforts to raise public awareness about depression have brought many to seek treatment. (Those efforts have also sold a lot of pills, but I don't want to get cynical.) It has lifted some of the stigma long attached to the illness, and it has taken us light-years away from the tired, simplistic Freudian and neo-Freudian explanatory blaming schemes ("anger turned inward"; "overprotective mothering"; "flawed cognitive habits") so long prevalent in the therapeutic community.

But maybe it's also fair to say that it has replaced those explanatory schemes with another that is, as its critics allege, not a little reductionist. Biological psychiatry is fond of likening clinical depression to juvenile diabetes: neurotransmitter deficiencies, its advocates assert, are no different from the lack of pancreatic insulin suffered by juvenile (or Type I) diabetics. Just as those diabetics require insulin to go on living, those with neurotransmitter deficiencies require antidepressants.

In some respects this is a useful analogy. It offers an easy-to-grasp model for depression—most people know something about diabetes. It tends to remove stigma—we don't blame Type I diabetics for their illness, after all. Beyond that, the analogy's usefulness dissipates rather quickly. For starters, you will find very few diabetics for whom insulin has failed. Meanwhile, media reports that antidepressants are effective for 80 percent of those diagnosed with depression come very close to hyperbole. In fact, "treatment-resistant" depressions like my own affect at least one-third of all diagnosed depressives.

The 1922 development of injectable insulin has saved countless lives—and since the antidepressant era began in the United States, in the 1950s, suicide rates have increased by 300 percent. (This may not, of course, be an entirely reliable way to measure the effectiveness of antidepressants; still, extensive studies indicate that melancholia accounts for two-thirds of our suicides; if antidepressant medications were widely effective, wouldn't the suicide rate be on the decline?) It's also true that depressives in the United States seek relief from "alternative medicine" more frequently than any other group of chronically ill patients in the country, save those who suffer from ongoing anxiety—which is itself frequently a precursor to clinical depression. Surely this also tells us something about the overall effectiveness of antidepressants.

So, I was learning, not everyone was listening to Prozac; or perhaps it simply wasn't speaking to thousands who wanted to hear from it. This underscores what is perhaps the most noxious effect of biological psychiatry: it has reduced the ancient melancholic narrative to one story. At the end of Hillman's lecture in Bozeman an audience member asked him to define the illness. For the first time all day Hillman seemed pensive and uncertain. He removed his eyeglasses and rubbed his eyes. He dropped his chin into his hand. He looked over our heads and out the window. Then he cleared his throat and finally spoke: "Depression," he said, "is hidden knowledge."

A stunned silence followed. Most of us in that room were "mental health professionals," practitioners and advocates of biological psychiatry day in and day out—and Hillman seemed to be saying that our pills and potions were suppressing something essential. What that might be, he didn't say, and it seems we were too astounded to ask. I think now that what so dumbfounded us was Hillman's implication: depression has its own narrative, and our medications are obscuring it. "Hidden knowledge" of some sort is the kernel of nearly every story we tell. The work of the plot is coaxing that knowledge into light, evaluating it, and trying then to integrate it into ongoing life.

This is the work that will teach us, as stories do, how we might live. But by and large biological psychiatry offers us just that one story. Surely you know it—you've read it, or seen it on television, or heard it from a neighbor or a co-worker, or watched a family member live it; maybe you've even lived that story yourself: the quest for the proper pill that will restore the life one was leading prior to the illness. It is a moving and compelling story, and I am grateful that so many of us have been able to hear it and to live it.

That is one way we might live. But we need more stories than just this one. Always and always, long as we live and breathe, this is what we need: more stories.

That fall I obtained a homeopathic materia medica, and I looked up "Calcarea Phosphorica," the constitutional remedy Dr. Beans had prescribed for me. Under that heading, the word "depression" appeared nowhere. Nor did "melancholia." Instead I saw this list of habits and traits which are, according to homeopathic theory, characteristic of this constitution:

- fear
- sensitivity
- helplessness
- hopelessness
- dissociation
- grief and despair
- low self-esteem
- mind wanders; mental confusion; memory weakness

These eight correspond pretty squarely with the *DSM* criteria for a diagnosis of clinical depression. But there were more:

- homesickness
- romanticism (dreamer/fantasy/wishful thinking)
- pessimistic
- desire for escape
- disengagement

- monomania (obsession at any hint of trouble)
- anxiety
- prostration of the mind from talking
- absent-mindedness
- dreams of cats
- craves acidic foods

When I saw Dr. Beans that August afternoon, nearly all these traits belonged to me, most of them since earliest childhood. Some were more recent: I'd mentioned to him that in the week or two before our appointment I had experienced insistent cravings for a plate of french fries served alongside a green salad, both drenched with vinegar. This was in response to his asking about my food cravings. He'd also asked, as the list would indicate, if I were homesick, if light bothered me, if I had difficulty talking with people; he asked what animals appeared in my dreams, he asked about my politics and my tastes in music.

As he asked these questions I wondered what he was about; no psychiatrist had ever asked them of me, which I took to mean that they had nothing to do with depression. But, he told me, my answers to questions like these told him something about the specific nature of my condition, about the ways my condition had intertwined with and then grown forth from my own nature. In that second list of symptoms the individual character of my melancholia came clear, indicating to Dr. Beans which "constitution" was mine. Those symptoms which might seem merely irrelevant quirks or idiosyncrasies, he told me, were the very life of my condition. Just like a person, he said, or an animal: some things are common to every member of the species. That, he told me, is where the medical model stops when it considers a condition like depression. "When you get right down to it," Dr. Beans had told me, "that's a pretty generic way to approach it. When you take into account all those quirks and idiosyncrasies, and add them to those generic qualities, that's what makes an individual. And that's sort of how homeopathy works."

"Constitutional theory"—the notion that each person and animal has a basic innate constitution—is at the center of classical homeop-

athy, and bears more than incidental resemblance to the ancient theories of humors and temperaments. All aim to get at the whole of a
person—the essence—not simply to treat the symptoms of an isolated "illness" in one or another bodily "system."

No wonder, then, that so many depressives seek out alternative
treatments like homeopathy, and that British psychiatrists are inclined to treat depression with homeopathy: it takes into account individual circumstances and preferences. In so doing it seems to
comprehend the essential nature of melancholia more readily than
the medical model does, without ever reducing the condition even to
such a label as "melancholia." This illness has a breathtaking circumference, striking body, soul, and mind, coloring everything seen
and experienced, and constitutional theory and humoral theory acknowledge that reach; at the same time, they recognize that to
each depressive the illness seems some portion of who you are and
where you live. This restores to us an ancient belief: melancholia is
minutely particular to each, perfectly adapted to its time, to its place,
to its host.

Constitutional theory and humoral theory restore to melancholia
an ecology: like the many melancholic variants observed over the
centuries, but now abandoned by the medical model, they give it a
place; they locate it precisely within the particular human ecology
where it manifests. But those who seek a homeopath hoping, as I
had been, for the rapid and effortless relief offered by antidepressants will be disappointed. Dr. Beans had given me to understand
that, rather like psychotherapy, it can carry into our vision things
long hidden, and will not magically erase our symptoms and restore
us to health. We will have to work at it. It will simply begin to restore to us the native balance of our constitution, and hopefully with
this balance restored we can see where that work lies and summon
the will to begin with it.

BUT FOR ALL THE CHAMBER MUSIC and lizards and remedies and new ways of thinking about depression, as autumn continued I went right along unraveling. Melancholia appears to originate outside the conscious mind, and the conscious mind appears powerless against it, so any notion of "self" as a cohesive and continuous being seems a fiction. Depression is a wholesale deconstruction, the perfect postmodern tale, featuring Mr. Shoulder himself as the unreliable (or is he?) narrator. It seemed some fable about entropy, and this was a story I didn't care to hear. So I became the consummate pack rat. I saved, dated, and filed away everything: the minicassettes from my answering machine. Receipts from every meal I ate out. Every letter or note I received. In my daybook I kept meticulous notes from every personal phone call I made or received. Evenings I sat down and wrote page after page in my journal, details of people encountered and conversations and the weather and films I watched and meals I ate. I wanted to erect this bulwark, wanted to keep close to hand any external, verifiable evidence of my existence.

Even retail therapy, shopping my way to distraction, was out. Every time I looked into a storefront window some voice whispered: That won't work. Nor will that. Nor that. Won't last. It is all in vain. And it was, and it always is; but I wanted the ordinary human pleasure of deluding myself, anyhow. It was autumn again, my favorite season, but this time around it came with no hope of regeneration behind or before. All was old and stale and futile, me most of all. This bottomless emptiness—that is to say, this nothingness—defined me.

This is the particular chaos of melancholia: it knows you. Meaning, it knows precisely how to undo you. Your mind becomes an instrument of torture, armed with a voice just like Mr. Shoulder's, a voice audible only to you, a voice that anticipates just where you would go to evade it and arrives there just ahead of you, always. Whether it was borne in your genes or through some horror in your childhood it seems it has grown up with you. It is a garment hewn precisely to your fit by some unearthly tailor.

So as the end of October approached, I was ready to follow Dr. Beans's advice and find myself a therapist. I had never put much stock in the "talking cure" for depression; to my thinking it was first and foremost a neurological problem. After the meds fixed that problem, I'd believed, then one could address other problems in therapy sessions. But all this unraveling was frightening me, so one afternoon in the third week of October, I walked up Higgins Street to my first appointment with Anita Doyle. In her office she pointed me to a rocking chair set beside the window. She sat down in another rocker, facing me directly. On the windowsill between us, there was a cobalt-blue bud vase with a single white rose in it. Out the window, the roofline of downtown Missoula and beyond that the mountains to the east.

She asked if I'd ever been in therapy, and I told her in the past I had heard too many platitudes, been told too many times that I'd get better if I'd just stop being so hard on myself. I asked if she considered herself part of any particular therapeutic school, Freudian or Jungian or any of the more recent ones. Nope, she said. "I belong to the eclectic school."

I told her of my dislike for such faddish nonsense as "rebirthing the inner child" and other New Age hokum.

"We should get along fine, then," Anita said. This is why I had sought her out: from what I'd heard from other clients of hers, she seemed intent on honoring life's complexities, which meant she was disinclined to employ the simplistic, gaseous formulas often volleyed about in therapeutic circles.

I summarized for her my experience with depression in the previous twenty-two months. Then I started to talk about work, and I went on and on about it. Told her about the way I felt compromised by my job, enforcing med compliance while I myself was off the meds, counseling clients about practical living when my own affairs were pretty much a mess. Told her I'd thought about quitting, but dismissed it: the job was financing my education, and if I left it now, I would be unable to pay for my final semester. Told her I'd had no other working life, and had no idea how I would go about finding one. Told her there was little chance that I was going to walk away willingly from the job—not now, when there was little else to tell me who I was. I told her about the hours I was spending in the basement, which in the past month had once again become a real problem. I was rarely at work now past lunchtime. Then I came home and wrote feverishly, or read—I had, in fact, accomplished most of my recent researches into depression on mental health center time.

"Hold on, hold on. Slow down for a minute," Anita said when I finally paused long enough for her to get a word in edgewise. "You've said a mouthful already. Let me respond to a little of it before you go any further. You've been resisting your depression for nearly two years now. What has that gained you?"

"Gained me? Is that a trick question? I'm not sure what you mean," I answered. "Well, I've still got the job, haven't I?"

"I suppose you do," she answered. "You will yourself out of bed and off to work every day. You try to will yourself to get in your five hours of billable time every day. There's something to be said for that. But sitting here listening to you, it's hard for me to guess what that something might be. Does your depression hurt any less because you're showing up in the office every morning? Does it make you feel victorious over it? Is it making you a better person? A better case manager?"

"How would I know?" I snapped. "Are you saying I should quit my job so I can find out?"

She raised her eyebrows. "Of course not. But ask yourself this: why do you go on trying to run away from it?"

"Jesus H. Christ," I said. "Are you telling me that I should just lie down and yield to what it wants?"

"What do you think that might be?"

I raised my hands, palms up, and shrugged my shoulders.

"You have to think about this," she said. She lowered her voice and spoke slowly and deliberately: "What do you think your depression wants?"

I squirmed in the chair. The answer seemed easy enough: it wanted my life, every portion of it, and nothing less. And was she trying to tell me that I was supposed to yield that? What did it matter what my depression wanted, anyway? Hadn't it got enough of me already? Wasn't I in charge here? Why should this depression get what it wanted, when I was getting nothing of what I wanted? I was flummoxed.

Anita remained still and calm. "Jeff, all I'm trying to say is, it seems pretty clear this is not going to just go away. You've been out there for almost two years in your hip boots, trying with all your might to push this river. It's a wonder you haven't drowned. How long do you think you'll have to push until it finally starts to flow the other direction? All I'm trying to suggest is, you can try to make some peace with it. The best place to start with that is to figure out what it wants from you, what role it wants in your life. Pardon me for saying so, but it doesn't look like you have much choice."

She was right. I needed reminding on this point. It had control of my life. I didn't.

"Tell me," Anita said. "In the last two months you've come across all this new information about depression. Have you changed anything about your everyday life as a result?"

I hadn't.

Anita raised her eyebrows. "Well," she said, "let's try something, then. Just think out loud, without lingering over every word. Try to tell me: What does this want from you? What direction is it taking you in?"

I thought I could answer that question. Looking back, I know that I might have mentioned that my melancholia, and the failure of the meds, had led me to all this learning already. But I couldn't see then what it all meant; I didn't for some time to come. This is where I think it's leading me, I told Anita: When I signed on to the job ten months before, I had signed up for disability insurance coverage. As you might have gathered, I am accident-prone, and I didn't want to end up bereft if I sustained some injury in the wilderness or on the sidewalk or on the basement stairs. Every month the premium was deducted from my salary. Recently I had begun to consider making use of that coverage. I wanted to work, and day after day I tried to will myself to it, but it did little good: my energy gave out, my concentration gave out, my memory ran out, my attention to detail ran out. I was no longer able to do my work. Didn't that mean I was disabled?

"It might or it might not," Anita said. "I know this job really matters to you. But to be honest, I'm not sure your depression cares that much about it. Let me rephrase my question: do you think your depression simply wants to put a monthly disability check into your mailbox?"

This seemed pointless. I reiterated for her the list of things depression had taken from me: the budding love affair, contact with people, my life's work, my pleasures in the outdoors.

"Do you think you can live without those things?" Anita asked me.

"I don't think I want to," I replied after some time. "Jesus God. I can't imagine life without them. What would replace them?"

"Do you really think it wants to take *all* those things, once and for all?" Anita asked.

For moments I sat silent as a stone. Finally, from outside we heard the university's bell tower chiming the hour. Our time was up.

Anita rose to her feet and grinned. "Well," she said, "you're off the hook. I'm just going to leave you with that question as a take-home, then. That is, if you're coming back."

I was relieved. I was tired of her questions. I shrugged my shoulders and gathered my things. I wrote her a check, and I stood there deliberating. Finally I made an appointment for the following week.

"Coming back for more, eh? Thought I might have frightened you off. Think about it," she said as I stood in her doorway. "You can go on fighting and fighting it, but I don't see that doing you much good. Maybe we can work on helping you find some ways to accommodate it."

The notion unsettled me. At one time, and not too long before, I'd have dismissed it out of hand. I never would have considered that depression might have some meaning, some message about the self or the world. That idea did not fit my model for it. But in the previous weeks I'd come across enough evidence to mistrust my own preconceived ideas about depression. I left her office, walked up Higgins Street, and went into a diner. I read the newspapers, drank some tea, scribbled into my journal. I remembered Hillman's words about depression being hidden knowledge, his implication that it had its own narrative thrust.

Now, what Anita wanted me to do, it seemed, was to make myself vulnerable to that hidden knowledge, try to bring it into the light, see what depression had to tell me. But what sort of story could this be? Look at the person it had made of me already—reclusive, shriveled and furtive, indecisive and stammering. What sort of life might such a person make for himself? To me melancholia felt not like narrative but like interruption, like severance—and to what end?

So I dragged my heels. I spent weeks, months, dragging my heels. That October evening I paid my bill, left the diner for home, and decided to stick to the alleyways; I did not want to see anybody I knew. I remembered my first weeks in Missoula, when I'd been exhilarated about living in a town where so many were working to make the world a better place, a town that wanted to usher in the "new paradigm." Some called Montana "the native home of hope," and in those days I thought I knew why.

But two years later, I had to wonder: what in hell was I doing in this home of hope, me with my unrelenting darkness, my brooding paranoia, my shifting glance, my sorry ass schlepping down the streets?

I wanted it to be this simple: I wanted to stand in this alleyway and shout, and be done with it. I would holler until my lungs ached, until they went leathery. Shout, if it meant I would see Mr. Shoulder get himself gone. Shout, and restore that thrum to my chest, the feeling that into my core I was solid and vibrant and belonged on this earth. I wanted to bare my teeth and shout away all this befuddled confusion, all this resentment and rage.

Shout, as if this eerie echoing down invisible alleyways were my true spoor. Shout, as if voice alone might restore my presence.

CHAPTER THREE

"IT'S IN YOUR BLOOD," my Grandma Thomas was telling me. I had taken the week off and traveled home for Thanksgiving. It was the first time I'd been back since my Christmas visit two years previous, right when depression was first setting in. She set a Tupperware pie keeper half full of her blackberry pie into the refrigerator, and moved across her kitchen, stopping by the stovetop to fetch the clean pie plates and then moving straight on to the cabinet where she put them back. There had been fourteen of us for dinner, and now Grandma and I were doing the dishes; the rest of the family was talking in the living room or off on walks up Stillhouse Hollow.

"Your granddad, I suspect, had a touch of it." She was beside me now with her towel, drying the gravy boat and then up on her toes placing it in the cabinet above the sink. "For no reason I could ever figure, sometimes he would just go out to the barn and hide there in the dark. He'd not come out for company and scarcely for family." She cleared her throat and began drying the coffee cups. "He'd just set in there and build birdhouses. He'd come in for supper and I'd look down the dinner table and he'd be staring off into space." She draped her towel over her shoulder. Two by two she carried the set of china coffee cups, which she reserved for holidays, over to the counter, and carefully put them in their box.

"It's in your blood, sure enough," she repeated, touching her hand to the countertop to emphasize her point. Grandma had been a meat cutter all her life, and her fingers were crosshatched with scars from cleavers and butcher knives; but for all that the only sign of her eighty-one years was her arthritic index finger, bent at the first joint. "No mistake about it." She looked at me, pursed her lips, and nodded. She lifted the box of cups and carried them up to the attic. During a phone conversation a few months before, Grandma had told me that if I would just get busy, my depression would go away. I didn't understand her reasoning: what with my job, and my studies, and my magazine work, I thought I was plenty busy already. But now she'd raised the subject again, suggesting that heredity had something to do with it, and this was a surprise.

Back in July I had finally come to understand that it was physical labor she had been recommending: my bookish and sedentary pursuits probably didn't seem much like work to her. For my Grandma Thomas was like her biblical namesake, Martha. She was a worker, as people at home said. She was a doer. She believed that hard work could antidote just about any ill to befall man or beast. Her own example might have been proof positive: apart from her asthma inhaler, Grandma required no prescription medications and scarcely took even an aspirin.

Martha had lived out her entire life on the riverfront. She had spent nearly fifty years here up Stillhouse Hollow, scarcely taking time away from her work to glance out the two kitchen windows— the north one looking out over the field where I'd run the dogs all those years before and into the forest beyond, the south one giving a view down the hollow and onto the Ohio. She'd been raised up on her family's seventy-acre riverfront farm in the village of Sardis, twelve miles south of Clarington. The youngest of nine children, from her early childhood days she tended to the berry patches; she fed and watered the animals; she milked the cows; she cooked and carried meals to her brothers out in the fields. She'd moved up Stillhouse Hollow with Grandpa in 1945; here she had raised two daughters, innumerable animals, kept her farmwork up to the minute, and cut meat for hours every day at the Thomas Meat Market in downtown Clarington. Grandpa had once told me that in his absence Martha could have kept the homeplace going and supported their daughters at the same time.

When she and my grandpa decided to sell the meat shop in 1962, Martha went to work for a friend who owned a grocery store in Powhatan Point, a coal-mining town on the river five miles north of Clarington. In 1972 the M&K was featured in a food industry newsletter. "Women's Lib Flourishes in Powhatan Store: Every Store Position Held by Woman," read the headline. Apart from birth notices and obituaries, it was the only time her name had been in the press. She was a little embarrassed by it, since she was by nature modest and did not think of herself as a "women's libber," but the article was very kind to her: "Mrs. Thomas," the article said, "the butcher and the head of the meat department, is especially popular with customers, who rave about her homemade ham salad and tasty bulk sausage. There is no meat cut she can't deliver." Fifteen years later, at seventy-four, still earning little more than minimum wage, she retired from the store to stay home and care for my grandpa after his stroke.

She might have retired, but she surely hadn't slowed down: she had prepared pretty nearly every bite of our Thanksgiving dinner. My mother and her sister had each offered to host our gathering, but to no avail. "The family's always had its holiday dinners here, and long as I live and breathe I don't see why that needs to change."

Every day she was up and working at the crack of dawn, and whatever the chore she would work alongside you without complaint, whatever your age, and keep up, too. But mostly now she worked alone on the homeplace, asking none of her grandchildren or neighbors for any help. Through the spring and summer she kept the acre of grass mowed. For the flat parts she had a riding mower; for the run banks and the steeper banks that started up the hillside, probably a third of the lawn altogether, she donned a pair of football cleats and started up the push mower. In the fall she continued with the mowing, raked leaves from the sycamores that lined the banks of Stillhouse Run, and worked the apples into jelly and applesauce and pies. All year round she quilted, and every week she spent two full days—by that I mean eight-, ten-hour days—volunteering her time at the New Martinsville Senior Center, working with men and women who in many cases were younger than she. Martha rarely wore makeup, and I'd seen her fingernails painted on just a handful of occasions, but there at the Senior Center she did the residents' nails. Whatever she did, she did it well: earlier that year she had been honored by the governor as the West Virginia Volunteer of the Year.

"Jeff, that goes down below. In the left-hand cabinet. Not up there." I'd been hunting above the stove for the wooden block where she sheathed her Old Hickory butcher knife. Turned out she'd spent a few moments standing outside: "Sorry to leave you here, but I needed to get some air. And is it ever nice out there," she said to me. "Once we get finished up, you ought to get out of the house and go walking."

There was a pile of dishes in the drying rack. She opened a drawer and pulled out a towel. "I'm telling you," she said, "it is in your blood. Here's my side of the family." She held up her hand and touched one index finger to the other, ticking off a brother, several nieces and nephews, and distant uncles and aunts and cousins remembered from her childhood, all of them prone to what she called "nervous breakdowns."

"And then there was Ruth. Oh Lord, poor Ruth." Grandma shook her head. She put down her towel and fingered the buttons on her red cotton blouse. Her sister Ruth had been two years older; they were inseparable as children and remained very close as adults. I turned away; there weren't often tears in Grandma's eyes and I knew she wouldn't want me to see. Aunt Ruth had been dead for two years. Since my grandfather died in 1987, Grandma had lost three siblings, and her closest friend had died the previous summer. Of her childhood circle Grandma was very nearly the last one left. I put my hand on her shoulder.

"Don't," she said. "Your hands are wet." She turned right around and handed me the cast-iron Dutch oven off the countertop. "This goes down in the root cellar," she said. "You'll know what shelf to put it on." The root cellar was where Grandma still kept her canned goods, and cooking implements she didn't often use; it still had a floor made from flagstones dug from the banks of Stillhouse Run, wooden shelves, and the cool, musty smell I had always loved.

Traveling from their home outside Louisville, Aunt Ruth and Uncle Harold had often visited Stillhouse Run, so I remembered her well. She was a gentle, restrained woman, who always seemed hesitant to speak. When she did, she tended to stammer, and there was always a slight tremor in her voice. She always traveled with her Scottish terrier, and she kept about her person an endless supply of red-and-white peppermint candies, which she was always unpocketing and handing to you, silently.

I came back up out of the root cellar and joined Grandma by the sink. "You know, even when she was well Ruth always stood with her back up against the wall. Like she'd just as leave be out of the room."

She went on: "I'm here to tell you, Ruth had some nervous breakdowns. She couldn't recognize any of us when she got bad off, and couldn't hardly talk either. First we thought it came on account of Mom dying but it kept right on with Ruth, for the rest of her life. She said over and over again that there was no good reason for it. She took nerve pills up until the day she died. She had the electric shock too, and had to go back in the hospital every once in a while, maybe every couple of years or so.

"None of it ever did really work for Ruth." She was drying off the silverware now, dropping the pieces singly into the sorting liner of her silverware drawer. "But she gave of herself to whoever needed her. Her church, her family, all sorts of people. Sometime I'll show you all the cards I got after her funeral. These were people I'd met just that one time, at her funeral—people she'd babysat with in the church's nursery twenty and thirty years ago, and their parents, and her pastors, and her neighbors. She touched a lot of people. She *gave*."

By now the dishes were all done and put away. "Well, that's a job well done," Grandma said. "Yep. It's all put to rights now." I had only washed the dishes; Grandma, nearly fifty years my senior, had done all the drying and putting away. She'd also wiped down the kitchen surfaces. She accomplished all this without ever appearing hectic or hurried. Now she carried all the napkins, towels, dishcloths to the laundry room downstairs, where she tossed them into the washing machine. I pulled a stool to the north window and sat there looking up the hollow.

I heard her come back up the steps and close the laundry room door behind her. "I sure do thank you for your help with the cleaning up," she said. I turned around. "This—this depression," she said. "If that's what they call it now. I know it's nothing easy to live with." She leaned back against the sink and crossed her arms. "I've seen it enough to know that. But you'll learn how. You don't have much choice, do you?

"It is in your blood. But so is the living with it." She moved her palm under her elbow. She rested her chin on her other palm. "You'll get through it," she said. "And if need be you just come on back home for a while."

Truth to tell, I was tempted. I'd flown into Asheville the Saturday before, and after spending the weekend visiting with friends, I'd rented an economy car and set out north by northeast across my home region. I went that day from the towering peaks and sheltered coves of the southern Appalachians up the Great Valley of Virginia into the Alleghenies, the familiar ridge and valley country that would stretch before me all the way home. In Wytheville I turned north and crossed ridge after ridge into West Virginia. I turned off the Interstate in Beckley and took smaller highways north and west across the state all the way to the Ohio.

I followed water all the way home. All the water here flowed just the way I was going, toward the Ohio. Following those bigger valleys—nary a road in West Virginia that doesn't follow some waterway—with the ridgelines on either side of me. The hollows tapering down their hillsides from sky to water, framing the runs and creeks that branched back from the river valleys, and then from the front receding—disappearing, really, back up into the mountainside.

I knew this country. The horizon truncated, so you couldn't see far into the future: a sudden rain squall could sneak up on you here, the clouds come barreling over the ridgeline sight unseen unfurling sheets of water from sky to earth. I knew this country: the rounded soft hills. The diaphanous blue haze, from all the water heaving off all these forests back up into the sky, rather faint that autumn day— the dry season here—but still here, and more so from afar, down in the distant hollows the one time I got a long view. You could almost hear the whisper of all that susurration. The air gone bluish: transpiration, and some wood smoke too this time of year; it would be chilly already up in the hollows.

This was home: moving through the water-softened butter-light of the late autumn afternoon. Out the window looking west leafless crowns of hickory, their bulb-ended twigs aglimmer with the sun slanting back of them; trees of ten thousand lights. The striped maples, stark naked up the hillsides, shimmering yellow brushes in the breeze. The oak crowns thick with their umber leaves clinging on until March. Along the streams, more and more as I neared the Ohio, the exquisitely mottled great sycamores: the bark sloughed off in irregular patches up the tree so that the gray-brown of the base gives way to the dappled trunk and then the brilliant bone white of the crown, that would steal your breath when set against a blue autumn sky or even a gray winter's morn.

The old houses stacked up the hillsides, the mobile homes along the road. The narrow shotgun houses in the old coal towns. All the churches, denominations both familiar and purely local, some in mobile homes, some clapboard or old brick, white steeples set in relief against the mountainsides. Roughly an equal number of bars. Rhythms of speech. Idioms people used when I stopped to get gas or buy a bottle of pop.

I wanted my eyes full of the landscape, I wanted its fiddle music and banjo tunes falling easy into my ear, I wanted the window down and I wanted that smell—fecund even in the autumn, rich with all the slow rot, all the water in those unglaciated highlands—the smell, that thick amphibian smell, filling the car.

Until that visit I hadn't known just how homesick I was. Plainly I ought to have known better, after Ann Arbor—but not only had I left again, this time I'd gone clean out into the far reaches of the Rocky Mountain West.

But there were plenty of reasons for me to like the West, and Missoula in particular. Rationally speaking, my homesickness made little sense. But maybe rationality has little to do with such matters. On that day I was reveling, vibrant for the first time in many, many months with some landscape. Like any landscape—and even more than the others—home is always interpreted privately, subject to no standards but one's own. All this marvelous narrow enclosure might strike a Westerner as claustrophobic. To me it felt enveloping. To some the moist air might seem weighted, turgid, suffocating: but to my eyes it lent some sort of inner radiance, as if every visible thing held some deeper hue, as if all that lived in this place held some soft glow within.

I suspect to many people Montana has some inner glow all its own. But something about these soft round hills and these hollows had a long hold on my bloodline and would not let go. For generations we had worked and played and lay in the shade or walked beneath the same trees, hearing the same birds call, living with all the other animals who seemed to prefer that landscape. The place seems part of the family. To this day we have a hard time leaving: my whole family is mostly still right there on the banks of the Ohio. You can draw a circle on the map, twenty miles across and high, with the river at its center, and within it live my mother, my father, my brother, both grandmothers, several great-aunts and great-uncles, many cousins. Even those who have moved outside that circle are mostly in Columbus, just a couple hours away. After my Ann Arbor fiasco, I ventured to North Carolina, which never seemed so far from home, and where I could find work that fit my particular qualifications, which were not in much demand back home in Monroe County.

But I had left Carolina too, moved to Montana, and reversed all my ordinary bearings: exchanged the wrap of humidity for the brace of western aridity, the muted light of the hardwood forest for the unsparing glare of the West. Moved to a place where the mountains were mostly bare rock or low-growing grass. Where hardwood trees were scarce and there was no autumn to speak of. Where the waters drained into a different sea.

I remembered my last long drive, to the Escalante River two months before. Since coming back to these parts I hadn't heard a peep from Mr. Shoulder. Did this landscape conjure some spell on him? In this truncate horizon, in all this water and rot, did he find it difficult to breathe?

Who knew? Don't get me wrong: I'm not saying one place or the other is superior. I'm only trying to tell you how I felt at home in one place, and not the other. What I knew that November day was this: something was restored to me, some shadow lifted. And this: I missed these smells, the colors, the light, the shapes of the trees, the enclosure of these hollows—all of them familiar to my blood for many generations. I was wondering: how in the name of creation could I haul such deeply rooted blood around in some new place and expect it to be contented there?

And if I was at home among these trees and hills and salamanders, some would say I was at home here temperamentally as well. It was once common to refer to the "genius of place," to contemplate the ways a landscape would shape the people it attracted and held to it. This quarter was once rather isolated, and is still often cloaked in mist and offers plenty of secluded spots for those who want to be spared the traffic and bustle of the world. On an overcast day, and there are plenty of them, these hills can feel kind of closed in, a little gloomy. It seems predictable, then, that the people of Appalachia are all the time described as "saturnine," both by those "outsiders" who loved these mountains and the people who came to learn from them and in some cases to live out their days among them; and by those who'd come only to try to haul these "contemporary ancestors" into modern America. (In the comments of this latter group the term "fatalistic" was usually in there too.) This happened from the first coming of outsiders to the region, and it's happening still: a book detailing a 1996 walking tour through the region's high mountains quotes approvingly such terminology to describe the people the author encountered.

Even granting that "saturnine" is a fairly broad term, it is better suited to describe one individual (and will quickly show its limits even then) than to categorize a whole region of them. I'm hesitant to generalize about any people, especially those I've lived among for most of my life: human nature in the Appalachians seems to me just as ornery and contrary, just as rich and contradictory as it must be everywhere. More than any other American region, Appalachia has managed to conserve some portion of its ancient past—its hand-work, its music, its stories, its religion, its traditions, its lessons. Even in the modern era these have been taken to heart by many thousands, native and otherwise—that Appalachian traditional music is played all over the world, for example, says enough: These traditions are not anachronisms, nor are they wishful thinking for ye olden days. These old notions still apply.

Even if there were anything especially "saturnine" or "fatalistic" about the ethos of this region, it seemed to me that people here knew that some manner of redemption was always near to hand. Often, finding that redemption entailed turning to tradition—to the landscape itself, or to music, or to work well done, or to God or family— to humble the inborn, intractable arrogance and selfishness of our species. These ideas don't agree with our modern American notions about human "progress," but really: has the human animal changed so much in the last century? These old ideas seem radical, in the literal sense of the word: they get at the roots of our dis-ease.

Now I knew I needed *something*, I wasn't sure what, but it seemed this place—the landscape, the people—could teach me. So when my grandmother extended her Thanksgiving Day invitation I was that close to taking her up on it.

To us, "nostalgia" signifies a rather sentimental attachment to the past, usually connected to "classic" television sitcoms or radio-station programming. But the older notion of "nostalgia," first described as a clinical condition by Johannes Hofer in 1688, was something very different: "grief for the lost charm of the Native Land, a continual melancholy, with incessant thinking of home." Of those who suffered it Hofer wrote: "They are apprehensive and find pleasure only in sweet thoughts of their fatherland." The prognosis for those so afflicted was dire. On the basis of his observations Hofer came to believe that "most of those who cannot return [home] . . . are driven mad." In 1847 the German physician Ernst von Feuchters-leben wrote: "That turn of melancholia which seems caused by homesickness often leads to suicide."

"Nostalgia" as a melancholic variant was apparently unknown before the European Age of Empire, when people by the hundreds left their homelands. Not long thereafter, Hofer and other physicians were diagnosing it in soldiers, sailors, expedition naturalists, navigators, students abroad, serving girls, and others who traveled away from their home regions. Into the early twentieth century, "nostalgia" continued to serve as a viable diagnosis; it received a separate entry in the eleventh edition of the Encyclopaedia Britannica, published in 1910.

But, as Virginia Woolf observed, and hardly in jest: "On or about 1912 everything changed." First, there was the reduction of all those old, particular melancholic variants to "depression." Given the biological emphasis of psychiatry in our own time and Freudian psychoanalysis before, it seems the gist of this whole century has been to remove melancholia from any broader context, to take it out of the larger world—out of human ecology—and refer it back onto the supposedly isolate self. So in our view, the landscape—even our native places—has no bearing on clinical depression. Add to that our belief that we should be willing to settle anywhere, that financial and occupational opportunity take precedence over attachments to place. The upshot: "The twentieth century has dealt with depression without returning to the concept of nostalgia, at least in any sense of a formal disease," according to Stanley Jackson's *Melancholia and Depression*.

Yet the anthropologists who study depression across different cultures maintain that the old diagnosis of "nostalgia" still has moment: "Refugee status is a powerful precursor and predictor of depression," wrote Kleinman and Good in *Culture and Depression*. And surely it still has moment in Appalachia too. In this century millions of Appalachian natives have left home to seek reliable work in urban industrial centers like Baltimore and Charlotte and Columbus. In Michigan I had known dozens of displaced Appalachian people, and I'd even met a few in Montana, and among us homesickness was rampant and grievous. "You can get us out of the hills," we'd say to one another, "but you can't get the hills out of us." Even in a time when you scarcely hear the word "homesick," in songs and stories from Appalachia it remains a recurrent motif. From the Carter Family in the 1930s to the Stanley Brothers in the 1950s to Dwight Yoakam in more recent years, there is no American music more homesick than Appalachian music. And if anything it is even more ubiquitous in the region's literature: a central theme in Harriet Arnow's 1952 novel *The Dollmaker*, in the poems of James Wright and Charles Wright, and in the contemporary fictions of Lee Smith and Fred Chappell and Jayne Anne Phillips and Sharyn McCrumb and Chris Offutt.

First I left home out of curiosity; after that I kept moving, largely because I believed I could remake myself, given the right geography. I suspect most Americans of the last couple generations believe this in some form: the self is protean, capable of remaking itself over and again. This is the very idea that undergirds the modern marketplace, with its sales pitch promising a new persona if only we purchase the right products. It drives the popularity of Prozac and other such drugs, for their ability to provide "cosmetic" personality makeovers. More than its antidepressant effect, this is what I treasured about Zoloft: for a time I was a new person. For seven months, I was truly "better than well."

It seems rather arrogant of us, believing that we can exile ourselves from nature without undue consequences, certain that we are not bound by any creaturely limits. Humoral theory and homeopathy and traditional medicine the world over aim to restore balance, not to enable us to overreach our limits. Surely their idea is right; surely the body, like any other landscape, has an elegant poetry of its own. By that poetry, the old concept of "nostalgia" makes perfect sense: we are, after all, animals, and animals have their chosen places. There is nothing sentimental about this: it seems to bear the weight of the generations, to express some evolutionary truth. Per-

haps some of us so deeply crave—need—the connection between animal and place that when our blood has begun to learn its way
around a given landscape, to banish it is asking for grief; perhaps attachment to place is so intrinsic to our species that if denied it will
express itself as illness.

Sociolinguists say that in any language the word for "home" is
the most poignant. It may be one of the ultimate mysteries, the way
that people and places conjoin. It seems indelible, but beyond our
comprehension, the way a place will fit a people to its liking and its
needs until some of those people—despite their belonging to the
most adaptable mammalian species—will feel settled in only one
place: Home.

Prior to this Thanksgiving visit I had never been away from these
green hills and hollows for so long. And for most of those two years
I had been clinically depressed. "It's in your blood," my grandmother had told me. There was much to like about her etiology. For
starters there was its simple truth: there was no mistaking melancholia's presence in both my family lines. She was right, too, if you considered this old notion of nostalgia: those family lines were all long
wedded to this landscape, and my blood seemed regulated to the water and the weather of this place, the smell of the trees, the way the
light fell on this landscape from one season to the next. By leaving I
had exiled myself from all these things my blood had been breathing
for several generations.

Perhaps this was the reason I couldn't keep the earth beneath my
feet in Montana; perhaps in some portion this was the way my life
had become untethered. Even in a place lively as Missoula, all the
way across the continent, I spent many of my waking hours trying to
keep in my life some essence of my home: listening to its music, reading about it, talking with other natives, and writing about it. My
bedroom walls were hung with pictures of the hills and forests and
creeks of southern Ohio and West Virginia and North Carolina. It
had always been so: nothing—neither my education, nor the pills,
nor politics—had ever taken me away from this place in any lasting
way. I don't think I will ever get to the bottom of my feeling about
this place. The diagnosis of "nostalgia" may seem idealistic or out-

dated; and perhaps nothing could be more anachronistic, more fatalistic—in short, more stereotypically "hillbilly"—of me than to say: this bygone diagnosis plays some part in my illness. Away from here I am sick into my bones for this place. This is what my body tells me: "nostalgia" persists.

After Grandma and I finished the Thanksgiving dinner dishes, I took her advice and went walking up the hollow. There I lifted from the banks of Stillhouse Run some pieces of sycamore bark. I placed them carefully in the breast pocket of my overcoat. Once back to the house I bundled them in a bandanna and packed them in my suitcase. As they grow and the trunk expands out of its old skin, sycamore trees shed bark. On the ground those shards of bark will slowly become soil, and that soil will be taken up into the tree once more to become bark, or leaf or twig. Or perhaps the loosed bark will want to root about in the soil, reaching down into the damp earth.

Those pieces of bark I carried back to Missoula might have been on the trunk when Grandpa and Grandma moved up Stillhouse Run; they might have been there when her other grandma, Bertha Dally, had died in her small house just across Stillhouse Run in 1950; they might have been there on some summer's evening with my Aunt Ruth sitting beneath; there when I lay out beneath that very tree as a child and imagined myself a salamander. They might have been there the day my grandfather died. Perhaps that trunk was the last thing he'd seen last time he looked out his window. To this day those small tablets of bark sit in my workroom window. I wonder still: is this the shape of the skin I have lost, or is it the shape of the skin I might grow into? No matter; I will be the last to know. They stay. Here on the sill they remind me: we carry within our blood wherever we go the memory of some long-familiar landscape, and that memory might save us, might settle us into some homeplace, and hold us there.

IF MELANCHOLIA WAS INDEED IN MY BLOOD, a family legacy, that raised some questions.

A. We don't have to start this story in a cave, but we probably could. "Nothing in biology makes sense except in the light of evolution," according to geneticist Theodosius Dobzhansky. So I ask you to picture the depressive on some ancient landscape. Nobody knows precisely how long there's been an us, a *Homo sapiens,* and nobody knows when melancholia first appeared either. We'd have a harder time figuring out that last one: this thing heavy enough to make the body heave and lurch downhill like a stone in a landslide, this thing with bone enough to carry another illness pickaback—it leaves no fossil evidence whatever. Only from the corpse does melancholia finally vanish.

I am none too sure, then, how to date this scene. But in the brain melancholia seems seated in the "reptilian" parts, affecting the "automatic" features that govern such essential genetic matters as food and sexual drives and self-protection. And it is spread all over the world, in roughly equal numbers. From these, evolutionary psychologists guess that it predates the hominid dispersion from Africa. So, just to be on the safe side, we'll set this scenario 60,000 years in the past, which is the latest possible date for that dispersion.

Our melancholic could be either male or female, though even in those times, according to evolutionary psychologists, it was more likely a she; as this unfolds I'm going to imagine our melancholic sometimes as male, sometimes as female, and assume she is suffering the classic symptoms: prolonged fear, sleeplessness, despondency, irritability.

All these add up to anhedonia. Perhaps she didn't call it that, but it's the simplest way I know to sum the various effects of that syndrome. There is no pleasure to be had. You know about hedonism. Imagine, if you can, antihedonism. Imagine: any conduit to pleasure is all plugged up.

Anhedonia. Pleasure gets a great deal accomplished for evolution—think of the orgasm, and what it's meant to assure. Perhaps the best motive we've got—and in our ancient friend there is none, nor any hope of it.

It is difficult to imagine the particulars of this life—the ways our ancestors fed and housed themselves—and they would vary enormously if we were to locate our scenario more precisely. On any continent, though, the mere matter of survival required considerably more energy than it does now: you hunted or fished or planted or gathered edible plants, or you and yours did not eat. Other things essential for survival—building and maintaining shelter, and keeping the village safe—took considerable energy too. And energy is another area where our friend is in trouble. If she were worried about her evolutionary fitness, it would come first on the list.

On this landscape, any sign of vulnerability could attract predators of all sorts, and she lacks the energy even to defend herself. So, naturally enough, she wants to keep all this hidden. But melancholia will out itself: your whole posture changes, and your manner along with it. People are watching you, you're sure of it, and that changes you too. And they would be watching: they need to know how much of their energy you are worth, and they need to know this very quickly. So the eyes are our first and most reliable judge of evolutionary fitness.

They look at you, and this is what they see: you are shrinking from everything. Careless, indifferent about work and play and food and ritual contest. There seems never to be enough territory for you—you sidle away from people, seek the farthest remove when attendance at any gathering cannot be avoided. The urge for solitude seems to be a driving force within you. Even—especially—when you are around people, you seem to be somewhere else. But where? Perhaps you are simply within some deep recesses of your own mind, but who can reach you in those remote precincts? More often than most, you slide your eyes across the horizon, sniff the air for the hint of predator or attack. Many of the threats you perceive will seem imaginary to the others, but you remain suspicious of the woods, of the desert, of the trail, of the night—you are suspicious even of those who have known you for years.

This, and many other things, will make you a pain in the ass to just about all and sundry. The village cannot count on you for anything practical and useful, and then there's your slouching retreating profile, your whole antisocial manner. You sit sullen and silent most of the time; if you speak at all it is generally to register some complaint, some dark insight, some dire forecast—apocalyptic bons mots are your conversational bread and butter. And if the neighbors are having a tough time with you, then more's the pity for your family. Your spouse is worried thin about how the family will get through the times ahead, given your disregard for work, and he is also starved for other attentions. When they aren't acting afraid of you, your children seem to find you a mystery: what are they to make of all this incompetence and uncertainty? It's the very last thing they need from you.

We might do well to wonder whether the melancholic would even have a family. What with this condition so evident to all, reproductive success doesn't seem likely at any time, in any place. In any village everyone would know how hard it could become to share quarters with a depressive. In any community with a long memory, this behavior would have been seen in your ancestors, and might have put something of a taint on your stock long before you appeared. And that mask of Saturn cannot form a come-hither look. Charm is absent, physical vitality more than a little lacking. None of the mastery of practical skills our evolutionary good sense would want to be very discerning about. In every particular, the message this one gives off is: don't breed with me.

Survival and reproduction are what evolution prizes most. And this ancestor was in no condition to compete for resources, not even for her day-to-day survival—let alone the future of her particular genetic inheritance. It would be hard to feel optimistic about it. The prospects for this character's survival—and looking into the future, the survival of her DNA—do not look good, not in any landscape.

B. And yet that DNA traveled for 60,000 years—assuming twenty-five years to the generation, that's 2,400 generations. We take that slouching and frightened figure from the ancient landscape and move toward the present day: for 2,400 generations his or her genetic essence survived battles unto the death over some woman or some man, or some stray goat or sheep, and likely over some other things too, so let's say a good many fistfights, Lord knows how many knives or bullets or scimitars or shillelaghs (who knows how much violence this character might have drawn upon his person); a few dozen stillbirths; countless wars; four-legged predators; an untold number of awkward accidents and preoccupied inattentions to basic survival matters; the occasional urge to suicide; the vagaries in available foodstuff owing to drought and flood and war and sometimes individual foolishness too; plagues and epidemics—for 2,400 generations this DNA has lasted through most everything life can hurl at a body.

Through all of this—and despite the anhedonia—this DNA has found some reason to keep coming back, over and again; all this time it's been coming,

C. And then one Sunday near the end of the twentieth century, a man sitting out by a garden and surrounded by splendid scenery and good friends notices that the things he feels attached to seem to be receding from him. He can still smell that garden, but in a one-dimensional way: the smell connects to absolutely nothing, arouses none of the pleasantries, none of the rich store of memory this smell usually carries to him. And he is not enjoying the company of his friends and their children. They've done nothing to provoke this feeling; he is usually quite comfortable with them.

And, as you know, I up and left that circle, and that feeling persisted and persisted. In fact it had been persisting for a long while, perhaps for 60,000 years, some part of the thread that tethers me to my ancestor there on that ancient landscape some 2,400 generations back.

How did we get from A to C? If it is such a threat to our everyday survival, not to mention our reproductive chances—how and why would depression remain in the gene pool?

D. It kept coming back clear into the present generation, and within fifty days of its most recent arrival had me tossing stones into a knapsack, throwing a green corduroy jacket over them.

Now the whole mystery deepens. Really deepens. "Suicide," Kay Redfield Jamison writes, "is as much wired into [depression] as myocardial infarction is for those who have occluded coronary arteries." Think of it: *wired into*. That's suicide, voluntary self-destruction, we're talking about. And there's no denying it: roughly one of every five depressives will eventually commit suicide. According to some extensive Swedish studies, depressives are eighty times more likely than "normals" to attempt suicide. It may be worth repeating in this context: melancholia accounts for some two-thirds of the suicides committed in the United States—where suicide is the eighth leading cause of death (and where death certificates, to suit the church or the family or the insurance policy, don't tell half the story). Recall its close association with all those chronic diseases—diabetes, coronary disease, high blood pressure—that are themselves leading causes of death. Then there is "suicide on the installment plan": an untold additional number of depressives, some clinically designated as such and some not, will self-destruct rather more slowly, by cigarettes or street drugs or whiskey or diet, or some combination thereof; tendencies to these habits are also believed to be heritable.

So for all its lethal inertia, for all its stupefied torpor, depression does make something happen: death. No wonder we think it perverse: it seems to operate wholly in defiance of all we consider "natural." So how do we begin to make any evolutionary sense of it? It removes from the gene pool many of those it inhabits—and yet it persists in our genes. Has been with us, near as we can tell, from the beginnings of human history. And in its everyday effects, depression appears just about entirely "fitness-antagonistic." It doesn't make any earthly sense.

Because it so defies evolutionary logic, a few evolutionary biologists are inclined to dismiss our centuries-old claim that it is inherited, and attribute depression instead to some as yet unknown and unseen virus. Of course, for most of this century we were far more inclined to attribute it to the way one was reared, to the home environment, than to genetics. This had much to do with Freud—but it also had the perhaps unwitting value-added benefit of sparing us the task of trying to make evolutionary sense of depression. Now, though, all our best evidence indicates that, however counter-intuitive it may seem, depression does have some genetic component. If none of your first- or second-degree relatives suffered from depression, you have about a 5 percent chance of developing it sometime in your life. If one of your parents suffered it, your chances increase to 10 percent; if that parent had his or her first episode before the age of twenty, your chances increase to 30 percent; if both parents suffered it, your chances are about 40 percent, and your chances also increase of incurring it in its "Severe" and "Recurrent" forms. Of course "environment" cannot be ruled out in these cases. Among identical, or monozygotic, twins—who share the same genetic material—even when they have been raised separately there is a 50 percent concordance rate for clinical depression and a 70 percent concordance rate for bipolar disorder, both rates significantly higher than concordance rates for fraternal twins, which seems positive evidence that the tendency to these illnesses is genetic.

Evolutionary scientists have in fact given a fair bit of thought to this matter: why is it that genes that contribute to psychiatric illness, genes that appear to be maladaptive, have not been eliminated by natural selection? Somehow in evolutionary terms depression seems to work. It persists, after all these millennia, and not only that; it seems to be on the increase the world over. Hence, as we understand genetics, we should be able to discern some survival value about it. In other words, this seeming predator must come bearing some gifts; it must be somehow "adaptive"; it must, via some anatomical structure or process, or through some behavior or another, make our organism more fit to survive and reproduce.

And it seems that certain manifestations of depression are clearly adaptive. Evolutionary psychology does not conceive of depression as biological psychiatry does; it casts its net rather more broadly, starts with the assumption that depression is a "heterogeneous illness," and aims to encompass the many symptomatic and neuro-chemical differences observed from one depressive to another, as well as the general circumstances that might occasion the illness. So evolutionary psychology includes under its "depression models" the variety we call "situational." And it is this sort of depression that evolutionary psychology can readily explain as adaptive, since in most cases it enables a person to survive in spite of temporarily compromised functional capacities.

Situational depression is, in these models, a "homeostatic regulatory process"—that is, its essential purpose is to conserve energy. Lacking the energy to accomplish necessary tasks, and trying meanwhile to hide the condition, the depressive sends a series of nonverbal signals—the slouch, the solitary behavior, the inability to concentrate on work—that will communicate that energy loss. If you don't have much energy, you figure out pretty quickly how to budget it, how to save it and where to spend it. We must be efficient—rather ruthless, really—about these matters. What would likely go first, according to the evolutionary psychologists, would be social contact of the casual sort, since it fails to yield "survival benefit" commensurate with the energy expended.

Those nonverbal signals also serve to elicit material help from one's kin and neighbors, so that basic survival needs are met without the expense of too much energy. (This, obviously, would have more application in the days before supermarkets and TV dinners and microwave ovens.) These models work very well to explain a first onset of depression that has external, easily identifiable causes: a loss of one's social, occupational, or reproductive status; the death of a loved one; interpersonal conflict that cannot be resolved; the loss of one's home or valued property; and so on. Typically those who suffer these time-limited, mild to moderate depressive episodes will return to active functioning levels and exhibit no further cycles of depression. Their depressions have served them—enabled them to efficiently focus energy, and to drop unrealistic wishes and goals or otherwise change their approach or attitudes. According to the British evolutionary psychiatrist John Price, "the adaptive function of depression . . . is that of assisting individuals in giving up 'attachments,' be they to things, persons, or status." A therapist might call this the "grief process." Once the situationally depressed surrender these attachments, the depression usually vanishes, not to return. Plainly, this variety of depression could confer survival and reproductive advantage, given the proper social circumstances.

And plainly, this situational depression doesn't much resemble what I've been calling melancholia. Evolutionary psychologists generally hold that these "situational" models explain only 15 to 20 percent of all cases of depression. As for the other 80 or 85 percent, there is no "apparent cause" for these, the severe and sometimes chronic conditions that frequently coexist with a melancholic temperament or with manic episodes. To explain the baffling genetic persistence of these, some look to "pleiotropy," which describes a situation when, as evolutionary psychologist Michael McGuire writes in *Darwinian Psychiatry*, "genetic information contributing to minimally adaptive traits may be carried along from generation to generation because such traits are controlled by the same genes that are responsible for an adaptive trait."

McGuire goes on to explain how this might apply to chronic and recurrent cases of melancholia: "Perhaps the clearest example of pleiotropy would be that of greater fecundity among females during reproductive years (the adaptive trait) coupled with late-life (post-reproductive) vulnerability to conditions such as depression (the minimally adaptive trait). In this example, late-life conditions would have a reduced chance of being selected against, while increased fecundity would ensure that the pleiotropic gene(s) will be present in subsequent generations. Similar interpretations have been offered for unipolar depression and bipolar disorder, where a greater-than-chance occurrence of highly creative persons (the adaptive trait) with these disorders has been reported." (Just in case you wonder: Creativity might be adaptive, McGuire cautiously suggests, because it may "foster efficient social navigation and increase mate choice options." But among evolutionary psychologists there is no sort of consensus about that.)

Should this model hold true, it obviously would not apply to all cases of severe and recurrent depression. Even in this model, which might help explain their ongoing existence, depression or bipolar disorder are not seen as adaptive. My own depression ("condition vulnerability prior to condition onset") seemed consistent with the "trait variation" model, which explained "chronic, treatment-refractive depressions" as the result of "chance effects of genetic mixing at conception or biased genetic information"—and I knew that depression was in all four of my family lines. According to Michael McGuire: "The [trait variation] model does not assume that depression is adaptive," and it's hard to see how it could: this sort of depression tends over time to decrease one's biological chances of survival. Because it is recurrent and hence offers slim chance of eventual reciprocation, in village life it would not elicit the altruism that situational depression inspires; and it seldom responds to the lifestyle and attitudinal changes that can ameliorate situational depression.

As for "dysthymia," the *DSM*'s poor cousin to the melancholic temperament—the state marked by chronic mild to moderate depression, usually coupled with "functional capacity limitation," "failed social strategies," and varying degrees of social isolation—evolutionary psychology also has no clue as to what might make this temperament adaptive.

Of course, these are not the last word on the matter. Some evolutionary thinkers, including Stephen Jay Gould, find "adaptationism" rather reductionist anyhow—a charge the evolutionary psychologists seem to have taken to heart in formulating their inclusive and broadranging models of depression. Others hold that depression and the melancholic temperament are "exaptations"—that is, genetic entities that were adaptive at some point in our evolutionary history, but no longer. Vestigial, in other words; a kind of emotional appendix. Others maintain that it is a mutation. Sensible as these views may appear, they have little support. If depression were an exaptation or a genetic mutation, most evolutionary theorists believe, natural selection would have done away with it long ago.

There may in fact be another reason why these phenotypes stay with us: geneticists refer to "assortative mating," the phenomenon whereby individuals with similar phenotypes tend to mate far more often than chance would allow. A person prone to depression is likely to couple with someone similarly predisposed—and it's been observed that this attraction can happen before there's been any evidence of the illness in either partner. Perhaps there is some special pheromone; perhaps melancholics give off a scent known only to one another. It makes for a wonderful accommodation: a person who knows your rather peculiar ways is drawn to you, and may have some clues about how to live with you, since there's every chance he or she has watched parents or grandparents live with it. It is, again, hard to figure why evolution has outfitted us in a way that seems to encourage and increase the ongoing life of this apparently "maladaptive" condition, but there it is.

No surprise: the last word in these matters belongs to Saturn. Worldwide 100 million new cases of depression are reported every year.

ON THE WINTER SOLSTICE, December 21, I found myself in the kitchen preparing a pot of southern-style black beans—nothing too complicated, but still and all the most elaborate dish I'd attempted in months. That evening I was going to a potluck gathering to celebrate the shortest day of the year. The last time I'd tried to attend a party, back in October, I'd gone stiff immediately upon entering the house and walked right back out without speaking.

So this was odd. But directly after returning to Missoula in early December I'd gone again to the music store where I'd bought the Beethoven quartets back in September; the store also sold jewelry and greeting cards and tasteful bric-a-brac, and I was looking for a Christmas gift for my Grandma Thomas. She collected animal miniatures, and had a particular fondness for bears. I spotted a figurine that I thought would be perfect for her, and I was bent down before the glass-fronted cabinet looking at it. Suddenly—I'd heard nobody approaching—through that cabinet a familiar face met my eyes. Those gold round-rimmed glasses, the calm blue eyes.

"Hey." It was Lisa. She smiled. "Haven't seen you in a while. How're those Beethoven quartets?"

"Oh my," I said. They plumbed me as little else could right then. What could I say? I shrugged.

Lisa raised an eyebrow and whistled low, shaking her head. "I know, I know. And how have you been?"

"Fair," I said. I shrugged again. "Just fair." Through the glass I saw her rest her palms on her thighs and push herself up evenly.

I straightened out of my stoop and met her eyes. "I spent Thanksgiving at home," I said, "and I just got back into town. I didn't want to come back. I won't be here much longer anyhow—I finish school in April and I'm off. Going back home. I'll go somewhere in those hills, anyhow." I couldn't believe I was talking like this. I'd spoken of this to nobody, wasn't even aware that I'd actually made any decision to go back home, and here I was telling it all to a stranger. Around this woman, it seemed I was always surprising myself.

Lisa told me that she was a native of Montana. "I think I told you I lived in Auburn, Alabama, for a while. But I didn't much like it there." In those years, she told me, she'd once vacationed in North Carolina—just a few miles north of where I was living at the time, as it turned out.

"I did like it up in those mountains," she told me. She slid open the back door of the glass counter and reached for the bear. "I can see how a person might get attached to them. So green, so many trees, so many plants of all kinds, so much water. Wonderful music too. Best time I had during my whole stay in the sweet sunny South." Her voice had a lilt, so that every sentence had its own melody.

She lifted the bear out of the cabinet and sat it before me. "It is a beautiful thing, isn't it?" she said. She ran her fingers over it. Again I noticed her hands, precise and elegant.

"You know, it's odd," she said. "I've lived in Vienna, and Salzburg, but I have never been so homesick as I was in Alabama, right here in the United States." She told me she was trained to teach English as a second language, and that's what she'd been doing for two years in Austria. After earning her master's in German, she was back in school to become teacher-certified, and was just now finishing up her student teaching. "I'll be able to teach high school German and English as a second language," she said, "but really I'm itching to get back to Europe." In January, she told me, she was going to a job fair in Chicago, for teachers seeking jobs abroad.

"After that, who knows," she said, almost whimsically. She looked down at the bear again. "It looks like a bear, not like some idealized, stylized version of a bear." She leaned back. "Nope, there's nothing cutesy about it. It has the specific look of a folk art carving, don't you think? Would it be rude of me to ask who you are buying it for? It's not for anyone who'd prefer their animals done up soft and cuddly."

She had a point. That didn't apply to my grandmother. I told her that I'd take it and handed her some cash. When she brought my change, I thanked her.

"You've never mentioned your name," she said.

My mouth was dry and I could feel my pulse pounding in my throat. I squeaked out my name and without another word said goodbye.

That was my fear, or my shyness; over the next few days I came to regret my abrupt departure. Lisa seemed like someone I could talk to, someone who put me at my ease—that is, until I started to think about what I was doing.

I wanted to see more of her, wanted at least to apologize for my rudeness, so the following Saturday I returned to the store and pretended to shop. It was just before closing time. Because it was right in front of the cash registers where Lisa was stationed that evening, I planted myself in the rock section. I was flipping mindlessly through the CDs when I felt a hand on my elbow.

"In this section, eh? You must be feeling better," Lisa said. She looked down. "Uncle Tupelo? They're great. A long way from those Beethoven quartets though, isn't it?"

My head dropped reflexively, and I studied on my boots for a moment. I felt my face go red, caught my breath, and willed myself to lift my head. I blurted out my apology for running off so quickly after buying the bear.

"Oh," she said, "don't think twice about it. I see that red face now. You're a bashful one, aren't you? That's what I thought. So it never crossed my mind you were being rude."

Before I could respond a co-worker walked up to ask if she needed a ride home. I gathered that Lisa had ridden her bicycle to work in the morning, before the snow began; it had been falling wet and heavy for five hours now and the streets were passable in a car, but would be treacherous on a bike.

I was about to do it again. I didn't stop myself this time. Before she could respond I broke in—rudely, yes—and said I'd be happy to give her a ride.

"Hmmm," Lisa said. "Are you sure? It's clear over on Poplar."

"Hey," I said, "that's on my way home, so why not?"

"Yeah," she said. "Why not?" She eyed me a little warily. I'd really surprised her this time; maybe I'd gone a little too far.

But she walked with me to the Toyota after she was cashed out, and we started up Higgins on the way to her house and somehow wound up instead turning west on Broadway toward the Forest Lounge, a working-class bar in west Missoula. A friend of Lisa's was behind the bar, and we each got double shots of whiskey on the house—scotch for her, Jack Daniel's for me. We sat down right there by the pool tables.

For hours we talked and sipped our whiskey. Lisa's friend kept our glasses replenished, and if there was anybody else in the bar I don't remember. We talked about all the usual things: our families and the places where we'd been born and raised. Lisa was from the small town of Belt, about twenty miles east of Great Falls, where the Rockies give way to the High Plains. We both preferred to write by hand, rather than at a keyboard, both of us partial to fountain pens, even though neither could afford anything more than a five-dollar steel-nibbed Parker. We talked about her teaching; we talked about music. Lisa's mother was a pianist, her father a fine baritone singer, and all her siblings played one instrument or another, and some of them several. A couple were professional musicians. I dragged out of Lisa the information that she herself played the violin, the piano, the flute, and the guitar, and had sung with several choral groups. Too, we talked about country music, and about the old-time Appalachian music she'd heard in North Carolina, and about the pop music of the 1970s that we'd both had a constant ear to.

I hadn't talked for so long in months. When the bar closed, I drove her home, and before she got out of the car she asked if I'd like to join her at the solstice potluck. I took my black beans, she took a pasta salad, and I enjoyed myself there, talked easily with people. It had been ages since I'd felt so much at ease with strangers.

After leaving that gathering we rode east on Highway 200 out to Gold Creek. We parked the car and walked into the forest; the moonlight spoked through the trees. We climbed the trail, the snow crunching beneath our boots, to the top of the ridge, where we got a clear view of the full moon. We did not touch and scarcely spoke. We just walked, on an old two-track logging road. The air fragrant with pine, winter-crisp. Absolutely still. The snow, laminate there on the ground, seemed to illuminate the sky.

Lisa's Poplar Street house was right at the base of Mount Jumbo, and when we got back to town she asked me in for brandy and cocoa. Small as it was, the house was uncluttered. Folk art paintings hung from her walls; a Czechoslovakian puppet dangled from a curtain rod. All about—atop her desk, on the bathroom counter, in the corner of the kitchen table—were beautiful, spare arrangements of colorful and oddly shaped stones. "They're from Belt Creek," she told me. "It runs past the house where I grew up and into the Missouri River." I didn't mention my own arrangements of turtle shells, oak leaves, acorns, chunks of coal, and now sycamore bark—the souvenirs of home that were all about my rooms.

We sat half the night on the hardwood living-room floor and talked. To my surprise I talked some about my melancholia. As it turned out, Lisa had endured melancholic episodes of her own, and had taken herself off Zoloft some months before. "It took away the depression," she said, "but it made me feel flat and metallic, like nothing could touch me or move me, and that worried me. I don't want to live like that."

I knew she was right; I'd observed a kind of impermeable feeling myself, when the Zoloft was working, but that was a big part of what I had welcomed about it. I told her that I wondered if I ever would have quit them if they had not quit me first.

We fell silent then. She stood to put on a tape. I snuck a glance at her bookshelves. Thomas Mann, Robert Musil, Thomas Bernhard, Ingeborg Bachmann in German; Alice Munro and John Berger and D. H. Lawrence and Willa Cather and Thomas Hardy in English. Lots of others I'd never heard of, in both languages. Out the corner of my eye I saw her walk from the stereo to her desk.

When she came back to the floor she had a book in her hand. "Can I read you something?" she asked. "You know Rilke, right? This is an earlier draft of the Tenth Elegy." She got a sheet of paper off her desktop and sat down in the armchair. "Would you mind to wait just a minute? I translated this in one of my German lit seminars, but I think I can do better now." She tapped her fingers on the arm of the chair. With her fountain pen she scratched a few words onto the paper. Then she cleared her throat and read:

That I someday, after taking leave of the unyielding insight,
    might lift my voice in jubilation and praise to assenting
    angels.
That then not one of the clearly struck hammers of my heart
    will fail
to break the silence because of faint-sounding, uncertain or
    ill-tempered strings.

That my streaming countenance make me more radiant.
That the hidden weeping should then bloom.

How you will be dear to me then, oh nights of despair.
Woe that I have failed to kneel before you, inconsolable
    sisters, failed to more freely surrender myself in your
    loosened hair.

We, who squander our sorrows.
How we look beyond them into the mournful passage of time
to see whether they might end.

But they are seasons of us, yes, our winter—
Abiding leafage, meadows, ponds, landscapes we are born into,
inhabited by birds and creatures in the reeds.

She finished, and I looked away.

"Oh," she said, "I'm so sorry." She left the room; when she came back she set before me another cup of cocoa.

Who was this woman? How had she known? This was just what I needed to hear, at precisely the right time, with the right metaphors to reach me: "They are seasons of us . . . landscapes we are born into . . ." It was a little haunting, yes—but mostly it was comforting: to be seen, to be comprehended in such a way.

On Christmas Eve Lisa was leaving for Belt, three hours northeast of Missoula, to spend the holiday with her family. While she was gone, I would feed her cat and collect her mail, so that morning I stopped by to get her housekey.

She poured me a cup of tea. "I just got off the phone," she told me. It had been one of her professors, offering her a job teaching English in Moldova for the George Soros Foundation. It was the first I'd ever heard of the place.

"Moldova is a former Soviet state—between Romania and the Ukraine in Eastern Europe." She drew her breath. "The capital city is in Chisinău, which is where I'd be teaching. The job isn't permanent—it starts in January and lasts about six months. I'd leave town on January 6." She looked at the calendar. "Jesus God, that's in two weeks.

"It's exactly what I want to be doing," she went on. She was thinking out loud, I knew. She had a big decision to make, and apparently she had to make it quickly. "It'll save me the trip to Chicago. And I've been wondering how I'd ever start paying off my student loans. The record store wage only goes so far, you know. This is a real stroke of good fortune."

I nodded and told her I was pleased for her.

She called Christmas morning and told me she thought she would accept the job. "But," she said, "it's been a hard decision to make."

She paused for so long I wondered if she was still there. Was I supposed to say something? Nothing came to me.

Finally she went on: "The timing couldn't be worse. I mean, three weeks ago I wouldn't have had to think about it. But now, it seems like—it seems like—" Her voice trailed off. She sighed and started in again: "I don't want to make any assumptions. But it seems that maybe this is something we've got started here. Something real."

She paused and laughed out loud. "Listen to me. Here I am almost thirty years old and I'm all twittery and nervous like some schoolgirl. Anyhow. What do you think about it?"

I could not stop to think, or I would never say it, so I just blurted on ahead: "You're right, this is something we've got started here, and I really don't think your being away for six months will make too much difference over the long haul. Of course you should take this job. We'll stay in touch while you're gone, we'll wear out our pens writing letters." For one perpetually in doubt and ambivalent about everything, including love, this kind of certainty was a real surprise. And where did this hopeful tone come from?

It was all new, so new that right after I hung up the phone the doubts began to swirl: my melancholia might undo this, as it had with Barbara and me. And what about moving back to Appalachia? And six months apart might be a good thing, for a couple that had been together for some time; but we were just starting out. Like nearly every one of my friends, I had tried this long-distance relationship thing before, and knew how it could unravel a relationship. Perhaps I should have waited, given the matter more thought, been more diffident.

That train of thought played itself out pretty quickly. Something here was different. Obviously, in just six months she'd be back in Missoula, so we weren't talking long-term long-distance relationship. But this difference went beyond that. I remembered our drive home from Gold Creek three nights before: we had ridden for miles and miles through a moonlit snowscape without speaking, and it had been comfortable. This gentle woman with calm eyes, elegant hands, and an ear for poetry had shared long silence with me, and easily. My mouth had spoken true.

EVOLUTIONARY PSYCHOLOGY'S "TRAIT VARIATION" MODEL, you will remember, "does not assume that [this type of] depression is adaptive," as Michael McGuire so gently puts it. But McGuire goes on: "This model . . . does not preclude the possibility that help will be provided by others or that persons who are depressed will attempt to act adaptively." I was absolutely blessed with help that fall: from Dr. Beans, from my clients, from Don and other friends, from Anita, from my family, from Lisa, from all the books I was finding. But acting adaptively? I wasn't ready for that one.

Surely McGuire is right: our depressed ancestor's neighbors must have helped in many ways—perhaps in part by finding something useful for her to do, something that particularly suited her nature. Perhaps filling such a role was the melancholic's "attempt to act adaptively." Those same almanacs, shepherd's calendars, health manuals, and learned treatises that provide us with an iconography for melancholia also suggest some of the ways our kind has adapted to the melancholic temperament and illness. Homeopathy and humoral theory held that we live best when we live faithful to our native constitution, and living in that fashion was thought the best chance one possessed of the melancholic temperament had to avoid the illness—so these publications counseled their readers about how to accomplish it. Since the documents I'm drawing from here—many of them cited in *Saturn and Melancholy*—were aimed at very different audiences, from the well educated to the peasant, they reveal a variety of roles the melancholic might fill, according to his or her station. And we can presume that these documents represent centuries of handed-down observation, folk wisdom, and scholarly ideas about the saturnine temperament and the depressive illness.

A goodly number of those broadsides and almanacs show a saturnine character manning some solitary outpost, a crescent moon above: the night watchman. This would fit nicely with his (and this one is always a "he") circadian rhythm. He was always up most of the night anyhow, and as a rule more alert and attentive then, if not more sociable. No doubt the solitary nature of such work appealed to him also. Then there was his loyalty. For all his indecisions and uncertainties otherwise, he was generally thought to be a loyal man.

And you want a loyal man standing guard for you. Well aware that he was not to the liking of many people, to those who showed sincere interest he returned ardent attachment—never, of course, the stay-right-at-your-elbow sort, but when he was on your side you always knew it.

And he treasured his territory; "guards it jealously" described his relationship to it precisely. How sure he was to look about him, to gauge his space when you walked up on him, trying to decide just how far he needed to be from you, and making sure he had sufficient room to maneuver. We might say today that the saturnine man had an extended sense of personal space, perhaps extending clean out to the borders, and he would protect it.

According to a number of elegantly designed contemporary studies, it is not the depressive who views the world with any marked bias, any "delusional overlay." Seems it is the "normal" who sees with bias, a "self-enhancing" bias. That is, the nondepressive tends to perceive both the self and worldly events with "an illusory glow . . . in an excessively positive light."

This last is not the man for your watchtower. These studies suggest that melancholics are more likely to give dead-on depictions of themselves, the daily news, and our prospects for the future. In place of the illusory glow, the melancholic character possesses what those same researchers are calling "depressive realism." That may be a gift to him or it may be a curse; all we can say is he is always alert for the threat, looking always as if he were under some siege, and since in his mind he has already played any scenario out to the worst possible case, he isn't likely to panic should havoc ensue.

So woe be unto any who haunt his watch. He wants no change coming his way, none at all, and he knows that change always arrives from across the border. So he's guarding it with a vengeance; and he is making that temperament useful for his community's survival.

According to evolutionary psychologists, the greater prevalence of depression among women has been more or less constant throughout human history. The literature bears this out. In these old documents, in representations of the illness we frequently see a woman alone and disheveled in her rooms, or alone in a crowd.

This woman might also be in a sitting room looking distracted, as in Lucas Cranach's "Melancholy," from 1528, with a cat on her lap as the children carry on raucously, looking well accustomed to their mother's undisciplined approach to child care. Or she may be about the sewing, as in a Dutch health manual of the sixteenth century—or, rather, the sewing is on her lap, elbows pressed into her thighs, her head bent into her palm. She is frequently seen tending to or collecting plants, as in the eighteenth-century German painter Eduard von Steinle's "Melancholy." Sometimes she is some manner of priestess or visionary or healer. If she appears with any partner in these illustrations he will appear melancholic too. Perhaps we've noticed "assortative mating" for a long while.

Le Blon's woodcut "Four Types of Melancholy," created in 1628 as the frontispiece for the third edition of Burton's *Anatomy*, illustrates one melancholic type with a monk reciting the rosary. Judging by all these old texts, Saturn was thought very likely to fit one to the shape of a religious. He was the god of "timeless wisdom" and "philosophical reflection," and seemed to endow his children with speculative and abstracted habits of mind. This held true from the classical era into the Middle Ages and beyond, when, as Le Blon's woodcut indicates, monastics male and female were thought predominantly of the melancholic temperament, and especially vulnerable to the illness. Anthropologists have observed that in a variety of indigenous cultures, among them the Alaskan Inuit and Australian Aboriginals, melancholics were likely to be installed as shamans or priestesses or prophets.

It seems too widespread to attribute this simply to the cherished Romantic idea about the mentally ill being somehow closer to God. Consider this from a utilitarian perspective; consider the community good. These contemplative roles called for solitude, and often required periodic ritualistic retreats from the everyday commerce of the village. So, the village elders could demand of the melancholic shaman or the medicine woman: Hey, last summer we sent you on a two-moon vision quest. And our harvest was better than it's ever been. How about a three-moon quest this time?

Don't get me wrong: I don't mean to imply that these people, whoever they might be, were greedy, or unkind. Not at all. Perhaps they were genuinely seeking some spiritual growth. But let's be frank about this—there's something to be said for a planned vacation from the melancholic type, and if extending it brings more whales or more corn or more game come fall, then that's just gravy. And truly, there was nothing unkind about it: the melancholic type was known to welcome the long spell of solitude. So this was your basic win-win situation.

And some evolutionary psychologists speculate that the "status improvement" attendant on being raised to such a position would increase reproductive allure enough to compensate for the obvious drawbacks of the melancholic temperament and illness. So perhaps these "promotions" would also help the community assure that this type stayed in the gene pool. This might be taken to mean that they wanted the melancholic around, even with all the trouble.

One of the keynotes of the melancholic temperament is its propensity for removal, for escape; recall what the contemporary humoralists refer to as the "avoidant" nature of the "inhibited" child. Often that remove is to the imagination, and living in the imagination, as many of these seem to do, might help explain the "creative" tendencies of this temperament; whether with voice or lute or pencil or brush, many of them seem bent on moving some envisioned world from the imagination out into the everyday world. The idea that the melancholic type was particularly well suited for solitary intellectual or creative endeavor goes back at least to the fourth century B.C. when Anstotle asked in his *Problemata*: "Why is it that all those who have become eminent in philosophy or politics or poetry or the arts are clearly of the atrabilious temperament, and some of them to such an extent as to be affected by diseases caused by black bile?"; it is seen again in Marsilio Ficino in the Italian Renaissance, and is nearly stereotypical still: the melancholic bard, the depressive keeper of the stories, the reclusive artist. And there's no question: from antiquity to the present, the number of the world's great artists and writers who've been of the melancholic temperament, or suffered from the illness, or both, is far too large to list here; but to give some idea I will limit myself to a few of the American writers and artists who were melancholic in one sense or another: among our poets John Berryman, Hart Crane, Emily Dickinson, T. S. Eliot, Randall Jarrell, Jane Kenyon, Robert Lowell, Edna St. Vincent Millay, Sylvia Plath, Edgar Allan Poe, Ezra Pound, Theodore Roethke, Delmore Schwartz, Anne Sexton, and Walt Whitman; among our novelists and playwrights Samuel Clemens, Ralph Waldo Emerson, William Faulkner, F. Scott Fitzgerald, Ernest Hemingway, Henry James, Herman Melville, Eugene O'Neill, and Tennessee Williams; and among our artists Ralph Barton, Thomas Eakins, Georgia O'Keeffe, Jackson Pollock, and Mark Rothko. (This list comes from Kay Redfield Jamison's *Touched with Fire*, which is essential reading for anybody interested in the matter of madness and the artistic temperament.) Such a list raises an interesting, if finally futile, question: what would the American museums or our literary canon look like had psychotropic medications been available 150 years, or even 50 years, earlier?

For such work, the melancholic was thought to be gifted with a penchant for solitude, with a ravenous curiosity, with a rather fastidious and perfectionist nature (recall the hedgehog), and with the ability to bring great concentration to bear on a particular subject—the sort of submersion into another realm that this character could sink into with relative ease. When immersed in such fashion, many physicians noted, the melancholic type seemed to evince a stamina otherwise missing from his character.

Wandering minstrelsy would be indicated, just for the long hours of solitude moving slowly about the countryside. Not to mention the long-observed saturnine love of music and story. Prized commodities, song and story and news and gossip. This would give the melancholic minstrel a means of support much valued by others: he comes to the village and in exchange for these gets his bread and board. In fact, those talents probably brought to the traveling minstrel a bounty of premiums—if long legend be any guide, sexual favors prominent among them. If this be true, the role might also impart some of that compensatory reproductive advantage. Minstrelsy would also free the antisocial saturnine character from living wholly within polite society.

The stay-at-home village bard or story keeper seems a fitting role as well. Illustrations of "Saturn's Children" from Germany and Spain and England show the saturnine type with a lute or some other musical instrument, and this character was thought to have a tenacious memory (for the things he or she wanted to recall, anyway). Such a role would, of course, suit a solitary nature, as well as one that sought immersion in something without the self: what else does story do, after all? And in story and song this character might even reveal a wit, a bent for humor, that was nowhere evident in your everyday contact with him or her. The melancholic temperament and illness seem inextricably woven into some of the finest comics of our century, among them James Thurber and Charlie Chaplin.

Art is useful—whether or not creativity confers any reproductive advantage, there's no mistaking our visceral and historical need for stories and songs and painting. It seems it must be wired into us. So the melancholic could bring the gifts of her temperament to something absolutely necessary to any community. The songs and stories of a people and their place are diversion, yes; but also they are instruction and worship: they carry tradition and history and place and ethics. They are in themselves a force of nature.

In times past, the scientist was thought just as likely a candidate for melancholia or mania as the writer or artist or scholar. (Of course, times past did not discriminate quite so finely as we do about what is "art" and what is "science.") Melancholia seems to have had some particular affinity for those who spent their nights gazing into the cosmos: when the seven liberal arts were apportioned among the planets, astronomy was placed under the aegis of Saturn because, according to Dante, it was the "highest" and the "surest" of the arts. Of course it also offered solitude and would be nicely fitted to the melancholic's night-owlish circadian rhythm. The practice of geometry was also thought to have a particular attraction for the melancholic type; if you see a character bearing a compass in any of those old health manuals, you can guess it will be the saturnine.

Biography would seem to bear these ideas out. Throughout his life Isaac Newton suffered bouts of melancholia: in 1662, just before his twenty-first birthday, he threatened suicide, and considered it over again throughout his life. It seems Charles Darwin also suffered severe episodes of depression. All his life Darwin suffered from some "unidentified illness" that caused violent headaches, pains about the heart, and a whole battery of stomach troubles, all typically preceded, then accompanied by, a severe depression. Biographers tell us he was full of gloom and misery for months before he finally embarked on the voyage of the *Beagle*. (Perhaps Darwin, like Melville's Ishmael and many other young men of the nineteenth century, was encouraged to take to the sea to remedy his case of "the hypos"; if so, perhaps in a roundabout way we owe the theory of natural selection, conceived on that same voyage, to a case of depression.) For eighteen months after his return to England, Darwin reported being "too depressed to read." And not for the last time. In 1959, the American physician and medical writer Walter Alvarez asserted in the *New England Journal of Medicine* that Darwin's symptoms constituted no mysterious illness; they were simply "the manifestation of depression"—which sounds very much like the "somatizing" today's anthropologists talk about.

According to the ancients, because of his close association with earth, Saturn also fitted those born under his influence to be out of doors, working in the soil, caring for animals, studying the natural world, working with wood and with stone. Of course, Kronos and Saturn were the classical Gods of Agriculture, their iconic symbol the scythe of harvest (and also of reaping the dead). We sometimes see the melancholic type depicted with that scythe, and later with a sickle; we also see him or her with a pickax, a spade, a rake, a hoe—any number of implements, and one clear meaning: this solitary earthbound type was very well suited to the garden. Many believed "hands in the dirt" a specific cure for melancholia.

Later illustrations show the melancholic type afoot or afield in the wilds. Abraham Bloemaert's eighteenth-century portrait of "Melancholy" is typical: a young woman sits on a stool, a botanical guide open before her, drawing pad leaning against the same tree that she will, we presume, get around to studying on if ever she lifts her chin out of her hand. Gardeners, naturalists, herb gatherers: the type was thought to have some particular subterranean affinity for plants. Interestingly enough, a plant biologist friend tells me that the "sadness of botanists" is still a commonplace in the field.

Some believe that among naturalists, Meriwether Lewis ranks with Darwin. On the Lewis and Clark expedition, he "discovered" and described three hundred heretofore unclassified species—178 plants and 122 varieties of fauna. His precise observations of wildlife and flora and his richly detailed writing make the journals of Lewis and Clark worth reading even without the plot; so it's a little disappointing that from time to time Lewis' entries will come to a halt, not to reappear for months, with no explanation offered. According to Stephen Ambrose, Lewis was in one of his fits of melancholia as the Corps of Discovery reached the Pacific, for of that momentous occasion—the mission accomplished—we have not a word from him. "Lewis had from early life been subject to hypochondriac affections. It was a constitutional disposition in all the nearer branches of the family of his name"; so wrote Thomas Jefferson, who was Lewis' mentor. Knowing of Lewis' fits of melancholia, Jefferson still had faith enough to put him in partial command of the expedition. We know how well placed that faith was. But it was life back in civilian society that Lewis found hard, as Jefferson realized: "after his establishment at St. Louis in sedentary occupations they [Lewis' "distressing affections"] returned upon him with redoubled vigor . . ."

Three years and a month after the Corps returned from the West, on October 11, 1809, Lewis was dead, a suicide, dogged by debt and political scandal—Jefferson had appointed him governor of the

Louisiana Territory, and Lewis made a botch of the job. Lewis had attempted suicide many times: hurled himself off boats and tried to shoot himself. This time, with a gun and a razor, he succeeded. Lewis started the job with the razor, hacking off great chunks of his flesh, and then put his pistol to his temple. To his servant, who came running upon hearing the gunshot, Lewis said, "I have done the business my good servant give me some water." Upon hearing the news his dear friend and former traveling companion William Clark wrote to a mutual friend, "I fear O' I fear the weight of his mind has overcome him."

The blueblood son of a Boston Unitarian minister, Francis Parkman had his own calling. In 1831, when he was eight years old, Francis fell ill and was sent to recover on his grandparents' farm in Medford, some miles outside of Boston. He wound up staying there for five years, infatuated with the woods of Middlesex Fells. Just before his return to Boston, Parkman had a kind of vision, and he spent the rest of his life trying to fulfill it. After his vision thoughts of the ancient forest, as he would write years later, speaking of himself in the third person, "possessed his waking and sleeping dreams, filling him with vague cravings, impossible to satisfy."

By the time he was a sophomore at Harvard, in 1841, Parkman thought he knew how those cravings might be met: he would write a history of the great eastern forest. He aimed to write, according to Simon Schama, "an American history with the forest as its principal character." Parkman's ambition is breathtaking still: he wanted to tell two hundred and fifty years of Euro-American history, and he wanted to speculate intelligently about the origins, habits, and character of the Native Americans on the eastern side of the continent. By his own edict he would use primary sources only. But his research would occasion what Parkman most enjoyed in life: long hours of walking in those forests. He began in earnest during the summer of 1842, walking from Boston into the White Mountains of New Hampshire; he also began to gather primary sources for his "History of France and England in the New World."

Before the next summer arrived, however, Parkman would suffer his first episode of melancholia. He was forced to abandon his studies for several months. Another of Le Blon's "portraits of the melancholic" is labeled "Hypochondriac": a man (need I mention the head in the hand?), with a towel about the forehead, dozens upon dozens of medicine bottles about, etc.: this was one of the oldest and best known of melancholic variants. To our ears a derisive slur, in Burton's time and for many years thereafter the term "hypochondria" was applied to cases of melancholia where the illness tended to present itself alongside a raftload of physical symptoms. It was thought just about particular to men. "Hypochondria" was Parkman's specific diagnosis; as it was Lewis', and it would seem to fit Darwin's case as well. Parkman's episodes were grueling, and they returned frequently. Along with the characteristic depressive mood he was stricken by arthritic pains in his knees, a racing heart, and, most markedly, an inability to bear the sun.

But Parkman continued his treks into the wilderness, trying to imagine his way into the forest of years past. He walked from his home near Boston to Lake Champlain, to Lake George, over and again into the White Mountains. He was painstaking and persnickety about his research; according to Schama, "Sometimes this naïve passion for authenticity, the need to hear a twig break beneath his foot as it had for Champlain or Howe, led him directly to disaster. In his wanderings he fell from sheer cliff paths; sank to his chest in swamp; was eaten alive by clouds of ravenous blackfly; and pitched from his flimsy canoe into the bone-chilling waters of the Magalloway. His body began to record these histories in scars, dislocations, dull muscular aches that in later life would cripple legs and arms."

In just about every way, Parkman fails today's standards of enlightened tolerance. He vehemently opposed woman suffrage; he loathed the Sioux people he lived among in South Dakota, while traveling the Oregon Trail, as "thorough savages." For all that, though, there is a rather heroic dimension to Parkman. His life was fairly agonizing: his elder son, Francis, died in 1857, and his wife the following year. Before and after these deaths he struggled constantly with melancholia. And yet, the life he made for himself. Without particular training, he became an accomplished botanist: turned his

Jamaica Pond property in Boston into an arboretum of sorts, bred a new variety of flower, the *lilium Parkmanii*, and in 1866 authored *The Book of Roses*, a classic of horticulture. In 1871 Harvard College hired him as a professor of horticulture, but Parkman was unable to adjust to campus society, and he left the position before the academic year was out. He continued with his extensive walking trips through the American forests, journeying all over Michigan and Illinois and Iowa and Pennsylvania and up to Nova Scotia and New Brunswick.

And he worked on his history. It was a slow process: Parkman was meticulous, and his encompassing project meant his research needs were exhaustive. Worse, there was his condition. Parkman's melancholia left him unable to bear even ambient sunlight, or to write with his eyes open, or to concentrate on any subject for more than a few minutes at a time. To accomplish any research or writing he would block the light from his rooms with impermeable blinds (which he designed himself) and work by candlelight. He rigged boxes of wood and wire so that he could write a straight line on the page while his eyes were closed. Finally, in 1892, fifty-five years after he'd conceived it, Parkman finished his life's work, which by then ran to nine individual volumes. He died the following year. Today, Parkman's history is one of the unheralded classics of American narrative prose. "[T]here was little on Francis Parkman's written pages to suggest a man stranded at the border of his sanity," writes Schama. "Whether dictated or painfully penciled along the wire guides of his writing frame, the end result was often expansive, thoughtful and elegant, and at times sardonic. Despite the periodic descents into anguish, in writing *The Conspiracy of Pontiac* (the first volume in the history) Parkman believed he had held at bay . . . the formless beast that stalked his footsteps in and out of the forest of his mind." In concluding, Schama says of Parkman: "Only in his blackness could he make those words live."

Horace Kephart's is a classic melancholic downward mobility tale. Kephart was born in 1862, in the Allegheny Mountains of Clearfield County, Pennsylvania. His forebears had settled the area in the

1770s, and in Horace's youth he heard from his grandfather endless stories of the pioneer days. In 1865 his father, a Church of the Brethren minister, returned from serving as a chaplain in the Union Army and uprooted the family to Jefferson, Iowa, still largely a frontier territory in those years. In that grassland Kephart was an only child, and had no neighbor children to cavort with. According to the writer Jim Casada, Kephart "traveled largely in the realms of imagination." During that secluded childhood, Casada says, "a desire for solitude, a craving for the quiet splendor of untrammelled ways, first became manifest in his soul." Kephart started college there in Iowa at the ripe age of thirteen; the following year, 1876, when the family returned to Pennsylvania, Kephart enrolled at Lebanon Valley College, from which he graduated in 1879.

He went next to Boston University for advanced studies in zoology, and while there began working in the library. He found himself enjoying this work wholeheartedly, so from that library Kephart moved in 1881 to Cornell University, where he served as head cataloguer under the renowned bibliophile Willard Fiske. Fiske fell out with the Cornell administration and, independently wealthy, moved himself to Florence, devoting himself to collecting Dante and Petrarch manuscripts and early editions. In 1885 Kephart followed, and spent a year in Italy learning from Fiske the bibliophile's trade. When Kephart returned to America he married Laura Mack of Ithaca and in 1887 the couple settled in New Haven, where Kephart had landed a job as assistant librarian at Yale College. But he tired quickly of life in New Haven, and began looking about for a position that would offer him the opportunity to pursue his deepest interest: the American wilderness.

In 1890 Kephart got his wish, when he was hired to run the St. Louis Mercantile Library. This was one of the best appointments in the nation: the Mercantile was the first library west of the Mississippi River, and was in those years regarded as one of the finest libraries in the nation. Kephart went about building its collection of western American pioneer literature—diaries and memoirs and travel journals—and along the way became an oft-consulted and oft-cited authority in the field. His assistant at the library, Clarence Miller, remembered him years later: "Kephart was easily the most brilliant man I have known, and almost as a matter of course, the least assuming."

Kephart held that job for several years, he and Laura had six children, and the couple became part of St. Louis' cultural aristocracy. Then something happened. "At the turn of the century," writes Casada, "Kephart's outlook upon life underwent a fundamental change. He became disenchanted with the basic context of his home life . . . He drifted away from his friends." According to Miller, Kephart was always "a withdrawn and baffling man who lived entirely in a world of his own"; but now, Miller said, "the aura of loneliness about him increased." He drew up an outline for a sweeping history of western settlement, modeled after Parkman's work (the Bettmann Archive portrait of Parkman hung on Kephart's office wall) and in the library apparently spent more time researching that project than attending to his administrative duties.

Then he began to spend weeks and weeks away from the library, on solo walking excursions into the Arkansas swampland and the Ozark Mountains. In 1901 Kephart inked the words "Songs of Barbarism" onto the cover of a small bound notebook. Inside he copied aphorisms and quotes from the usual Romantic suspects—Wordsworth, Shelley, Byron, George Eliot. But Kephart copied in more passages by far from the work of literary naturalists: Lewis and Clark, W. H. Hudson, George Catlin, Richard Jeffries, and, of course, Francis Parkman. The overarching theme of that notebook, according to another biographer, George Ellison, was "the decadence of an overly civilized, material, urban life and the corresponding virtue of a more-or-less primitive style of existence."

Kephart was, in a sense, trying to live in both these worlds. It couldn't last long. In the fall of 1903, according to Miller, the library's board, "alienated about Kephart's camping trips," fired him. Just before Christmas, Laura left him and moved back to Ithaca with their children. By April of 1904, Kephart was in a St. Louis hospital, the victim of a "complete nervous collapse." His father came West and removed Kephart to the care of his family, now living in Dayton, Ohio.

As he recuperated, the forty-two-year-old Kephart came up with a plan: he would move to the most remote wilderness in the eastern United States. That would be the southern Appalachians, and Kephart arrived in western North Carolina in the fall of 1904 and found himself a secluded corner of primeval forest, land that is now within the Great Smoky Mountains National Park. Of that move, Casada writes: "He immediately found the solitude and tranquility he had sought. The peacefulness in turn provided him much-needed surcease from society's strictures. Arriving in Dillsboro, North Carolina, apparently in a perilous state of health, he soon settled down on nearby Dick's Creek. Living in a tent, Kephart had ample opportunity to begin what would become a career devoted in large measure to the arts of camping and woodcraft."

Kephart had found his niche, and he went native in a thoroughgoing way. He studied local plants, local dialect, local crafts, local cooking, and he made himself part of his community. He turned his back-to-the-land lifestyle into an authoritative volume of practical woods wisdom, *Camping and Woodcraft*, first published in 1906, and in print yet today. It is a stunning, encyclopedic work of woods lore, still current even if our tent-making and camp-cooking technology is rather different. *Our Southern Highlanders*, published to great acclaim in 1922 and still held to be among the finest books about the people and landscapes of the southern Appalachians, also remains in print.

Once he moved to the Smokies, Kephart's restlessness ceased; he stayed in the mountains for twenty-five years, until his death. From his writing—contemporary "outdoorsmen" considered *Camping and Woodcraft* their bible—he had some modest fame; he was asked to plot the path the Appalachian Trail follows through the Smokies. In the 1920s he lent his considerable influence to the movement to establish the Great Smoky Mountains National Park, writing innumerable letters and articles to generate support for it. Privately Kephart was ambivalent about the idea—he knew that turning this wilderness into a national park would dispossess hundreds of his neighbors of their land, and he knew that the tourist trade sure to follow a national park would spoil the character of the area. But he also foresaw logging and mining enterprises working in nearly every watershed, and came to feel that a park was the only way to save any portion of it. Today one of the peaks in the Smokies is named Mount Kephart.

On an April morning in 1931, Kephart died in an automobile accident as he was driving a winding mountain road home from his bootlegger's place. His funeral, held in a small town near the Smokies, was filled to overflowing by the local people. "I owe my life to these mountains," Kephart wrote in his later years. Downward he traveled, and landed right on the landscape that would save him.

All of these are only models; they are only stories. But sometimes stories are all we have. Sometimes they are all we need.

Don't get me wrong: I'm not trying to imply any rigid determinism, and I'm not claiming any superiority for this temperament or illness. Every priest or watchman or gardener or naturalist was not melancholic. Nor was every melancholic a poet or painter or visionary. I don't read these stories that way. What they offer are hints and suggestions, based on centuries of observation. To me they are a guide for the uncertain: you might recognize yourself in that portrait of the saturnine temperament, and perhaps that would help you find some place for yourself. It is a heartening thing to contemplate: our kind has always been adaptable, flexible, and creative enough to accommodate, and even incorporate, this strange temperament and illness into our communities.

And I'm sure that Parkman and Kephart, and all those melancholic writers and poets and musicians and composers, were not unique among their contemporaries. In the long-ago days before the Psychotropic Age, this was what people did, artists and astronomers, farmers and the mothers of children: they made a life with melancholia. They adapted to it.

Of course, that didn't often cure the condition; but what would? No matter what they did or what honor their work brought to them, melancholics never seemed very happy, if you want to use that word; or "satisfied," if you prefer that one. But with such work perhaps

they found some blessed immersion, which seemed as near to fulfillment as they could approach.

More stories: some Jungians, who assert that the "collective unconscious" is a kind of evolutionary adaptation to the ontological mystery of life, hold that our folklore tells us about the function of
depression. They claim that the many mythic "journeys to the underworld" arise in part from the melancholic experience, and make
some sense of it. Consider the Sumerian story of Inanna (the Assyri-
ans knew her as Ishtar), the Goddess of the Above. Recorded on
cuneiform tablets in the third millennium B.C., it is one of the first
written stories we have. This alone should attest to its import; too,
this "story motif" is found in folklore the world over. For reasons
that vary from one version to another, Inanna is made to journey to
the Underworld. On her departure from the Above, all the creatures
forget how to procreate, the rain ceases and all plant life falls dead.
    Once in the Underworld, Inanna is made to disrobe, layer by
layer — as if she must shed the familiar self. Then she is summoned
by Ereshkigal, the dark Goddess of the Underworld. Ereshkigal calls
Inanna "sister," and in her Inanna seems to glimpse some shadowed
version of her self. Ereshkigal hangs Inanna from a peg—stripped of
her ordinary identity, her customary garments, and having envisioned that disquieting doppelgänger so many melancholics are ac-
quainted with, Inanna is left alone—for all intents and purposes
dead—in the Underworld. And months later Inanna emerges newly
formed, a wiser and more enduring woman, and all life returns to
the world of the Above. Then there is the story of Persephone, the
Greek Goddess of the Underworld: without her yearly, season-long
visits to the Underworld no earthly plant life would sprout, no animals seek mates.
    To the Jungians, the lesson of such stories is this: melancholia-like
descent is necessary to the individual, and plainly—nobody eats
without it—to the larger culture too.

•   •   •

One story or another; and it's all just guesswork, really. Oh, this melancholia is some wild thing, finally, predatory and unfathomable; ultimately as unknowable to us as the wolf and the whale. We can't figure its place, and we go on trying to be entirely shed of it; and yet it goes on and on, indifferent to our judgments, making its own place. Calling us, it would seem. Down those 2,400 generations it has come back and back and back, finding reasons to endure even through the anhedonia; and calling us, it would seem, to something.

Calls us and calls us and calls us; and are we listening?

ROOTS ARE ETERNALLY HELL-BENT. You see them in the forest, spidering out from atop stones; you see them in desert canyons crevassing down between the walls to some small trickle; you see them arching over swamp water; but for all these local variations they are single-minded: without fail they will descend. Descend into the dark earth, and shape themselves into long tongues to tangle and twine and branch toward water. Hell-bent they are, but for good reason. All these splendid adaptations—all these shapes they take as they reach into the unknown—accomplish their aim: to draw life from the dirt.

On December 29, I walked out the back door of my building and headed down to the riverfront path toward Lisa's house, where we were going to celebrate my birthday. Just past the Higgins Avenue bridge, right out from the summertime swimming hole, a gathering of ducks made a circle on the water; all about them the river was iced over. One after another they left that circle, amidst a great rustling of wings and honking and squawking. As one departed, another would return.

For a long while I stood there and watched them. All that day I was full of a welling gratefulness. Now there was this much tangible life before me: the night before, Lisa had returned from Belt, and we'd made some plans. Since regular telephone communication would be expensive, and the postal service rather unreliable, not to mention slow—mail from Moldova to the United States, she'd learned, could take four weeks to arrive—I would get an Internet account at the university and for the six months of her stay we would stay in touch by E-mail. Thanks to its benefactor and guiding spirit, George Soros, the school in Moldova was outfitted with the latest computers. E-mail would be free to both of us, so thanks to this new technology, we would be able to court in the old-fashioned way; by correspondence.

In the week before she left for Moldova, all sorts of magical things would occur: we would spend New Year's Eve soaking in the pools at Hot Springs, Montana; the next day, a glorious Rocky Mountain winter's day, clear and sunny, with the mountains towering all about us we brought in the New Year driving back to Missoula and singing along with the Carter Family and Elton John. And as we lay in bed early in the morning of her departure, over the radio would come one of those late Beethoven quartets, Opus 135.

Not so long ago, I had avoided the bridges that crossed this river; just four months before, I had planned to drown myself a few miles downstream. It seemed that was some other person. A very lucky man is what I was, walking in that December dusk, having survived another year, almost in spite of myself, and here I was walking under the sign of Saturn, already out in the southwest sky, shining full in the peak of his season; and I was walking once again along the Clark Fork River, taking it in, and when I arrived at my destination we would celebrate. I was grateful: I was walking somewhere, and when I got there the door would open and the smell of warmth and food would flood out into the night and this clear-eyed, evenhanded woman, this smart and sane woman, would embrace me.

The shape of the root is where diversities draw together and make something new: it is where soil and water and light join to make wood and leaf, to make nut and fruit and flower. All this life begins in one place: beneath the earth.

"NATURAL HISTORY." I relish this old-fashioned phrase, have since I first heard it. I like its implication: Nature is *story*.

Modern psychiatry still uses the term "natural history," to describe the course of a mental illness unimpeded by "effective medication"—by which is meant pharmaceuticals or electroconvulsive therapy. This "natural history" would be melancholia's story, told by its own self in collaboration with those it inhabits. Whether or not this particular usage of "natural history" would apply to my own case is a matter of interpretation. The American psychiatrists I'm familiar with don't consider homeopathic remedies "effective medication" for mental illness, since the remedies don't meet their definition of "effective": they don't offer rapid elimination of the symptoms. To me it seemed that if the remedy worked, it would shift the narrative of my melancholia in some "effective" manner. Some homeopaths agree with that.

Others contend that the remedy only meant to restore balance sufficient to help me integrate melancholia's narrative into my own. Maybe melancholia's story would not be changed, and I was the movable object in that relationship; in that case the remedy might engender some shift of my perspective, and make for a kind of merged natural history.

For who knows where melancholia's natural history leaves off? There seems little question that, as Kay Redfield Jamison puts it, the melancholic view of reality "looks out onto the fleeting nature of life, decay, the finality of death, and the finite role of humans in the universe." Vanity, vanity, all is vanity. This outlook must follow from melancholia's very biology: it is some part of what makes its story move; it is some part of its natural history. We might say that melancholia raises the same sort of questions that Job addressed to God.

For there is something divine about it: omnipotent and omniscient—and mysterious too, accomplishing so much even while shrouding its cause, its purpose, its origin, its precise location. No wonder we finally flung up our hands and explained it by pointing in an offhand way at Saturn, that old dark god reigning in the cold distances of the firmament and in the fearsome depths of the earth.

And it humbles us still. Sure, we can shape some personal response to it, turn our ear to one story or another; but on the whole we cannot comprehend it. It survives—nay, it burgeons—in spite of all we do against it. It does so with the apparent blessings of God, or whatever entity we appoint with evolutionary design. And more than once it had crossed my mind: melancholia survives not simply with their tacit blessing but, worse, because our creators are indifferent. Or because they are sadistic. Faced with all this we might respond like Job and question everything. Question the wisdom and compassion of any divinity that would appoint creation with such an entity; or, if we are pantheists, question the wisdom and compassion of any creation that would appoint some fair part of its creatures with this suffering. Suffering that seems without cause, without justice, without mercy. Suffering that makes some of us remove ourselves from that creation.

We can't see the point of melancholia, nor of mosquitoes; and yet, who among us wants to live in a world where the point is so meager that our humble race could grasp it? And out of the whirlwind God answered Job, and he lifted Job's eyes from the narrow slit of his own suffering: "Where wast thou when I laid the foundations of the earth? Declare, if thou hast understanding."

Could a human even imagine, let alone comprehend—let alone make manifest—the wonders of creation? What do you know, God asks Job, you or any other of your kind? "Hast thou perceived the breadth of the earth? Declare, if thou knowest it all."

Lewis Thomas writes that if charged with designing creation, modern humans would fail to advance life much beyond one-celled organisms; raw nature progresses by trial and error, Thomas knew, and he thought our species too devoted to mechanistic perfectionism to make much progress. Too, we would want a creation perfectly fitted to our purposes and prejudices. In the late 1990s it appeared that genetic testing of embryonic infants would soon be possible. These tests would ostensibly reveal to parents and physicians a child's pre-dispositions to various illness and disease, the sort of body type he might grow into, the sort of intelligence she might possess. A 1997 survey asked a number of young couples: if genetic testing were to reveal that your newborn-to-be has a 50 percent chance of becoming obese, how would you respond? Fully three-quarters of those couples said they would choose to abort the fetus.

On hearing tidbits like this I am grateful that until very recently, the ultimate genetic destiny of the human animal has been in some hands other than our own. If evolution has taken such a shine to melancholia, there must needs be some breathtaking elegance of design and motion about it. Some beauty we are blind to.

It seems to fit, to serve some purpose, even if it is absolutely un-fathomable to us. No landscape—not even the saturnine one, with all those solitary types about—can exist unto itself. Each is singular and also each is webbed with every other, and the removal of any risks all the rest. They join together, and when we lift our heads from our own private landscapes we know it. We belong to something larger.

We know that, but dimly; and everyday life mostly conspires to our forgetting it. Each one of us, every single two-legged landscape, every lizard leaning into the sun, every shedding sycamore—any one of these, any one of us, any landscape at all; all these, and our sum total too—this whole blue and green and brown spinning orb—all of this, every last atom of the creation points finally to the beyond.

"Then Job answered the Lord, and said . . . what shall I answer thee? I will lay mine hand upon my mouth." Natural history is story; story requires storyteller, author, creator. We read in this story, the Book of Creation, and we come to the last chapter of our comprehension and still the unread pages are thick beneath our hand. May we go on trying to turn them, and may we go on mostly failing at it. Because its tale could end only with the unanswerable questions—Creator? Purpose?—because without fail it makes us to raise our eyes and gaze toward something beyond human comprehending—"natural history" was long synonymous with "philosophy."

BOOK III

WAYFARING STRANGER

I am a poor wayfaring stranger
While travelling through this world below
And there's no sickness, no toil nor danger
In that fair land to which I go

I know dark clouds will hover o'er me
I know my pathway's rough and steep
But beauteous fields lie out before me
Where God's redeem'd their vigils keep

I'll soon be free from ev'ry trial
This form shall rest beneath the sod
I'll drop the cross of self-denial
and enter in my home with God

I'm going there for to see my Saviour
Who shed for me His precious blood
I'm only going over Jordan
I'm only going over home.

—Appalachian folk hymn

CHAPTER FOUR

MAYBE THE ROOT had been drying out all that time, and I hadn't even noticed. Maybe the remedy slipped me. Maybe it was my customary cycle, the solstice-time onsets, reasserting itself. At any rate once more it was my time to sink. Lisa left town the first week of January, and I sank for a few days, and the melancholia slipped in right beneath that, and then it stayed. All the month I pitched and lurched.

My tongue stobbed dry to the roof of my mouth. In bed at night I lay on my back rapping my knuckles against the cinder-block wall. Pueblo kept her distance, retreated into the cubbyholes and far reaches of the basement. Never mind the weather: in my head it was July once more, and then it was August. It was back to those months, as if the autumn had never happened, and after a few days more it was some month I'd never seen on any man's calendar.

And then it was still that month, and it was also, in the world outside, Monday in the second week of February. I finished my lunch, washed the dishes, and trudged out the door to my weekly appointment with Anita. On the Higgins Street bridge I looked down at the Clark Fork. It was frozen over, with tablets and clots of ice piled atop it. I looked up Hellgate Canyon, and could see no further than a quarter mile in that direction. The inversion was back. And so was Mr. Shoulder, his familiar belch and smirk fully intact. Wherever he'd been, he came back with a new tactic: it seemed he was storing away my every sentence, casual and otherwise. Then, minutes or hours or days later, he'd play it back to me, slanting it this way and that, the deconstructionist of my dialogue, parsing it to a razor's edge to prove all the ways I'd unknowingly revealed myself as a fool, insensitive and offensive in an absolutely offhand manner. Typically Mr. Shoulder would then supply the smarter response, the more witty repartee, the more thoughtful reassurance.

I was across the bridge now. On the sidewalk I held my body close. If anybody jostled me I might whirl on them, swinging. The goddamn bicycles whizzing past on the sidewalk, blurs of hard-bodied exer-nazis in that silly yellow Lycra. Don't they know what the hell the street is for? And all the fucking dogs in this town. Piles of turds everywhere you look.

There was no sky. Smog shrouded the peaks of Mount Sentinel and Mount Jumbo. Cloud cover just above my head. The air reeking of sulfur. Mr. Shoulder might have been about some good with this latest project of his, but I wondered why he waited until it was too late to point out my conversational shortcomings and mistakes. Why didn't he show up when I needed him, and feed me my lines when they might have done me some service?

Since in my mind's ear I had to hear repeated three or four times every sentence I uttered, I had gone just about entirely silent. So on this February Monday I dreaded seeing Anita. I was stalled and stagnant. In our last three meetings I had mostly sat silent in the rocking chair, staring out the window. When I could talk at all it was about leaving my work. I knew I couldn't carry on with it any longer, but I couldn't make a final decision about it either. "You need to make a plan, set a date to turn in your resignation, then one month later you walk away," Anita had told me in mid-January. "The longer you stay with it, the more likely you are to break down altogether."

In spite of her counsel I was still trying to hold on. I just could not muster up the focus to think it through; it was one of the biggest decisions I'd ever faced, and I wasn't sure I was in any condition to make it. And what if I quit, and then got better? Wouldn't I be sorry?

I finally got to Anita's office. I took my seat by the window.

"Look," Anita said as she sat down. I turned to face her. "Let's save your money. Right now whatever is going on is more than you can make sense of. You're angry, and you're frustrated, and it's understandable. You had that remission, you traveled home, and you fell in love—you had your own life back for a while—and now the depression is back again. And now your life is gone again. No wonder you don't want to talk."

She reached into a canvas shoulder bag that was propped against her chair and slid out of it a paper-clipped sheaf of paper. "I've photocopied this for you. Take it home and read it. Think about it. Maybe it'll shed a different light on what you're going through. Call me when you feel like talking again."

She handed it to me. The title page read, ominously enough, "The Dark Night of the Soul." I raised my eyebrows. Anita explained: it was a chapter from Evelyn Underhill's *Mysticism*, first published in 1911. "It's one of the most hardheaded, concrete studies of Christian mysticism that I know of. If nothing else, I think you'll appreciate the clarity of her writing and thinking."

I made my way back down Higgins Street, stopped by the office to sign myself out, and walked home to read the chapter. Underhill used the word "depression" only once, but just then I wasn't too concerned about clinical precision. She described the "dark night": a time of "characteristic pains described by almost every expert who has written upon this state of consciousness. Desolation and loneliness, abandonment by God and by man, a tendency of everything to 'go wrong,' a profusion of unsought trials and griefs."

Underhill discussed at length the various mystics and saints who had suffered this "dark night." She quoted Teresa of Avila: "As long as this pain lasts we cannot remember even our own existence . . . all the faculties of the soul are so fettered as to be incapable of any action save that of increasing our torture. Do not think I am exaggerating; on the contrary, that which I say is less than the truth, for lack of words in which it may be expressed. This is a trance of the senses and the faculties, save as regards all which helps to make the agony more intense."

Sounded familiar enough. But there was something new here. Underhill accounted for the dark night thus: "We may see it, with the psychologist, as a moment in the history of mental development, governed by the more or less mechanical laws which so conveniently explain to him the psychic life of man: or with the mystic himself, we may see it in its spiritual aspect as contributing to the remaking of character."

She went on: "[the] consciousness, overstretched, breaks up, and seems to toss the self back to an old and lower level . . . it is a state of disharmony; of imperfect adaptation to environment . . . [it is] the intervening period of chaos between the break-up of an old state of equilibrium and the establishment of the new . . . the Dark Night is a phase of growth largely conditioned by individual temperament."

"A phase of growth"? Of *growth*? This withering, shrinking, re-tiring state, this death-in-life? I'd just accustomed myself to the idea of "adapting" to it; this idea went far beyond simple adaptation. I could scarcely believe what I was reading. Here were these wise men and women—John of the Cross, Meister Eckhart, Catherine of Siena, Teresa of Avila, Jakob Böhme, and many others—describing how their melancholic episodes threatened their faith, spawned doubt, and made it difficult to pray. What mattered most to them—the ongoing presence of God—had vanished. Yet in time they had come to see this estrangement as a necessary stage.

But was it available only to mystics and saints? While I was no sworn atheist—if I ever gave the matter any thought, I suppose I con-sidered myself a pantheist—I had no idea what it meant to live with faith in something I could neither touch nor see. According to James Hillman, "theologizing" depression can falsify it, by leading one away from "discovering the consciousness and depths [depression] wants." But I was by then fairly certain that melancholia could re-make me, in one direction or another; if it was a falsification to let it guide me toward some "new state of equilibrium," then I was will-ing to start living falsely.

I remember very particularly that week, the sense of hope these new ideas brought. I walked to the library that evening and wrote Lisa a long e-mail quoting from Underhill and those saints. We wrote back and forth about it for days. My calendar for that week at work shows a full schedule, and more billable hours than I'd put in for some time.

But that Friday, I was summoned to a meeting with Peter and the Director of our agency. Before the Director was an outlay of graphs and photocopies. I was soon given to understand that these were to document my workplace demise in an official way. First the Director showed me the billable hours charts I had lately been tossing into the trash: since September my billable hours were at a paltry 60 percent of the shop standard. The Director had asked one of the secretaries to check my daily service reports against my client charts, and of course she'd found that my progress notes were several weeks behind. If we were audited soon by the state mental health department, or by Medicaid, my poor productivity and record keeping would present the agency with problems aplenty. The Director told me that none of my clients or colleagues had complained—not since Donnie fired me, anyway—but still, things couldn't continue like this. Peter nodded his head gravely.

The Director went on to tell me that they believed I needed closer supervising for a while, and he laid out their terms: every day, first thing in the morning I would meet with Peter and present him with my schedule for the coming day. At the end of the day I would meet with him again to see how closely I had followed my schedule. Before that meeting I was to sit down and complete all my progress notes for the day, and at those end-of-the-day meetings I was to present that paperwork for Peter's approval. If I was feeling overwhelmed, the Director told me, I could arrange a different work schedule, and for a few weeks he could put me on 60 percent time— since that seemed to be the level at which I was functioning—with a corresponding reduction in my pay and benefits.

"And I'll expect you also to meet with me, here, in this office, every Friday at 4 p.m., to review your progress," the Director said.

I nodded my head. The Director's office was right at the top of the building, and it gathered all the heat from the waiting area and the three secretaries' desks and the "bullpen" where the case managers' cubicles were. It was always stuffy in there. I rubbed my sweaty palms on my pant legs.

"Okay," I said. "I'll go along with that." There was no argument to make; I knew my performance warranted such measures. I pressed my palms to my thighs and started to rise in my chair.

"Whoa there," the Director said. "Hold on just one minute, Mr. Smith." He reached into another file folder and grabbed out an oblong slip of light-blue safety paper. He rolled his desk chair toward me, leaned from the waist like a blackjack dealer, and flung the paper onto my lap like a bad card. I looked down at it. It was a check. Made out to "Cash," it drew out of an agency account the sum of one hundred dollars. It was dated January 20, three weeks earlier, and it was signed by me.

"What do you know about this?" the Director asked me. I was studying on the check closely, my head bent over it as if it were some inscrutable text. "Did you write that check?"

The handwriting was plainly mine. But I held my peace. In the whole office area there were no walls, and if all else was quiet, everyone in the building could hear what transpired in the Director's office. And right then all was quiet: the secretaries answered the phones in hushed tones, and for a change several case managers were at their desks, finishing up their paperwork for the week. It seemed everybody must be listening, and I wondered how much of this had already been whispered about within the office.

"It doesn't make any sense, Jeff." The Director bent his head over his coffee cup. "Any thief would have taken much more. You know damn well there's usually a couple thousand bucks in that account— and if you took this chance, for no more than a hundred lousy dollars, well, all I can say is you're a pretty stupid criminal. And if you *did* do this, you've done nothing whatsoever to hide your tracks, and that would have been easy enough to accomplish. If you really did this, it doesn't make a bit of sense to me."

Nor did it make any sense to me. But I had done it: had written the check against an account that was available for lending money to clients who were in need. It was for clients, not staff members, and while it might have been permissible for me to borrow from that account, I hadn't even asked. And the real kicker was that I hadn't needed the money in the first place. Then I made no attempt to replace it before I was found out. What had I been thinking?

The Director lifted his coffee cup to his mouth, pursed his lips as if to drink, and eyeballed me over the rim of the cup. Then he stopped himself and set the cup down. "You've always struck me as a man of principle and conviction," he said. "This doesn't look like your work, but it sure enough is your handwriting." He lifted the cup to his lips and once more he glowered at me over its rim. "There's no mistaking that, is there?"

I tried to formulate excuses or explanatory schemes but none came to mind. My mouth was dry. All I could think was: Anita was right. Back in December I had paid for my final semester of school. I no longer needed a full-time job. I could have quit then. But I had hung on anyhow, and why?

The Director folded his hands together behind his head and leaned back in his chair. Peter was watching him intently, and I realized that he had no more idea than I about what would follow.

The Director leaned back into the meeting. He gathered back into their manila folders the billable hours charts, the check, the paperwork audit, and the plans for my closer supervision.

He crossed his hands on the desk. "Why don't you take the weekend to think about what you want to do, Jeff," he finally said to me. "We're going to have to call our attorney about this check business, and if that looks okay, I still think you'll need the structure and oversight we've laid out here." He tapped his finger on the folder. "If you'll agree to those conditions we'll work with you."

"And feel free to call me," Peter said, "if you need to talk about it. I'll be home all weekend." I stood up to leave but before I did I gave the Director a good long handshake, and for some reason I bowed in his direction. Then I turned to Peter and I clasped his hand in a standard businessperson's handshake; then I slid into what we called in my youth a soul shake, hands bent at forty-five degrees and palms flush together; then I interlocked bent fingers with him; we finished off with the Flintstones' Water Buffalo shake, our thumbs hooked together and our fingers flapping like wings as we lifted our hands towards the ceiling. Peter was grinning broadly. Even the Director, who generally laughed at nobody's jokes but his own, laughed. It was the first time in weeks that I'd made anybody laugh.

But very likely I misunderstood their laughter. It seems to me now that theirs was the tinny, hollow laughter one forces when one has no idea how to respond to some just-witnessed act that is utterly discordant with the situation at hand. The Director and Peter must have wondered—you must be wondering as you read this—and I am wondering still: had reason finally abandoned me altogether? Was I so far immersed in that parallel universe that such a sobering event could not rouse me, couldn't get me to face with some dignity the consequences of what I'd done? I could scarcely recall, let alone explain, writing that check, but there was no doubt I'd done so—and even without that, my recent work performance certainly called for drastic action. Yet there I was, at the close of the most distressing meeting I'd ever been called to—I was this close to losing the only career I'd ever had—and my response was to bow like a mandarin and offer this foolish, childish handshake.

I think it's true: by the time of that meeting I had finally arrived in the place where, despite the occasional remission, I'd been bound for all these months: the real true netherworld. Call it what you will—dissociation, insanity, meet punishment, a healthy response to the Puritan work ethic, the natural progression of my illness—but on that day the evidence became overwhelming: I was no longer capable of navigating aboveground.

I went home to my basement room, put the phone beside the bed, set Bach, Arvo Pärt, and Shostakovich CDs into the disc player, and pressed the repeat switch so they would play over and over. I lay there on the bed, sweating. I was ashamed of myself, more ashamed than I had ever been, for betraying my employers, and I was frightened to the core. Perhaps the agency would prosecute me. My mind latched on to this: I saw myself on trial, and firmly in jail, all for one hundred lousy bucks. What sort of person would piss away his life's work in such a fashion?

And I thought about my financial situation: I had savings enough to last three or four months, but would I be in any condition to return to work once I exhausted that money? With such a tainted work history, with such narrow professional experience, having no handyman skills whatsoever—and in such an unstable condition—would I be able to find another job? Why hadn't I pursued the disability insurance? For weeks now I'd been mostly incapable of carrying out my responsibilities. I *was* disabled.

I had to wonder: had I stayed on the medicine, or gone through with the electroshock therapy, or waited to try the new pill my psychiatrist suggested, would I be in this position?

Around midnight, 7 a.m. Lisa's time, I called and told her about the meeting. "I should have faced up to this a long time ago," I said to her. "The job has had the better of me for months."

I was prepared for her to end our relationship right then. Instead she softly said: "You know you need to leave that job. I know you need to leave that job. Anita knows you need to leave that job. Maybe this was the only way you could do it. I wish I were there. Your life is falling apart, and I'm thousands of miles away."

We talked a while longer, and for a time I felt better, but shortly the knot of nausea was back in my stomach. I didn't sleep that night, for imagining myself in jail, or in the poorhouse. I had disappointed so many people. My mind whirled and whirled, from one sordid possibility to another, and then it whirled to the lack of possibilities I had beyond this job.

I did not eat or leave the basement all weekend. I had some truth to face. Apart from the money issue, I couldn't offer the Director and Peter any hope that my work would improve. I'd been trying for eight months to will my way through it, and to no avail: melancholia, I had learned, isn't readily subdued by application of will. My only chance for timely improvement was to resume the medications, and hope that one of the new antidepressants would prove effective in a lasting way—and with my history the odds on that seemed pretty slim indeed.

Nor did I want to prevail on the Director's mercy and ask for a second chance. Why did I merit one? Once again I wished I had listened to

Anita, and got out by my own druthers before anything like this happened. I thought about the clients whose company I would miss, but these days I was little good for them. They deserved and needed better; it was time for me to take my rightful place with them, as a peer.

Practically speaking, leaving this job would be a foolhardy gesture. But practicality had little bearing on my circumstance just then. It looked as if Anita was right: the longer I stayed, the closer I had come to losing my faculties altogether. I had some grappling to do, a grappling that, or so it seems now, I could not attend to so long as I went on trying to maintain my workaday life. I was worn to my nubbins. And perhaps those odd gestures following the meeting in the Director's office were my awkward and discomfited way of bidding farewell. To the netherland I was a-going, and it seems those gestures, however inappropriate to the occasion, also had about them the giddy relief of surrender after a long siege.

So on Monday morning I walked into the office, confessed my wrongdoing and repaid the money, tendered my resignation, and said my goodbyes.

And then I went into retreat.

SUSAN SONTAG HAS WRITTEN: "Precisely because the melancholy character is haunted by death, it is melancholics who best know how to read the world."

Well, maybe so maybe no. But reading is one thing; day-to-day living something else altogether, and in this art, from the majority view, the melancholic has generally been found wanting. "A man becomes a tyrant when, whether by nature or by manner of life, or both, he is a drunkard, voluptuary, and melancholic." This from Plato's *Republic*, written in the fifth century B.C. A text from the third century A.D., attributed to the Roman physician Soranus, describes the nature black bile conferred as "crafty, avaricious, despondent, misanthropic, and timid."

Like Lucifer, by his own doing Kronos/Saturn fell from the heights of divinity into the depths of hell. In 1156 St. Hildegard of Bingen, a physician as well as a composer and mystic visionary, wrote in her medical treatise *Causae et curae* that before the Fall human nature had been uniformly of the sanguine humor. But at the very moment Adam partook of the apple, she writes, "melancholy curdled in his blood, as when a lamp is quenched the smouldering and smoking wick remains reeking behind."

While perhaps one could adapt to it, with few exceptions the atrabilious complexion was thought sinister, if not utterly diabolical. In the fifteenth century Nicholas of Cusa wrote that black bile caused the "pestilential" vices: "usury, fraud, deceit, thieving, pillaging, coveting." Some quotes culled from *Saturn and Melancholy*, having originally appeared from the second century to the sixteenth in almanacs, shepherd's calendars, and household health books:

- "The planet Saturn is the highest and greatest, and the most worthless . . . hostile to our nature in every way."
- "Saturn is the planet of wicked and worthless men who are thin, dark, and dry, and wear unclean garments."
- "Corresponding to the nature of the god, the nature of those born under Saturn is dark, coarse, and heavy; melancholy and miserly. They speak one thing with their tongue and another with their heart; they are solitary, silent, and dull."
- "They are foreign to all public affairs and prefer to lose themselves in secret contemplation."
- "They have all evil things by nature."
- "In the hour of Saturn"—that is, at dusk—"Jesus was betrayed and delivered to death"—by Judas Iscariot, who because of his deceit, avarice, and eventual suicide was put forth as an exemplar of the temperament.

We know already what Hildegard made of the melancholic temperament; here's what she thought of the illness: "melancholia was Adam's punishment" for eating of the apple—"his gall was changed to blackness and his melancholy to blackness"—and therefore "had to be borne by the whole race." Melancholia came forth from Original Sin, then.

The acquaintance with death Jamison and Sontag allude to can inflict a particular passion for despair; melancholia's relentless fear and hopelessness breed an apocalyptic cynicism. Life is empty and meaningless, melancholia tells us, and who knows the best way to reckon with that? Into the Middle Ages many Christians held the illness responsible for and sometimes identical with "acedia"—a sort of spiritual torpor, a seemingly willful indifference and ambivalence about one's faith. Acedia was suffered by Chaucer's Parson in *The Canterbury Tales*, and by the residents of the fifth circle of Dante's Inferno. It is worth noting: acedia was a cardinal sin. Yielding to the temptations of melancholia was akin to yielding to more red-blooded desires, to covetousness or lust; it would seem that melancholia was common enough—and if not common enough, then dangerous enough—to warrant such attention.

Today we know that incarcerated criminals typically have drastically low blood serotonin levels, leading some to suggest that increased dosages of Prozac might reduce the crime rate. The point is, very quickly any consideration of melancholia will move away from biology and reckon with the ontological questions it raises; any illness can force us to contemplate our mortality, but in its effects melancholia is perhaps the most existential illness we know.

That February, I had little awareness of this. I had heard nothing of the spiritual approach to melancholia implied by the chapter Anita gave me from Underhill. Frankly, up to that time I had never considered the illness in any sort of philosophical way; it was a biological problem, period. In fact, in my eight years of working with the mentally ill I had heard no inkling of this tradition.

As it turns out, to this day, in cultures the world over, melancholia is often received as a manifest of the sacred, an instrument of divinity. Whether we find in it the machinations of divinity or of biology, that nebulous entity the soul—by broad report, and even by secular types—seems to be the organ (if you will) most affected by melancholia. And so the Pueblo peoples of the American Southwest, and the Ibans of Malaysia, and the Yoruba in Nigeria, and the Balahis in India—indeed, almost all indigenous peoples—attribute melancholia to "soul loss." Some cultures nod to the way melancholia's circumference ignores the distinctions we in the West attempt to make between "body" and "mind" and "self" and "soul" by referring to melancholia simply as "soul sickness." The American philosopher and psychologist William James (himself a melancholic, and his father, brother Henry, and sister Alice too) devoted a couple chapters of *The Varieties of Religious Experience* to the "sick soul," which in James's description sounds very much like melancholia.

If it thefts souls or renders them "sick," melancholia might well turn us to evil, as was long believed; but because it renders this existential despair, it has also long been thought to develop and nurture faith, to spur conversion even in the most unlikely, as Leo Tolstoy's autobiographical *Confession* testifies. And among our spiritual traditions it casts a broad net: according to Gananath Obeyesekere (the same anthropologist whose research reveals across non-Western cultures a predominantly "existential" approach to the illness), since depression teaches that "hopelessness lies in one's own lot and in the nature of the world, and that salvation lies in understanding and overcoming that hopelessness," a depressive is likely to make "a good Buddhist." And recall that among Muslims, as Byron Good wrote, melancholia is thought to have "profound religious and personal significance."

And those medieval mystics who suffered from the "dark night" were by no means the first Christians to reckon with melancholia. The Bible is rich in stories that suggest or address it: there is the story of Job (which, to be diagnostically precise, would have to be called a "situational" depression—that is, his melancholia had clear causes); there are the Lamentations of Jeremiah; there is Nebuchadnezzar hiding out in his cave, eating of the grass; there is the story, in the Book of Kings, of David playing his harp to soothe the melancholic Saul; and several of David's Psalms allude metaphorically to the death-in-life of his unwilling journeys to Sheol—that is, to the Underworld; and there is the story of Jonah in the belly of the whale. Some medieval commentators suggested that Jesus himself was a saturnine figure. They cited the purported season of his birth, when Saturn rules the sky; his rebellious, sometimes truculent way; his (at least as the Bible renders it) monastic nature; and his oft-expressed desire for seclusion. And of course for several centuries it was believed that anyone so wise and so cryptic must have at least some touch of the melancholic about him. Among early Christians, the fourth-century Egyptian Desert Fathers developed lists of Scripture readings to comfort melancholics.

Another Christian tradition posits that melancholia, or at least a state very much like it, is a "divine gloom," a necessary step on the mystical journey. This widespread idea, apparently first articulated in the sixth-century writings of Pseudo-Dionysius, held that the religious must learn to maintain faith in the utter and prolonged—perhaps even terminal—absence of God. The idea persisted into the fourteenth-century British mystical classic *The Cloud of Unknowing* and on into the lives and writings of the late medieval monastics and mystics Underhill mentions in her chapter treating the "dark night of the soul."

About the same time the great Spanish poet and mystic John of the Cross was writing in his classic memoir, *Dark Night of the Soul*, of his own spiritual reckoning with this melancholic-seeming condition, Martin Luther was himself in the clutches of another melancholic fit. He was thirty-two; the year was 1517, and he was a monk in the Augustinian order. Since his twenties Luther had suffered from episodes of what sounds to us, and to latter-day clinicians such as Erik Erikson, very much like clinical depression. In those episodes Luther was particularly haunted by a question melancholia might well raise for a believer: how can one whose deeds and thoughts are so base and unworthy be forgiven, redeemed, and loved—"justified"—by God?

Now the fit was upon him again; this time, though, Luther had his revelatory "vision in the tower": "I have faith, and therefore am justified." Shortly thereafter he nailed his Ninety-five Theses to the door of the Castle Church in Wittenberg, and the Reformation began.

For centuries prior to this, artists had tried to classify the apostles according to humoral theory. Typically they painted as the melancholic the apostle John, which seems appropriate enough for the purported author of the rather saturnine Book of Revelations. But already, in 1526—less than a decade after Luther's "revelation"—in his rendering of the apostles, Albrecht Dürer overturned that tradition and painted Paul, already considered the tutelary genius of Protestantism, as the melancholic. One glance and you know: he holds open the Book and it seems he has been in dialogue about it with the gentle-looking John; but as you approach the scene, he alone meets your glance, the skeptical and imperious glare out the corner of his eye stopping you in your tracks. The association persisted, because it fit: of all the biblical writers, the often cranky, occasionally tyrannical and apocalyptic, always opinionated and conservative Paul is perhaps the most perceptive about the ways the self—the ego, as we might call it today, or the "flesh," as Paul was wont to call it—has to obstruct our spiritual longings; a very saturnine—and Protestant—preoccupation, this. (To be fair, Paul was also the author of the gorgeous and wise familiar lines about love in I Corinthians 13, and numerous passages of extraordinary delicacy and compassion.)

To this day Paul's writings are central to Protestant beliefs and practice. And with the Protestant emphasis on an unmediated, personal relationship with God, it's easy to see how melancholia was particularly suited to them too. With the self, rather than an institution, at the center of one's relationship with God, Protestants have long thought an unceasing, incisive, and unsparing measuring of the self essential to faith—witness all the conversion narratives and "automachia" written by the early American Puritans. (One could argue that these were the progenitors of that most durable American literary genre, the memoir.) And as we know, this ever-plastic entity melancholia would lend itself very nicely to this very sort of self-examination.

And for many years, melancholia was a substantial part of the Protestant tradition, prominent in the writings of Wesley and Calvin and in Bunyan's *Pilgrim's Progress,* where the pilgrim must traverse a very melancholic sort of "slough of despond" before he can find salvation. In the early 1700, Cotton Mather considered melancholia a prevailing, endemic affliction among the New England Puritans. In the 1770s, Mother Ann Lee established in the States the mystical Protestant sect the Shakers; she had originally conceived of Shaker principles and practices—a rather monastic sect, to be sure, with a somewhat perfectionist work ethic and a fairly melancholic appreciation of raw nonhuman nature and the redemptiveness of garden work—as she emerged from a nervous collapse. Into the nineteenth century and the Second Great Awakening, melancholia continued to be prominent in American Protestantism. William James drew liberally on the Protestant "conversion narratives" to make his case that the sick soul was a necessary tonic for his own (as James saw it) overly optimistic, "healthy-minded" times. (It's worth mentioning that James penned most of *The Varieties of Religious Experience* in 1902 as he lay abed in his own "neurasthenic chamber.")

But James's eloquent and penetrating study of the sick soul was its last widely read manifestation in Western cultures. All those sweeping cultural changes, already underway as James wrote, gained full force in the first two decades of this century; and not coincidentally, most of our twentieth-century thinking about the sick soul has drawn on Freudian psychoanalytic theory, and then on biological psychiatry, neither of which give much credence to the soul.

Of course, we could easily dismiss all this history as an anachronism. As Henry Adams suggested, for thousands of years religious preoccupations framed the world for many people, just as science, commerce, and the dynamo frame ours. Surely this inclined men and women of the past to offer up theological interpretations and responses to melancholia, just as we explain it as an anomaly of brain chemistry. In his medical history of melancholia and depression Stanley Jackson writes: "By the turn of the century, religious melancholia as a distinct disease, or even as a subtype of melancholia, had essentially disappeared." Today the only mention of "religion" in the *DSM* is as an adjectival prelude to the word "delusions."

I grew up in the northern limits of the Bible Belt, and in my youth I heard plenty about Jesus and the Bible, and attended services with

my family at the brick Methodist church on Main Street in Hannibal. It was a calmer church than it had been in my Great-grandfather
Dally's time, to be sure. It reflected the way our village had changed,
and changes in the larger culture too: we heard gentle sermons urg-
ing us to be pious and decent, and we sang dull, major-key, piano-
based hymns—contemporary Protestant church music—from the
Methodist Hymnal.

But into my teens I also attended many services in the country
churches, with my rural classmates and then with my "youth group"
friends. Those country churches were seldom part of any national
congregation; the preachers were seldom ordained graduates of divinity schools. More often they were farmers and coal miners and
other laypeople from the community, who preached not from notes
or a prepared sermon but, seemingly, from memory or inspiration.

Their oratorical gifts were impressive; the congregations rarely
drifted off into head-nodding, as so often happened in our town
church. I recall sitting spellbound one Sunday morning in one of
those country churches as my math teacher at the local high school,
a quiet and unassuming man at school, rose to the front of the
church and preached a convicted and emphatic sermon, relying just
about equally on anecdote and Scripture, about loving thy neighbor,
and about forgiveness—important virtues in a rural community
where everybody knew everybody's business.

For a while I studied those preachers closely. Given our history, it
was natural for my family to harbor some hope that with my regard
for books and music I would enter the ministry. There was another
reason they thought me suited for the ministry: very early on it was
clear that I lacked "common sense." Even on the riverfront, where
by my childhood most men had left farming and other household
economies to take on well-paid factory jobs, the old local necessities
of self-reliance and resourcefulness still mattered a great deal. The
highest praise that could be bestowed on a male there was to say that
he had "a lot of common sense," meaning generally that he was
handy with all matters mechanical and practical. A problem solver.

The mark was on me pretty early: I had no common sense. I
could scarcely keep my spider bike in good repair. Meanwhile my

brother Jim, before he was six, had taken apart our family's lawn mower, piece by piece, and put it back together impeccably. My father was fond of telling anyone who listened that our mower ran better than it ever had, and that Jim would grow up to be a better mechanic than he—high praise indeed, since Dad was widely acknowledged as one of the best mechanics in the county.

I was nine or ten then, and could do nothing thought useful. So I seemed destined for the ministry or some other occupation where common sense was not required. It must have heightened my family's hopes when, a couple of years later, I involved myself with an interdenominational "youth fellowship" group. We met every Monday evening, all carrying our copies of The Way, a translation of the Bible with a vaguely psychedelic-looking cover and a sort of blue-denim tone to it. It was 1975, and I realize now that our group was an offshoot of the Jesus Freak/*Godspell*/*Jesus Christ Superstar* syndrome— the Christ-comes-to[from?]-the-counterculture movement of those years.

Well, I don't think any of us attending those Monday night meetings in Monroe County, Ohio, considered ourselves "hippies" or "freaks." I know there were some whose faith was heartfelt—some of them are back in Monroe County now, serving as pastors in one church or another. Our high school music teacher was the group leader, and he was a good folk guitarist. We opened every meeting with a couple of songs, often with one or another of those old folk hymns, and then we did some Bible study and discussion, and then we closed the meetings with more singing.

I enjoyed those meetings, but I can assure you my attendance had nothing to do with "faith." I might have had some vague ideal of being "good," and thought I might get some rules for that or at least brownie points for being interested; but it was more about music, and a sense of community, and meeting girls—there were always plenty of girls at the meetings—the usual teenage preoccupations.

These were pretty shallow reasons, so I wasn't likely to hold out when alternatives presented themselves. Mostly, though, I was a curious and horny teenager, and it was the 1970s, and I was supposed to Do My Own Thing. I was beginning to sense that being a practicing Christian might interfere with that. So at the start of my sophomore year in high school I quit the youth group, went all the way to the other side and became one of the unrepentant "freaks," one of the cynics and know-it-alls and would-be artists and poets and potheads. We all lacked common sense, and had little interest in athletics or cars. We stood in the high school hallway reciting lines from old Dylan tunes, acting out skits from *Saturday Night Live*, then in its mid-1970s heyday, and generally plotting our escape to some place where our lack of common sense and manly bluster wouldn't consign us to the margins.

In college I found that place, and I also found less craven—not to mention more pretentious, which may have been the point in those years—reasons to reject Christianity. In a sociology class my first term I learned that Protestants were responsible for just about everything an intellectual ought to despise about contemporary America: bland suburbs, shopping malls, the work ethic, conventional morality. Later that year in a literature class I was introduced to Albert Camus and Flannery O'Connor and Eugène Ionesco and Jean-Paul Sartre; we discussed "existentialism" and "the grotesque" and the "absurd."

I was enthralled to be in a place where simply *being* seemed to matter so much, where one could dwell, near as I could determine, just about full-time in the rarefied world of abstractions and concepts, and scarcely had to reveal what one could not *do*. My first college girlfriend was the daughter of a Presbyterian minister, and she was studying to be an opera singer. Vicki was a good person, and deeply so, steady and guileless. Sex was fairly new to Vicki, and we would roll and thrust on the floor of my dormitory room, scuttling across the linoleum floor like a pair of sand crabs, then up against the wall for a while, and finally on that small iron-framed institutional-issue bed; and then, as was her habit, she would fall asleep.

Soon as Vicki began to doze, I would get up off the bed and sit down at my desk with Dostoevsky or Camus open before me, jotting in my notebook well into the small hours of the morning, the filterless Camels piling up in the ashtray beside me.

One night Vicki aroused from her slumbers, swept her thick hair off her face, and softly asked what in the world I was doing at my desk at three in the morning. I harrumphed, irritated at the interruption, not to mention the fact that she had little interest in my philosophical questing. This last I attributed to her Christian faith, and I wanted to bring her around to seeing the light—that is, of course, the light I saw. Which was: There are no answers, only more questions.

I slid my chair back a little and crossed a leg over the other knee, keeping my thighs together. Here one could sit any way one chose. When I sat this way back home I'd been called a "pussy." I harrumphed again. Her question demanded a short answer, but I was too puffed up with my contemplating to realize that. I lit a cigarette and blew the smoke into the small cone of light from my desk lamp.

"Many, many years ago," I started, "Socrates wrote that the unexamined—"

"Yes, I know. Not worth living. What did he have to say about the sleepless life?" Vicki shot back. Without another word, she rolled over and back into sleep.

Our relationship didn't last long after that night, and who could blame her? It was the comfort of abstraction I craved—and there was something exhilarating about it too, a purity and elegance of thought or phrasing I'd come across sometimes in my reading that would make my heart pound. Anyway, it was abstraction, its comforts and its exhilarations both, that I craved, maybe more than I did the warm body beside me in bed.

I didn't give much thought to the matter, but if asked I'd have probably said that individual Christians might be good people, but the faith as a whole was malicious. Just look at what had been done in its name. By avoiding it, I stayed on the right side, as I imagined, and as long as I was right, I believed I need not trouble myself about my soul. So I marched and shouted and wrote letters for all the "right" things—nuclear disarmament and social justice and U.S. Out of North America and Anybody But Reagan and saving the environment and equality for women. Politics mattered, art mattered, music mattered, philosophy mattered, but religion? What did that have to do with anything?

In Ann Arbor I began to feel some interest in spiritual matters, and for a time I attended Buddhist services in a gleaming modern temple. This was nothing like "religion": I left those services feeling calm, cool, and cerebral. This was what I wanted. Immediately I drew up my absolutes: "Belief cannot be about emotion," I remember telling my friend Rob. I never discussed this with any of the monks or teachers, and not even with the other attendees; unlike the churches I'd known, there was nothing social about these gatherings. Most of us were educated whites, and there was no congregating together after services were over. We left the services one by one, two by two, quietly and quickly, as if afraid to disturb whatever peace the others had gained in the hour of meditation and chanting. To my friend I extolled the virtues of Buddhist detachment, in the half-assed way I understood it: you do away with desire and with personality.

Rob, a poet who'd attended Quaker boarding schools and colleges, was quick to respond. "Well, sounds to me like its appeal to you is pretty simple: you don't have to feel like a human being."

Of course, Rob knew this was not the aim of Buddhist practice; he also knew me well enough to read my character perfectly. Being right was what mattered. Remote was the point. In North Carolina I became an environmental activist, and I allied myself with groups who believe that anthropocentrism, or human-centered thinking—the idea that the natural world exists mostly to serve human ends—is largely responsible for the demise of our environment. Like most other environmental advocates, I charged Christianity with being chief sponsor and advocate for anthropocentrism. On Genesis 1:28, which appears to give humans "dominion" over the rest of creation, we lay the brunt of the blame for human abuses of the environment.

During that time I also managed the homeless shelter. I worked day and night with Christians of every stripe. I saw the love and generosity and selflessness many of them offered to human need and suffering. On an everyday basis, I saw faith in action, and I gained a new respect for the faith.

But still I held Christianity, and particularly Protestant Christianity, accountable for environmental degradation and the displacement of Native Americans and the oppression of women and the materialism of our culture. I'm still inclined to believe this; my foolishness was that I looked at the ways humans have fit Christianity to their purposes and assumed that represented the true arc of the faith. I assumed this, and put myself in the way of nothing whatsoever that might contradict or even complicate that view. Not even the Bible. Particularly not the Bible. I had so many relevant things to read, you know.

LATE FEBRUARY. The inversion hovering over us still. This was the season when my calendar emptied out. The snow spread like a slate. I turned facefirst and walked into the headwind. I took off my cap and let the wind blow my hair. I spoke into it: I want to be scoured by this season.

For this was the season when I lay awake in a sweat, worrying about money, worrying about jobs, worrying about what I had done, worrying about what I would do, worrying about what I would be.

One by one the pieces of my life had gone pendant and then fallen forth. The pills would not help; nor could I do anything for myself. I didn't have the resources or the endurance to outdistance melancholia on my own. I had clutched tightly as I knew how, but my "self" seemed gone from me now. What happened next was this: I withdrew from the world. I read. I walked. The meaningful drama here happened elsewhere. Some place that resists drama, resists scene, resists words. This was the season when life emptied out, when all the ways I had of knowing my self were gone, when my self would brook no façade, when my self became a shape I could no longer maintain.

This was a real problem. The preachers my generation listened to told us: Be Your Own Best Friend. Actualize Your Self. Realize Your Self. But now that self had become its own torture chamber. Regret, guilt, blame. The idea of "realizing" or "actualizing" this self made me think of a boil in need of lancing. It had become the obstacle. All

I wanted was some self-esteem. The antidepressants had given me more self-esteem than I had ever known before, and all I'd had to do to merit it was swallow a pill or two every day.

This is what I wanted. But melancholia will tell you something entirely different about this "self" and what it needs. And that bewildered me. One way of thinking, one way of imagining, one way of telling my story to myself was gone. It had shaken right out of me. And now I had to find another. It seemed the whole way was cleared for it: I had no job, no obligations, nothing but time on my hands, supporting none but myself and a slender cat. I missed my work, missed joking and commiserating with my clients, but I knew this was right, however it had come to pass. All I *had* to do in those months was revise the essays I'd written in the past three years into a thesis. What I had was time to contemplate, and room to walk, and I needed the both of them.

Perhaps that self was not for now full of kind regard for its person; but it was still full of something; it was full of itself. And little else. And that self followed me everywhere, by turns shapeless and piercing, uncertain and specific.

Mostly, unforgiving. My mind unreeled an endless spool, I became a bean counter hoarding my transgressions. It would not stop.

Finally I phoned my friend Tony Sayer. Tony was a Methodist minister in Asheville; he had been my supervisor at the homeless shelter. Tony and I could talk politics, and we could talk music, and we could talk books. Tony read everything, it seemed, and he remembered verbatim passages from his reading, and recited them with great relish. Obscure and difficult German theologians, David Foster Wallace, Wendell Berry, Eugenio Montale, Alice Munro, Leslie Marmon Silko.

So I found it easy to talk with him. "I know this," I had said to Tony: "I am nobody's victim. All my messes are my own doing. There is nobody I need to forgive but myself. So how do I do that?"

"You know," Tony said, "you can be exasperating." He could also be blunt. "You just refuse to accept forgiveness. That's the whole problem. If you choose, you can go on believing that you are so flawed, put together so poorly, that whatever comes next is just the natural progression of your doomed and damned character."

"Show me evidence to the contrary," I said.

He came back low and gentle: "Nothing I could say would convince you anyway. What would? Listen, it's really about as simple as this: you have got to get beyond your Self. Centered. Ness."

I heard him take a swallow of his Coke. I had a question ready for him but he wasn't done yet: "Part B of my answer: you will never effect any of those transformations on your own. Certainly not. I'm not sure that any mind—any intellect, I should say—can be the organ of a transformation like that."

He paused, took another swallow of Coke, and went on: "Do you have any idea how arrogant it is to reject forgiveness?" He paused again. "That is the real gift of Jesus—we are forgiven, one by one, because with him human flesh is capable of rising above its ordinary selfishness, its ordinary preoccupations with itself. And when flesh does—as it will—follow its own desires, you are forgiven. You don't need to linger over it, you don't need to assume that you are one and the same with your sin, now and hereafter. And you, sir, you see fit to reject that.

"You put your particular sins, in other words, even above Jesus' ability to forgive them. Seems to me you think they make you special. Do you really think they are so unique, or even especially interesting?"

Tony laughed. "No, no, erase that question. Clearly, you do think so, or you wouldn't insist on telling this one story over and over again: how I am fated to fail you. I am *worthless*, you keep saying. I can't *do* anything, you keep saying. It's just as bad as pride, I'd say, your obsession with your sins and shortcomings: just as self-important. I'm not saying that you're wrong: you might well be worthless. Maybe you can't do anything. Maybe you don't know anything.

"Maybe you are empty, or worse than empty: full only of yourself. But what does all of that matter anyhow? Living in faith requires none of them. You worship a graven idol, and that idol is your self. You need to get out of your own way. Forgiveness—for you, forgiving yourself—will relieve you of that burden. What's the point of refusing forgiveness, except to feel unique, self-important? You are human, remember? Or are you? And what humans need most of all is forgiveness. Here's my advice, old friend: put your self in the hands of something bigger and wiser than you."

Something was required of me, it seemed, and I had no idea what it was. I saw the truth in Tony's words but did not see how to put it into practice. Now I was getting a sense of what a faithful response to melancholia entailed, and it seemed beyond my resources.

Sometime that winter, my friend Robert Clark mailed me an anthology of nineteenth-century American poetry. There were long sections of poems by Melville, and Emily Dickinson, and many poets to discover too. I was listening then to a lot of traditional Appalachian music, and the volume also included some of those ballads, as well as a small selection of nineteenth-century folk spirituals, songs similar to "Wayfaring Stranger."

In those old gospel songs, and in the air around those old country churches at home, and there in my aunts and great-aunts and great-uncles and grandparents and parents, the self is the least of it. In quiet and unassuming ways such unfashionable spiritual practices as obedience, restraint, humility, and discipline were ongoing practices for my grandma's generation, and for some of their children too. They observed Lent, giving up for those six weeks things that really tempted them: candy, bread, junk food.

I had never observed Lent in any way. But now I was beginning to think the old-time religion was by no means merely conformist or pietist; instead, in its own way it seemed genuinely countercultural. It had no odd clothes or brand names or theme songs, no decade named for it, but more than most of our so-called countercultural movements this one stood, quiet and firm, foursquare in the way of the true icon and underpinning of our republic: the self.

An interviewer once asked Bob Dylan if he was happy. To which Dylan responded: "These are yuppie words, *happiness* and *unhappi-*

ness. It's not happiness or unhappiness, it's either blessed or un-blessed." And I was starting to see his point. "Happiness" is a mat-ter of situation, circumstance, disposable income, self-satisfaction. Feeling "blessed" is a choice we are free to make regardless of in-come or race or gender or size. Considering oneself "blessed" is a way of receiving the events of one's life with equanimity and grati-tude.

To me this is what songs like "Wayfaring Stranger" express. Change your life, those songs tell us. Surrender your pride and self-absorption, and walk in submission and sacrifice. The saints and mystics cited by Underhill said much the same thing. According to the British mystic William Law: "All the disorder and corruption and malady of our nature lies in a certain fixedness of our own will, imagination, and desire, wherein we live to ourselves, are our own centre and circumference, act wholly from ourselves, according to our own will, imagination, and desires." Thus to Law the dark night was "when the deepest root of all selfishness, as well spiritual as nat-ural, is to be plucked up and torn from us." Catherine of Siena be-lieved that the necessary work of the dark night was "digging up the root of self-love with the knife of self-hatred." These are old, old ideas about the self, ideas that inform nearly all the world's spiritual traditions. They say that the self has its limits.

Theirs is a message of hope, about the peace that follows from maintaining an awareness of the humble place of the self in the order of things. I had seen plenty of people at home and elsewhere who lived that message with intelligence and presence, sincerely and thoughtfully, who met you clear-eyed, with love and forgiveness and generosity. This message is simple, solid bedrock; it is at the center of Jesus' teachings. It is a message meant to unravel, and unravel me it did.

And a lot of these songs had to do with walking: and walking was what I was about that season. As a child I had walked constantly and joyfully; even when all my classmates were driving to school I walked. This befuddled the menfolk in my car-obsessed home region;

I went for nearly two full years after my sixteenth birthday without obtaining a license to drive. That March I took up regular walking again.

It was another of those times when things seemed to converge: I got to reading about walking, and in Bruce Chatwin's *Songlines*, I read that for centuries a pilgrimage or walkabout was thought highly specific for melancholia. And I could see that: it had always made for a useful balance for me: when walking I could ruminate, could recite or sing; but any preoccupations, self-absorptions, flights into the abstract, could be shattered in an instant: by the play of light across a meadow, by a mound of carpenter ants along the roadside, by a tree, by a circle of people standing in a yard.

I read about the "walking meditations" of the Tibetan Buddhists; I read of the Catholic faithful in the American Southwest spending Holy Week en route to Chimayo, the old mission in the New Mexico highlands. Chatwin tells us that among the Sufi, *siyahat* or "errance"—the action or rhythm of walking—is used as a technique for dissolving the attachments of the world and allowing men to lose themselves in God. A Sufi manual cited by Chatwin, the *Kash-al Mahjab*, says that the Sufi dervish aims to become a "dead man walking": one whose body stays alive on earth yet whose soul is already in heaven. Toward the end of his journey the dervish becomes one with the Way—becomes, that is, part of the landscape over which he or she is passing. I looked once more at Thoreau's essay "Walking": "I would fain be assured that I am growing apace and rankly, though my very growth disturb this dull equanimity—though it be with struggle through long, muggy, dark nights or seasons of gloom."

I read about the Eastern Orthodox pilgrim who walked thousands and thousands of miles across old Russia chanting to himself the Jesus Prayer: "Lord Jesus Christ, have mercy on me." He chanted to still his mind, to silence his self; he aimed to internalize the prayer, to make it resonate with his heartbeat so that in every breath he would sense the presence of Jesus. Measuring his mercies into his stride, into his breath, into his pulse, he aimed to free himself from awareness of the self and its limited concerns and desires.

Then there is Saul of Tarsus: literally blinded by the light that showed him his sin, he became a stranger to himself—he became the man we know as the Apostle Paul—while walking the road to Damascus.

So maybe walking would be my spiritual practice. This was how I passed my boyhood, and I had acquired no useful skills since. But I could do this: I could walk. I needed to rethink my life and I wanted to do it head-on, open-eyed and firm of foot. In those old gospel tunes, "stranger" and "pilgrim" are synonymous: "Wayfaring Stranger" is often sung as "Wayfaring Pilgrim." Because he or she has abandoned the comforts and securities of selfishness the pilgrim becomes an eternal stranger: forever without fixed quarters, living on faith.

The self is the least of it. The pilgrim knows this—or seeks with his walking to remember it. How would I know myself now? As a man who walked. As an empty man who walked.

So I prayed for poverty then, and loose limbs.

SUNDAY, EARLY APRIL, and I'd been up before sunrise, preparing for a day-long walk. I'd spent the week in Hot Springs, Montana, housesitting for a friend. And walking, walking, walking. Every day I had taken one long walk or another. Today would be my longest, and in the dawn I lounged on the porch with my tea and a smoke, and then another.

When I left the house the sun was barely up over the Mission Mountains and the air was still and pleasant. I walked down the dirt streets of Hot Springs. I turned hard left onto the road I'd be walking all day long. Sage and shortgrass meadows on either side of me now, the sage a sweet prickle in the nose. There on a fence post a western meadowlark—her favorite sign of spring in these parts, Lisa had told me the night before—all gloriously gold-breasted, the head arcing gently with every note of its ascending melody; a herald. The change is upon us.

Lisa and I had talked a couple of times that week. It was a delight to hear her voice, her laughter—we were fortunate to have E-mail available, and we wrote daily, but finally it left us a little hungry. An expensive indulgence, no doubt, but we had much to discuss: a couple weeks before, we had decided that before she returned I would move into that sunny house on Poplar Street, she to join me on her return, and the two of us—and Pueblo too—would make a home together. I cannot explain why I didn't hesitate about this. Things had happened fast with us, at least by my usual timetable; now, she'd been gone for three months and all that time things between us got easier, more natural—we were relaxing into one another, and I wasn't inclined to question it.

Right away we were planning the garden we would put in. It would be the first garden I'd had since I left North Carolina. I planned to begin working on it soon as I returned to Missoula: over the coming weeks, I told Lisa, I would dig some raised beds on the south side of the yard, plant some sweet peas along the fence so their flowers would climb there, and put in a compost bin. Above the doorway, we decided, we would hang Emily Dickinson's words: "I dwell in possibility / a fairer house than prose."

"Possibility"? Me? For the first time since I'd moved West, I would be out of the basement. And what about this: I was going to stay on in Montana. Through my two and a half years here, I had never called Montana home, never given myself over to it in the way one must to make a home of a place, never given myself over to the vicissitudes of its weather, to the peculiarities it spawned in its natives.

But it seemed I was ready to try. Spring came here a full month later than it did at home. There were precious few hardwood trees, and not much water, so there was very little to come green. I was walking uphill, and left and right of me were those meadows of sage and grass. As I climbed up that slope that April morning, I realized that for the first time I did not look at this landscape and wish to see green everywhere. I saw green, yes, in the pines on the mountainsides; but here were browns and golds and granites too. This is how making a home begins: we look upon a landscape and see what it is, rather than what it is not.

Now I crested the hill and saw for miles and miles below and before me a valley and ranches off in the distance. I stopped there on the crest and rolled myself a cigarette. Throughout my life the walks I had most admired were along streams, in the valleys. I'd never much sought the long view, the ascent.

In the Mission Mountains, off in the distance, there was every day a little less snow down the mountainside, a little more of the rock showing. Everything all about was atremble and waiting to take on another shape. It was the season of coming forth into the world, scrappy and ragged. Ragged but right, the old hymn says: but right? What is right? Being true to one's nature? Or submersing it entirely? Could any faithless shape like my own ever steady itself into trust?

I lifted my head. I was in the open with the day's light full on my face now. I pulled down my boonie hat and kept on walking along the ridgetop. Even going downhill into the valley I was in an openness unimaginable in the Appalachians, breathing in the Rocky Mountain springtime, looking out over the horizon before me: with its gentle undulation, its subdued colors, its sky. And all day I was walking in it, trying to imagine how it would feel to belong here.

Ten hours later I reached the crest of that same hill, coming back to Hot Springs just as the sun was beginning to go down behind the Cabinet Mountains. In recent weeks I had begun these walking sessions, walking meditations of a sort; I was also arising early and spending an hour reading the Bible and then in silent meditation. I would breathe slow and deep and careful and try to still my mind, try to empty my head of its ceaseless rattling. Try to fill myself with love, or gratitude or blessedness.

But there was something I wasn't getting. In my last session with Anita, two weeks before, I had been carrying on about my inability to feel better about myself. Finally she asked me: What would it take for you to feel redeemed? How do you imagine that happening?

I'm sure I crinkled my brow and looked befuddled. So she repeated herself: "Being redeemed, to you specifically—feeling that your self is something other than stupid and doomed—what would it mean?"

Redemption? I was dumbfounded. I scarcely thought about such words. But it seemed she was on to something: redemption was exactly what I wanted. How could I ever feel redeemed? I tried to imagine it. Finally I told her that I would feel redeemed if I could be somebody else. Perhaps a different species altogether. If I had to be human, I didn't want to be this particular human.

"That's not a valid answer," she said. "Try again."

So I told her that I would feel redeemed if the pills would work again. I was not being facetious. Perhaps one of those newer antidepressants would have just the right touch, like a key fitting the slot and the tumblers dropping into position just so. I wanted this now because when the antidepressants were working, I had little concern for my sins and shortcomings. What was done was largely irrelevant. Things were good right now, in this moment, and it seemed they would remain so. For as long as the antidepressants worked, that feeling stayed around. And I wanted it back.

Now I made my way down the hill and sat on a stone. Here on the ground the light was russet. From the meadow a sage grouse called. I looked in that direction. A ray of sun fell across the field and in its light a bleached pile of bones shone. I moved to them: apparently this was where local ranchers disposed of coyotes they shot or trapped. All around this boneyard there was a circle of flowers. At one time I had known myself by my desires, and fulfilled them as if commanded to, and mourned their absence sourly—considered the loss of them worth losing my life for. I had known myself by my work, and then that was lost. Now I knew myself by my shortcomings, real or imagined, and it seemed I did not want to yield even the idea of those. Verily, my grief was my self. But at least I knew that grief, at least I could name it for what it was, and make its presence tangible. To yield it, to contemplate the death of this self, frightened me to the quick.

I walked away from the flowering boneyard, crossed the road, and started down the slope. Just below me at the edge of my vision a blue streak into a sagebrush. Mountain bluebird, the blue of a mountain lake, the first blue in the eastern sky just before the sun slides up into it.

I stooped into a crouch and stilled myself. How to make the apparently isolated story of one invisible life, with its perplexing desires and compulsions, fit into the larger ongoing story of unfolding creation? How do we negotiate between biology—what is given to us—and spirit—our yearnings to rise above the often selfish demands of our bodies and minds? The bird sat there in the sage, its morning-glory blue resplendent against the lambent teal of the sage. How to pierce the cocoon of my self?

The sun was slanting into its last long rays. The bluebird flew off. The light was receding, and the warmth following with it. The smell of the earth went up as it always does in the springtime dusk. I started on down the slope. All above me every hour of the day, while I repeated to myself this one ongoing flashback featuring my own inadequacy and foolishness, there was this great drama of the sky, the endless narrative of the animals: all about us, all is story. Regret cements us within one set piece. It makes for an unchanging landscape, a short-sighted monochrome; if we dwell in it we fail to yield to that story. What did my wrongs, my faults, my incompetencies have to do with the circle of life all about me, with the comings of this or that season?

For now—just as my foot falls again onto the Montana earth, and far as I know at this instant not another moment beyond that—for no reason I can discern, my story is some part of all this unfolding going on all about me. As long as I regret, I will myself to remain outside that story.

Forgiveness, according to some, is at the very center of Christianity. It offers us a liberation from the self that would hold its own hurts and failures above all else. Holding the self above all is a kind of death, as it isolates us from creation going on all about us. Forgiving gives us a different death of the self, one that would restore us to creation. It is literally a rebirth: freeing us from seeing creation through our desires or our projections or our regrets, the resurrection of forgiveness enables us to see the heaven that our earth is, and to find our place in it.

This was the death of self that I needed. The literal meaning of "conversion" is to turn toward, and in that Montana dusk I finally turned myself toward death. This is where my walking had brought me, and I wanted to go on walking now, walking to discover the cartography of my inward journey, walking to discover how that map would join me to these outward landscapes. I wanted my walking to work loose all that was superfluous—to tremble free all that was withered. I wanted my walking to soften me, to fit my shape to yield, even if it was the ongoing emptying out into the darkness that we call a nervous breakdown.

"Walk hard, and regret nothing." This is what I aimed to do. This line from a Charles Wright poem ("Depression Before the Solstice") I had a couple of weeks before copied out into my commonplace book. It was the necessary condition of any pilgrim: to regret nothing. The past will never again be ours, and the future belongs only to God, or the unseen force of Time—whatever you prefer to call it; this moment is all we have.

"Wayfaring Stranger" refers to "the cross of self-denial," and even before our self-obsessed times the work of forgetting the self was known to be difficult, a cross we will drop and remind ourselves to pick up hundreds of times daily, a struggle to be enacted in nearly every breath. I knew I would find this hard: it would require imagination, and discipline, and restraint; on the whole, it seemed to run precisely counter to my own nature. But to bear that cross would mean to be born again, to be born into wholeness. It means to yield to some will larger than our own.

Now the great robe of light in the sky was loosening its last cinches and wandering further west. I started for the house. I wanted to stop my wallowing now and I wanted to start walking. I prayed: this stranger here, Lord Jesus, this pilgrim: pardon his trespass.

To bear that cross, to forget the self, means to walk hard, and regret nothing. Such walking turns loose a chorus of glossolalia: the tongue of the foot sole traces its kisses across the sod; the tongues of grass moan into the wind; the tongues of trails wind into the mouth of the dark woods; the root-tongues of the oak sink and spread beneath the soil. All these tongues sing both blessing and curse, praise and doubt. They sing true to the story that is creation. And here I was, my tongues giving off their own tunes, one small moving smudge in the corner of the horizon, walking westward, all tongue now singing the dimming of the day, this moment, this footfall, and nothing else. And therefore everything else.

"And Jesus said unto him, No man, having put his hand to the plow, and looking back, is fit for the kingdom of God." And the tongue of the gospel plow sings its own song: Preacher said I had to repent, So right down the aisle I went.

"Take my yoke upon you," Jesus said, "and learn of me; for I am meek and lowly in heart: and ye shall find rest unto your souls.

"For my yoke is easy, and my burden is light." I put my neck into the yoke, and I walk where that old song leads: Put your hand to the plow, that tongue sang, And hold on. Hold on. Hold right on. Don't look back.

CHAPTER FIVE

MARTY WAS THE FIRST ONE AWAKE in the Bison Valley Group Home, pulling on the chain by his bed that set off the hallway buzzer. I was in the kitchen getting breakfast foods out of the cabinets and the freezer, glancing out the window as the May morning came to Missoula.

I had walked my way back into the world. I'd finished my graduate program in late April, and the following weekend I started to work for the home health care agency that hired me out to this group home. The agency allowed us to set our own schedules, and I had arranged to work fifteen-hour days on Saturdays and Sundays, trying to keep my weekdays free for the gardening work at Lisa's— soon to be our—place on Poplar Street.

I reported for work at seven on Saturday mornings, to this small ranch-style house in a residential neighborhood behind Kmart. The residents were men and women, mostly in their twenties and thirties, who had sustained traumatic brain injuries, just about every one of them in an auto accident. During the week each one had a daily routine: they went to school or to sheltered workshops. But for all the best efforts at rehabilitation, most of these men and women would never again live independently.

My morning task in the group home was to wake up the men, then shower and dress them according to their plans for the day— the staff would accompany some of them to ball games, some to the park, and some to church; occasionally family members would come to take them home for a visit. Once they were all seated at the kitchen table, I would then fix them breakfast. I entered Marty's bedroom and he raised an arm off the bed, grinned at me, and grunted a hello. I smiled at him, raised a finger to my lips and pointed at the other bed, where Marty's roommate was still sleeping. He nodded his head. In addition to their physical injuries, most victims of traumatic brain injuries suffer from short- and long-term memory loss, so establishing new relationships or learning job skills is nearly impossible. Many of them also suffer hallucinations and severe depressions; in fact, all of the Bison Valley residents were on antidepressants. Most of them had to use body language to communicate; their injuries nearly always had taken speech from them, and because of their memory losses even those who still had free use of their hands were mostly incapable of learning sign language. But many of them went on trying to speak, and often seemed to believe they'd been perfectly clear when to our ears what emerged was more often a series of grunts and groans.

Marty's Attends was full. I pulled on rubber gloves, removed it, and cleaned him with a warm washcloth. I rolled off his condom catheter, wrapped a towel around his waist, and carried the bedpan to the toilet. Back in his room, I pulled a wheelchair to the bedside. I bent over Marty and he put his arms around my back. I lifted him off the bed and maneuvered him into the wheelchair. Of the seven residents here, six required wheelchairs. Although their injuries had seriously compromised their arm strength and coordination, only one of the residents had an electric chair. None of the others could afford one—they cost roughly as much as a new compact car. The house had conventional narrow hallways, leaving scant width for two wheelchairs to navigate, so there were many mishaps, which often led to wheelchair-to-wheelchair shoving matches.

I pushed Marty into the bathroom, set him before the mirror, and pulled the door to. I got out his electric razor and began shaving

him. Like most of the men here—and there was only one woman—
Marty was young, still in his twenties. On his dresser were pictures
of his child and his ex-wife; driving home from work one night six
months after he graduated high school, Marty had been hit head-on
by a semi. His wife was five months pregnant at the time. In the immediate aftermath of such an accident, it is hard to know what sort
of life the victim might be restored to; so it is hard to know whether
the heroic measures that saved Marty's life were a blessing or a
curse. Four years after his accident, the Marty his family had
known—by all accounts a good-natured country boy—was a distant
memory. And it seemed, understandably, that families preferred the
memory to the present reality, so they rarely visited the group home.
In the aftermath of our residents' accidents their spouses had all filed
for divorce.

I slid back the plastic shower curtain and set Marty's shampoo
and soap in the shower rack. I wheeled him from the sink to the
shower area, and I bent over to lift him out of his wheelchair. From
here, holding Marty in my arms, I would walk him up a ramp, guide
him down into the shower stall, and then maneuver him into the
shower chair. The shower chair had wheels on it, which should have
locked but didn't, and the shower floor was often damp. Damp or
dry, it was always a hair-raising chore, getting the residents into that
chair. Marty knew just how vulnerable he was here. The week before, when I lifted him out of his wheelchair to start the transfer into
the shower, he had pressed his palm into my shoulder blade and
made two loud, monosyllabic grunts that I couldn't quite make out.
His tone was urgent, and I feared that I had hurt him somehow, so I
lowered him back into the wheelchair to see if I could read his lips.
I had no luck with that, so I continued with the shower. When I
moved to lift him out of the shower chair and back into his wheelchair he repeated this request, or whatever it was. When we finished
the shower I reported all this to my shift partner, a woman whose
one year of experience at the group home made her the senior staff
member.

"He's asking you to kill him," Tammy told me. Marty was smart.
It wouldn't have been hard to accomplish his death during that

transfer from his wheelchair to the shower chair: a slight slip would have sent him caroming off the walls and onto the floor, headfirst. And nobody would have suspected anything: the whole procedure was so awkward, so strained that it would have appeared accidental.

On this Saturday as we moved into the shower Marty repeated his request. To be frank, I had a hard time denying him: what did he have to look forward to? Depression as I knew it was the least of Marty's afflictions. In time each of my episodes would subside and I would resume some manner of meaningful living. But every morning for the rest of his life Marty would be attended to by some stranger like me. It was sobering work. After I finished my morning routine at Bison Valley, I went on home visits: first to see Douglas, a man rendered quadriplegic in his mid-twenties, in a rock-climbing accident. I'd get Douglas out of bed, fix his breakfast, clean his apartment, do his laundry, and visit with him until noon. I'd spend the afternoon making similar home visits, with stroke victims, accident victims, and diabetics who had suffered amputations. Cooking meals, cleaning house, doing yard work; whatever needed doing is what I did. At five I'd return to the group home to help fix and serve supper, give evening showers to those who preferred them, and then help the residents into bed.

At 10 p.m. I clocked out for the day and went home. It wasn't hard to find this sort of job in Missoula: as medicine is increasingly able to help the victims of such traumatic accidents survive, the direct care field is a growing one. I treasured the work. In our residents' lives there were few tactile, tangible pleasures, and I could let my hands communicate to them comfort and soothing as I washed their backs or lathered shampoo into their scalps. There was the leisurely pace of the weekend days: I could cook up a big breakfast of eggs and pancakes and bacon and hash browns. I could take them to Wal-Mart or to a movie on a rainy Saturday. I could drive them out to see the scenery. For them, these were rare pleasures.

I'd always enjoyed these work situations where one of my jobs was to make a place—a homeless shelter, a group home—feel and work like a home. And I had none of the responsibilities of a case manager. That was a good thing. I was an entry-level worker in this field; to me fell the most menial tasks. And that was a good thing too.

For the first time in months I felt useful, doing what I knew I could do: offer support and try to lift spirits; and I could remain calm in the crises that often arose with seven adults living together in a very small house. To feel capable is no small thing. I was making money, sure, and I needed to; but I also got to serve other people, and that was a real blessing, a tangible step out of my self.

On the first of June I would move into the house on Poplar Street. It was full of light, surrounded by black walnut trees and lilac bushes. It would be an end to my basement dwelling. And now there would be a garden there.

I walk, and I love to raft or float a river, and I garden; that is about the extent of my outdoor activity. I don't fly-fish, I don't hunt elk, I do not rock-climb; I don't golf; I don't ski. In recreation-mad Missoula I felt a bit like a freak, but none of your high-risk adventure sports for me: give me a garden and I am fulfilled. And in this case I was making something for the life Lisa and I would have together.

There hadn't been a garden on Lisa's place in many years, so there was some soil-building work to be done. There was a suitable garden spot on the south side of the house, a nice flat rectangle with good exposure and drainage, and there was a small terrace up the hillside where I could dig a bed for herbs, and several spots around the house where I could dig flower beds. I borrowed tools and started the work in April. Then I set about trying to build the soil, trying to get the right mixture of humus and plant nutrients, making it friable, arable, and robust without using chemical fertilizers. I had decided to make two four-by-fifteen-foot raised beds for our vegetables. With Lisa's reel mower I cut the grass close to the dirt as I could. Then I used a mattock to work loose the sod, trying to retain as much of the topsoil as I could. This work might have been easier with a rototiller, but I wanted to make the garden with my own hands, and I wanted to sweat. I piled the pieces of sod behind the house so that I could use them to start a compost pile.

After I had the sod cut and moved, I used the mattock to work loose the top foot or so of soil. It was full of stones. I pried and lifted and carted them off in buckets. Then I set about double-digging. Raised beds make possible intensive gardening: in those deep beds of loosened soil, roots can spread downward, and deeply, rather than horizontally, as they will in shallower topsoil. Consequently plants can be placed closer together than in a conventional garden; in many cases you can fit twice as many plants in the rows of a raised-bed garden. Deep, rich, loose soil is absolutely essential to the project. I was happy to make it ready. I spent three days doing the double-digging, spading the loosened topsoil into a wheelbarrow and then using the mattock and spade to loosen the subsoil. Then I brought back the wheelbarrow and restored the topsoil. This done, I dug a trench three feet deep and three feet wide between the beds, using that soil to build up the raised beds on either side. I brought the sod back in the wheelbarrow and upended it into the bottom of the trench, starting our compost heap.

Once the beds were double-dug, filled, and raised, I had a truck-load of composted sheep manure delivered and spent another day hoeing and raking that into the soil. Next I went to work on the terrace, uprooting dozens of knapweed plants, a so-called "invasive exotic" that is taking over many thousands of acres in Montana. When the terrace was cleared to the ground I readied that space for the herb beds I planned to put there. Then, since the raised beds were near the trailhead up Mount Jumbo, I installed a fence around them to keep dogs and deer out. I planted the sweet peas along the fencerow, hoping they would grow, twine their tendrils into the fence, and be in full flower by the time Lisa returned the last week of June.

I might have been the saturnine character in one of those old broadsheets, working the garden with my hand tools. The smell, the sight, and the feel of healthy soil is one of the most sensuous experiences I know. After working in the garden on Poplar Street I would go to campus to write Lisa about my progress with it, my body pleasantly heavy with fatigue. There was much to anticipate, and from one day to the next there was much to relish. My weekday life, centered on the garden and reading and writing, had a slow and simple rhythm; and I was deeply engaged by my weekend work. I also knew now what I wanted—and how new, how welcome this warm flush of certain and specific desire—I wanted to sit still and settle in there with Lisa.

Along about mid-May I had all the beds ready. In Montana, with the arid climate and short growing season, gardening wouldn't be so simple as it had been in the Ohio Valley and in North Carolina, where, by comparison, it seemed one could sit on the porch in spring and spit seeds in the general direction of bare dirt and have a lush garden come August. In Montana, a gardener needs locally adapted short-season varieties and you must plan the garden with care. As you would anywhere—but it's even more critical here since the plants have to accomplish their life cycle in a fairly short span of time—you must orient the beds to make the most of the summer sunlight.

I talked with local gardeners, and I perused seed catalogues from local distributors. The genetic varieties sold in the national catalogues were adapted to longer seasons and wetter climates, so would fare poorly in Montana, if at all. I drafted and redrafted diagrams of the beds. E-mails went back and forth as Lisa and I discussed what we would plant. I set about buying the seeds and the starter trays, and I wrote out a planting schedule: first the lettuce and salad greens and radishes and turnips and carrots. Then the potatoes, cucumbers, broccoli, and snow peas. Last, just before Memorial Day, all danger of frost (mostly) past, I would put in the tomatoes and then the squash, beans, and corn. These last three would all grow together. I planned to plant the corn in circles four feet in diameter, setting three wooden stakes out in a triangle around each circle and tying them together at the top, tepee style, to serve as bean poles; on the ground I would plant the zucchini, giving it the room it needed to spread. In this way all three of these would get all the sunlight and earth they needed, in just four square feet of space.

But all that was still to come. On the morning of May 18 I was in the garden, seed packets for radish and carrot and turnip and salad greens in a box, yardstick and trowel and watering can at my side.

Before anything could go into the ground I had one last thing to do. For generations, before more precise testing was available, farmers relied on this very simple test as a reliable arbiter of their planting ground. You want a rich, deep taste, not too bitter and not too sweet, but maybe just a little sweet. So on that morning, the sun up but not yet risen above Mount Jumbo, the smell of lilacs all about me, I knelt there in our garden and I cupped my hand into the dark earth and raised a palm's worth to my mouth, and lo, it was good.

PERHAPS THERE *IS* SOMETHING intrinsically spiritual about the melancholic experience. You might recall that the evolutionary psychologist John Price believes the adaptive function of depression is to enable us to let go of worldly attachments; precisely what most spiritual practice aims at. Cultures the world over have treated it with spiritual rites and ceremonies; even now, the accounts of those for whom antidepressants have done their magic sound rather like conversion narratives, speaking of "miracles" and of "rebirth."

It seems those who wish to investigate the biological location of the soul could do worse than study melancholia, since for so many that elusive indefinable thing is precisely what seems to absent itself when the episodes strike. Given its cynicism and the self-absorbed despair, no wonder melancholia has always been suspected of having truck with evil and sorcery and blasphemy; it's no wonder acedia was one of the cardinal sins. There is something here that reeks of sulfur and brimstone; Sartre said, famously, *"l'enfer c'est les autres"*—hell is other people—and other people are hell to a melancholic; but the true hell of this illness is its endless self-absorption. *"L'enfer c'est* moi" is its motto. This is the leaden weight of melancholia, and here is its shear and its stab; here is the rent out which all buoyancy leaks. This wants escaping—but from the prison of *moi* there is little escape. We know that nothing worldly, nothing that pertains to the self—no workplace promotion, no well-received novel or painting—will diminish melancholia by much or for long. If at all. It defies ambition; it defies self-making by spending; it defies radical individualism; it makes monkeyshines of "self-realization" and "self-actualization" and "being your own best friend" and "following your bliss."

Its abiding notion—that the self as given is inadequate, and can be made full by nothing wordly—might explain why for centuries, and in some quarters to this day, our European and aboriginal ancestors saw melancholia as an instance of grace, a nearly unmatched opportunity to learn to reach beyond the self to restore a lost soul. And like some spiritual principle, it stands opposed to the great icons of our age: the machine, the marketplace, and the self. It lends itself to one of the cardinal sins of our secular times—a crime against the divinity of Self. Acedia was an apparently willful refusal to surrender to faith. Our fetishes are "happiness" and "self-esteem," and melancholia appears willfully opposed to those too.

Our spiritual approaches to melancholia seem to me among the most creative adaptations our kind has yet made to an entity whose nature sometimes appears wholly malevolent, wholly at cross-purposes with humankind. And though we hear little of them these days, the idea seems too apt to vanish altogether. In 1964 the Trappist monk Thomas Merton, who considered John of the Cross something of a personal hero, wrote of the "dark night of the soul" as if it were still very much with us: "It is a confrontation, sometimes prolonged, with an astounding recognition of the otherness of the self . . . [In the dark night] we begin to go out of ourselves: that is to say, we are drawn out from behind our habitual and conscious defenses. These defenses are also limitations, which we must abandon if we are to grow."

Nor is such talk limited to clerics and philosophers. In the early 1990s Harvard sociologist David Karp compiled a kind of ethnography of the melancholic subculture. Rather than rely on psychiatric data or clinical impressions of depression, Karp interviewed fifty melancholics, among them students, housepainters, unemployed waiters, and travel agents. In a postscript to the book that presents the results of his research, *Speaking of Sadness*, Karp—himself a depressive for over twenty years when he authored the book—writes that "the primary change in my thinking has less to do with society exactly than with a heightened respect for the value of spirituality in responding to sickness." More than anything else Karp learned from his fieldwork, "the claim of several respondents that the agony of depression has been instrumental in their spiritual growth" took him by surprise. "One unanticipated aspect of depression revealed in the interviews is the connection between depression and spiritual life . . . although questions of spirituality were not in my head when I began interviewing, I was quickly sensitized to the depression/spirituality link."

Some of those Karp interviewed were successfully taking antidepressants; the spiritual approach appears to be compatible with medications. Another point worth noting: according to Karp, "there was far more interest in Buddhism among this group of fifty Americans than chance alone could possibly explain. When I admitted my ignorance about Buddhism, several explained in nearly identical words that they found valuable its tenet that 'pain is inseparable from life.' "

Of course, that idea is present in Christian teachings too, and in recent years a number of leading Christian pastoral counselors— from Catholics and Episcopalians to evangelical Protestants—have developed Bible study programs outlining spiritual approaches to depression. It is easy to see the appeal of such approaches. Accepting melancholia as a kind of spiritual mentor offers a creative way to respond to it—"creative" used here to indicate the antonym of "passive." Approaching it in this way, we have no choice but to engage with it.

Such an approach can help us negotiate the strictures of biological determinism—and teach us to put temperament to the best possible uses—and the ephemeral satisfactions of protean seeking after "self-esteem"; which is what most faith practice aims at anyhow. "Our journey," wrote Merton, "is from the limitations and the routines of the given which confronts us as we are born into it without choice—and to the creative freedom of that love which is personal

choice and commitment. Paradise symbolizes this freedom and creativity, but in reality this must be worked out in the human and personal encounter with the stranger seen as our other self."
Melancholia forces that "sometimes prolonged, often astounding"
encounter with that stranger, that other self. In my case his name was
Mr. Shoulder.

That encounter cannot be passive. The practice of surrendering
the self, requiring as it does ongoing attention and mindfulness, can
only be passive—entirely given to us—on rare and blessed occasions.
Most of the time we must work at it. And the protean, store-bought
self will not do. One must meet with the self as given, and not evade
it. Mother Ann Lee told the Shakers: "A thing or a person is good in-
sofar as it is what it is meant to be. Do be natural. A poor diamond
is better than an imitation."

Nor can we simply accept that self as given; we must make a confrontation with it, as Merton says, and mostly we must do it alone.
You've got to walk that lonesome valley, the old gospel song says,
And you've got to go there by yourself. This confrontation seems
necessary in all our spiritual traditions, and perhaps melancholia
helps effect this negotiation; perhaps its very biology bridges body to
soul, or self to spirit, if you prefer it put that way.

As it turns out, the Bible doesn't much support the idea that humans
have any "dominion" over creation. Nowadays, most biblical schol-
ars feel "dominion" is a mistranslation; in the original, they say, the
concept was closer to "stewardship"—that humans have a responsibility to take care of creation, in perpetuity, for future generations;
and apparently most Christians these days prefer the "stewardship"
idea. They point out that there are two creation stories in the Book
of Genesis. The second is often overlooked: "And the Lord God
formed man of the dust of the ground, and breathed into his nos-
trils the breath of life; and man became a living soul." Even if the
language of the translation isn't "inclusive," there is nothing of
"Adam's rib" male primacy here, and there is nothing of human su-
premacy: we are made from the same dust as all else, and vivified by

the same breath of God that inspired—in the literal sense of the word—all the other animals, all of creation.

This is pretty close to what I had always believed: all life is one. This was a Christianity I could give myself over to.

So this melancholic landscape had changed again: now I saw it all set about with prayer flags and wailing walls and stations of the cross, and across the ground the footprints of the pilgrims who walked this way before me. That May I told Anita that I resented the idea that I might somehow need God, when so many others seemed to walk about sanguine, autonomous, and whole. To our next session she brought Merton's *Thoughts in Solitude*. "The spiritually poor man loves his very insufficiency," she read to me, and "the value of our weakness and of our poverty is that they are the earth in which God sows the seed of desire." She paused, turned a few pages, and then read this: "Poverty is the door to freedom, not because we remain imprisoned in the anxiety and constraint which poverty of itself implies, but because, finding nothing in ourselves that is a source of hope, we know there is nothing in ourselves worth defending. There is nothing special in ourselves to love. We go out of ourselves therefore and rest in Him in Whom alone is our hope."

And who knows better his very insufficiency, his very poverty, than the melancholic? Neither Tony nor Anita was trying to make me into a self-despising Christian; I think she knew how all of this fit the particular structures and needs of my own melancholia. She taught me how to turn toward it. I am a little awed yet by her insight, the way she found for grace to get to a locked-up spirit.

So when I walked that May I whispered to myself this chant of unbecoming: Melancholic, unform thyself. What is superfluous is my will, my desire, my ego. Annihilate the self and do away with separateness; annihilate whatever comes between me and God—which can now and forever only be me.

In these four months I had lost my place in the world. So I still called my melancholia "walking death"—but now I accounted the death part of it differently. This death was a yielding; I would, like any pilgrim, surrender my affairs into the hands of God. Walking death it is: I will know better this walking death; may it keep me walking, a little unraveled always.

THAT SPRING record amounts of rain fell on Missoula. Upslope from our garden site Mount Jumbo turned green; across the Clark Fork the west flank of Mount Sentinel greened; all the rain made the year's pollen crop a rich one, and then I fell into hay fever. I sneezed and I sniffled and I worried. And I worried some more: that the lack of sun would inhibit the germination of the seeds, that they would rot right there in the soil.

Merton wrote of the "dark night": "The transmutation of the whole man is required here—not a careful and departmental cultivation of that which we like to call his 'spiritual' side." I understood Merton to mean that our conversion will reformulate us, transform us entirely, that the "spiritual" must inform my moment-by-moment living. I felt plenty spiritual after my morning prayers, but out in the world it was a challenge—then, later, still.

I was still doing my weekends for the home health care agency, and picking up some overnight shifts at the group homes, filling in for people on vacation. My weekdays were still mostly free for walking and reading and writing and working in the garden. Once the danger of frost passed, I'd transplanted herbs from starter trays into their bed on the terrace: catnip for Pueblo right at its near edge so that she wouldn't traipse over the other plants getting after it; rosemary, tarragon, basil, borage (but no hellebore), lavender, chamomile, lovage, and so on. Up the hillside from the terrace I had planted a long quarter-moon of sunflowers and beneath them I planted scarlet poppies.

I was starting to see Merton's point: faith enters into absolutely everything. I'd never thought of it this way before, but now I realized that a gardener of whatever stripe begins in faith: that this small seed, flesh of last year's plant, will find its proper depth and orientation in the soil, receive enough water, resist whatever ails it. At first there is nothing but a plot of bare earth and the gardener's imagination: sketches on graph paper of what belongs where, and the winter months perusing seed catalogues, conjuring up visions of the harvest. Then there is the bodily labor of preparing the garden, in the late winter or early spring, making faith tangible, manifest, concrete, mixing in new compost and manure—their rot assuring a deep rich soil bed.

Then the careful planting, and then the watering; we can labor only so much, and beyond that our gardens are dependent on forces we cannot control. You can have all the best books, the finest tools, the finest seed stock; you can apply all the lessons of science and all the lessons of those who have gone before. But putting that seed into the ground is still finally an act of faith: that some set of forces will conspire to yield up once more food or flowers or greens or herbs.

It requires some imagination, and some faith, to maintain our hope that the garden will blossom. It was some miracle, Jesus turning the water into wine at Cana, but, as Wendell Berry has written, "the real miracle is the way water and dirt becomes fruit and wood." It is no miracle if the outcome is a foregone conclusion, if we wrest it entirely under our control. Surely a large part of what pulls any gardener to the soil is that mystery, the creative work of imagining and the mental gymnastic of maintaining faith.

That spring, as I waited for the first sprouts to appear in our garden, I needed assurance so badly that I came very near to taking up my trowel and scraping away the dirt to see if our seeds had in fact taken hold. This desperate act might have given me assurance. But it would also kill off the seedlings. In any situation, I was starting to see, like consequences follow from acting out of fear and faithlessness. Which was exactly how I had lived most hours of my life.

The only bridge from my cynicism and fear to faith was, it seemed, in the imagination. This new approach to melancholia required imposing one set of explanations and expectations and understandings for another. Hopefully it would manifest then in the world, and one set of actual responses and earthly conduct would in time replace another. But it began in the imagination. This may have been why I found this spiritual approach to melancholia so elegantly suited to the condition. Melancholia happened for me largely in the imagination. The "leap of faith" is imagination vaulting over and beyond "proof" and "reason"; and if faith is an act of imagination, then it could meet with melancholia, at least in my case, right where it lived. And it might transform that landscape yet again.

The sun shone for three consecutive days over the first weekend in June. I had just moved into the Poplar Street house. I spent Saturday and Sunday at my work, and when I stood out in the garden early on Monday, the morning sun bathing my flesh, rows of sprouts were showing themselves. Sweet pea vines were up out of the ground and twining their way into the fence.

There would be more fear in my life, and soon: in less than three weeks Lisa would return and we'd start our life together in this house. There would be joy, but I was nervous about it too. "Ah, intimacy," Tony said when I confessed my fears to him. "You might have a problem with that, but I guess nobody's ever been close enough to you to find out."

I laughed; no denying that.

"Well," he went on, "you've just finished with another master's degree. Now you're starting a terminal Ph.D. program in life. That's what intimacy will do for you." I knew from his tone that he was not being cynical.

But I was ready to try; Lisa would be home in just a few days. In my mind's eye I saw her graceful, precise gestures, heard her even voice, felt the peace of her eyes: she was full of grace, and I knew by then that whatever faith we possess shapes our graces as we move. I wanted this life here with her; I wanted that grace in my own gestures. I could name what I wanted—which was a start, anyhow. To tell you the truth, reader, as I sit here some years later remembering it, imagining you hearing this story, I am still a little red-faced. It is such a conventional, pastoral, prototypically American story: first the woman, then the church, then the garden, saves the man from himself. He runs like any bourgeois philistine from his encounter with nothingness. It wasn't intellectually reputable; there was nothing ironic or hip about it, nothing smart, nothing unique.

Exactly. "Pride goeth before a fall." It was as if my melancholia caviled at my every pretense and distance and finally would allow none of them. In my adult life I had thought of Christianity as a retreat from the everyday struggles of life into comfort and assurance, a retreat that offered a life-list of dos and don'ts to simplify life's ambiguities. I believed it offered a final and absolute answer, one that promised a certain final outcome if one simply followed its rules.

Religion, as Marx famously said, is an opiate—it is comprised of worldly institutions formed and administered by human beings, who do from time to time require simplicity and ease. But far as I could tell, faith—the encounter with mystery—was no opiate. It was no substitute for my antidepressants. Faith requires the utmost in moment-to-moment consciousness, a willingness to exercise imagination and to displace the self and its desire for instant gratification and sure bets. Make no mistake: for me this would be an ongoing struggle, learning how to avoid the cheap, cowardly out of cynicism.

Into my adulthood I fit the profile of Kagan's "avoidant" children: it was always my inclination to solve a situation by moving away from it. With earthly attachments—intimacy, and responsibility, and the like—I'd never done so well. My predilection was for flight and avoidance—fleeing off into the abstract, into the ether and vapor, and not into the soil and muck of an honest reckoning with life on some concrete and earthly terms. It was the weight—the lead—of melancholia that finally brought me into that soil, and then held me there. Something had to do it.

That Monday in early June, I was surprised over and again: the garden was coming up. For the first time in months, years, I would have changed places with nobody. I was struck with the paradox of it all: I had committed to the death of my self. Yet the aim of that death was to make me become more real and more present inside my skin; to incline me away from my habitual ambivalence, nostalgia, and regret. Needless to say, this was very different from the death-in-life of melancholia.

There was still melancholia, of course, with its parallel landscape. But this act of imagining leapt some gap, straddled those two landscapes. The Bible tells us the true name of God is "I Am"—that is, the eternal present. Living in faith is living in that present, and remembering that Moses found God in the darkness, that Jesus spoke of conversion as an anointing unto darkness. It seemed only faith, the imaginative leap into that darkness, could begin to move this melancholic beyond his self, to join up with the present moment of creation unfolding all about him.

On the summer solstice, a year after the start of our story, I turned over a bucket and sat atop it out by the garden. "Pilgrimage is necessary," wrote Thomas Merton, "because we have to come to the end of a long journey and see that the stranger we meet there is no other than ourselves—which is the same as saying that we find Christ in him." I had met with that stranger, and now would walk with him, rather than away; or so I hoped; or so I prayed.

As the sun dropped behind the Bitterroots I stood from my bucket, walked away from the house, and started up the mountainside. I walked that night by the light of the stars, and trusted them to guide me home. A walk is breath; a walk is a pulsing, our feet falling in perfect iambics through earth and air, each foot sole a perfect copper conducting from one element to the next that same pulsing that shines the stars and shimmers the night air.

I walked, and I sang into the night air lines from "Wayfaring Stranger," hearing in the ancient drones of its melody the thrum of mystery, the bittersweet vibrato of ongoing creation. "I'll take the cross of self-denial," I sing, "and enter in my home with God . . ."

I walk: and the next step is to fall down, down on my bended knees, down onto my praying ground.

BOOK IV

HOME

What's best in me lives underground,
rooting and digging, itching for wings . . .
—Stanley Kunitz

CHAPTER SIX

ON JUNE 28 I met Lisa's plane at the Missoula airport, with a bouquet of wildflowers from our garden in my hand. She had boarded her first plane in Vienna twenty-five hours earlier, but she looked absolutely fresh in her blue flowered summer dress; and again her smell, of rosemary and daisies. Back home we had dinner waiting: a salad of Buttercrunch and Deer Tongue lettuces, mixed with turnip greens, and arugula, some mint and edible flowers—calendula and nasturtiums—on top and tossed with a feta-garlic dressing. The main course was a tomato-zucchini tian with rosemary, dill, and chives. Poppies and Indian paintbrush and lupine fluted out a vase on the table.

Some of these things had come from the garden. We lit candles and sat there eating and talking far into the night, about the home we would have. And we did make a home. That summer was a rich time: our lives began to intertwine. I met Lisa's family, and her friends. In a brief time my life enlarged. My own circle of friends took warmly to Lisa. Many evenings that summer the house on Poplar was filled with her friends, or mine, or some combination of the two, and guitars and singing and laughter and food and wine. Some afternoons we would spread blankets on the lawn and serve up large salads from the garden. We'd sit in a circle and laze in the sun and talk, musicians and painters and social workers and pastry chefs and activists and former clients and writers and fathers and mothers and children.

Lisa returned to working at the music store and I kept up my weekend work with the home health care agency. At home together we worked in the garden, watering and weeding and planning the things we'd do differently next year; as dark came down—very late in the Montana summer, and I was glad for it now—we'd sit outside and watch the sun drop behind the mountains or we'd sit inside and read to one another. We listened to a lot of music; she showed me her favorites, I showed her mine. We had a peace and an ease with one another that I'd rarely known with anybody.

Sounds idyllic, don't it?

Maybe it was more peace and ease than I could stand. For alongside the above, rather impressionistic narrative of that summer there is another, one set in that ever-capacious, ever-expanding parallel universe of the melancholic landscape.

The history of "love melancholy" is as rich and ancient as "religious melancholy," and has been used to explain just about every variety of love and eroticism. Except, of course, the "lived happily ever after" sort. Burton devoted a full one-third of his *Anatomy*, the equal to a full tome in itself, to this melancholic variant. The stories are mostly what you would expect: melancholic states brought on by unrequited love; or by separation from the loved one (the wives of soldiers and sailors being particularly prone to this); or by the death of the beloved. Under this category also came melancholic states of unknown cause that expressed themselves through romantic or erotic obsessions.

There was an interesting tidbit or two in all this love-melancholy history. "The best possible remedy for melancholia is coitus." This would-be pickup line is in fact the opinion of the noted seventh-century Greek physician, Paul of Aegina. The notion prevailed for centuries, and was even recommended by Saint Hildegard of Bingen;

some benefit must have been observed. (In light of that, it's interesting to consider that our leading antidepressants so effectively inhibit orgasm that physicians routinely prescribe them to treat premature ejaculation in "normals"; in fact, they cause "ejaculatory failure or ejaculatory delay" in over half those who are taking them—including women, in case the *PDR*'s terminology makes it uncertain.)

Then, in general, under "love melancholy" comes also the particular difficulties melancholia makes for in an intimate relationship, because of that fearful, jealous, withdrawn, pessimistic nature. "They are never in favor with woman or wife," says one of those old health manuals of the saturnine type. My story fits best in this particular category. Some may be from Mars and some from Venus, and that might explain something about what happens in intimate partnerships—but some of us are from Saturn. That changes the story a little.

This parallel love-melancholy narrative started even before Lisa and I sat down to dinner together the evening of her return. Missoula's airport is about five miles west of town; out on the strip before we even got back to the downtown area, I saw blue lights in the rearview mirror. I made my way across the lanes and pulled onto the shoulder.

We sat in the swirling spray of blue light. On her side of the car Lisa sat still and grinned slightly, nervously. I reached into the glove box. I handed my license and registration to the officer now at my window.

"I'll need to see proof of insurance too," he said in a flat military monotone.

"Sure," I said. Nonchalantly I reached back into the glove box. I kept the certificate in a blue plastic pouch, and I handed it over to him. Yeah, "sure." With money being so tight, I sweated that insurance payment every month. More than once, I'd been tempted to take my chances and drive without it.

"Jeffery, you were going fifty-three in a thirty-five zone," he said. He appeared to give the matter a moment's thought, and then I watched a spasm of hilarity seize his features. "Are you dyslexic with numbers, by any chance?" When he stopped laughing he aimed his flashlight at my documents.

"Really?" I whistled. I tried to joke: "I didn't know this old car would move that fast."

He shone the flashlight into my face. "If you doubt my word I'll show you the radar readout."

Don't ask me why, but my next thought was, maybe this guy has a romantic heart. "Officer, I was just at the airport picking up my girlfriend here. This is Lisa Werner." I turned my face out of the flashlight glare and looked over to her. She smiled at him.

"Good evening, Lisa," he said. I heard his flashlight click off.

I looked up at his badge. "Lisa, meet Officer Reilly." He wasn't grinning, so I got on with my story. "She's just come back into town after six months of teaching in Eastern Europe." I paused, and then decided to make myself plain: "It's been a long time since we've seen one another. We're on our way home, and I guess I lost track of my speed."

Officer Reilly's face was still a blank. He bent down to look down the front seat. He smiled over at Lisa. "Ma'am, may I see your airplane ticket?" Lisa didn't flinch. She reached into the back and I heard her moving her things around.

"Jeff," I heard her say. She was leaning into the back of the car, and I didn't understand the rest of what she said. I looked over at her and she was trying to turn on the dome light.

"It doesn't work," I was saying, but just as the words left my mouth up alongside my ear the cop hit his flashlight switch. I jumped. The car filled with light.

"Thank you, Officer Reilly," Lisa said. She turned sidewise and reached into her bag and got out her ticket.

"Dome lights are real cheap, son," the cop said. "And pretty easy to install." He took her ticket and my license, registration, and insurance certificate and gathered them into a bundle. "Thank you, ma'am," he said, looking across the front seat at Lisa. Then he turned a glare onto me. "You stay right here, Jeffery."

He went back into his car. He was gone for a long time and I sat there trying to wipe off my sweaty palms. Then he was back. "Son," he said, "I do understand your hurry to be home, but eighteen miles over the limit, inside city limits, I can't let that go by."

So he wrote me a ticket, to the tune of $128. Which was about what I made in a weekend of work. I couldn't even get us home, on this of all evenings, without untoward incident.

And untoward incidents kept happening. Being a careful, graceful person, very precise in her movements and actions, clumsy accidents rarely befell Lisa. I observed this very early on, and it seemed to inspire in me a clumsiness beyond even my own previous level. In fact, as we washed the dishes after dinner that first evening, I dropped a Bavarian beer glass to the floor. It had been in her family for generations. Lisa said, "Oh, that's okay, it's only a thing."

A couple of evenings later I dropped a china serving platter as I carried our spaghetti to the living room, where we ate our meals. Pasta and sauce and shards of china went everywhere. Lisa stood up from her chair. "I'll get some forks and we'll eat off the floor," she joked.

I scorched meals from family recipes that I had fixed successfully dozens of times in the past. I couldn't even pop corn without filling the house with smoke. I set about to make Lisa some brownies one evening, set the oven to the wrong temperature—I was only off by about 125 degrees—and burned them to a crisp. I broke more dishes.

I'd go to the attic to get a book out of the boxes I had stored up there. Lisa got used to seeing me return with my forehead dripping blood after having bashed my forehead once again on the attic beam.

Obviously, even on my own I could make a decent chaos; then it seemed my force field affected even inanimate objects. One evening I plugged in the floor lamp, and the plug burst into a brief flame and then the lightbulb cracked and blew shards of glass all across the living room. One morning, I switched on the computer and before I even touched the keyboard, first one file, then another vanished until the entire hard drive was gone.

Tell me something, reader: is this any sort of person you'd want to live with? In all my life I had never been so inept. It is true that I had never been the most capable, handy guy you knew, but now I felt sure that Lisa must regard me as some domestic Jonah.

For it seemed it was just me. In the car I'd put a cassette into the machine and seconds later hear the crinkling sound of tape being wound into the machine's innards. I'd extract the cassette, with its yards of now-ruined tape dangling, and a few minutes later Lisa would slide in another tape and without fail it would play flawlessly, front side and back. Our bathtub plugged up. We borrowed from Lisa's brother-in-law Ron a plumber's snake to clear the line. I worked it down through the stagnant water and into the drain, pushing it just as far as it would go. The water stayed pooled and scummed up there around my wrists. I pulled the snake out of the drain and as I drew it out I saw that the spring had lost its tension, effectively ending its useful life.

Or almost. When a friend of Lisa's stopped by later that day, we told him about the problem, and he worked the snake down into the hole, same as I had, and *whoosh!* the water went right down with the snake. Bryan extracted the snake and handed it to me. "Well," he said, "it got that job done but it's not good for much more."

I was a household hazard and I knew nothing useful. I didn't know what Lisa was thinking, and it didn't matter what she told me, but I was convinced she'd seen enough already, and would be asking me to leave shortly.

Then there was my jealousy. This is a notable melancholic quality—the jealous lover being, along with the monk and the hypochondriac, another of Le Blon's "Types of the Melancholic," on the frontispiece of Burton's *Anatomy*. Experts past and present will attest to it, and I did nothing that summer to disprove them.

Late in July, Lisa's friend Marina needed to buy a dress for a wedding, so she asked Lisa to ride with her to Spokane to look for one. Glad to have the house to myself for a few hours, I spent the morning listening to music and writing. At ten I walked to the store and bought flour and yeast; I wanted to bake some bread. I had enjoyed baking bread ever since college, but since melancholia had begun two years before I'd baked none. Lisa said they'd be back around 5 p.m.; I wanted to have a fresh loaf awaiting them.

I wanted to show Lisa, after the past few weeks, that I could at least do this much right, was at least this useful. I chose an old favorite, wheat bread with oatmeal and hazelnuts. Except that when I began to turn the water into the flour the wooden spoon snapped. I replaced it with another and went on stirring.

When I rolled the mix out onto the baker's table it looked pathetic. Too dry, I thought. I added some water, I turned the dough, and I kneaded and kneaded—a task I customarily relish—and nothing improved. So I returned it to the bowl and stirred in some more water. Now the second goddamned wooden spoon broke. I turned on my heel and threw the handle across the house. Pueblo beat it the hell out of there.

I gouged my fingers into the lump of dough and plucked out the bowl of the spoon. I turned the dough out onto the baker's table, and started in to kneading again. "Furiously" would describe my kneading style right then. The dough lopped off into large chunks; it just would not meld together. I put it into the bowl again and stirred in some more water, and set about stirring with a metal slotted spoon. We were now all out of wooden spoons.

My first turn with the metal spoon and it lodged in the dough. The handle twisted. Now it too was ruined. Why did I think a metal spoon would work where a wooden one would not? The longer I thought about it, the stupider I got. I got out a grocery sack and threw the dough into it, then all three spoons. Rolled the top down tight and carried it out to the garbage can. I lifted the lid, threw in the sack, and slammed the lid back onto the can like a cymbal.

I did not want to sit around the house waiting for them to return, with nothing accomplished. I cleaned up my bread-making mess, taking care to leave no signs that I had even tried. By now it was getting on toward four. I got on my bicycle and took a long ride up Hellgate Canyon; I got back at five-thirty and there was nobody home, no messages on the machine. I was more restless than ever, and now I was worried too: what if there had been an accident?

Then it crossed my mind: perhaps she hadn't gone to Spokane at all. Maybe she had just gone off visiting some man somewhere. She'd lived in Missoula for ten years; surely she knew plenty of them. What if Lisa had seen enough of me already and had decided to try her luck elsewhere? It would be an understandable response. I was frightened. I had to get out of the house. So I took off again, this time walking—trotting, really—up the side of Mount Jumbo. I flat out ran clear across the mountaintop, trying to chase off this anxiety. Came down off the trail in another part of town.

From the light I guessed it was along toward seven. I was calmer now. I meandered home. Still there was nobody there, and still there was no message on the answering machine. I tidied up the bookshelves, putting books back and aligning their spines into orderly rows. I straightened up around my desk, got the next morning's work organized and ready to go. I swept the kitchen floor. I did all this without thinking. My mind was seized with one question: where is Lisa? Now they were three hours late, and still there was no message.

Strange that she wouldn't have called. Unless she's too busy with someone else. It would help if I did something else, something noisy, so I could ignore the silent phone. I started vacuuming; and I was working on the bedroom floor when Lisa and Marina came into the room.

I cut off the sweeper. But I didn't move. Lisa walked across the room and kissed me. "Hey, sweetie, cleaning house?"

My gorge was stuffed with words. I could taste bile just in back of them. Not a good time for me to speak. But still I had to communicate it somehow, didn't I? I looked long and hard at the clock.

Lisa handed me a book. "Look what I found."

It was one I'd been wanting. I mumbled some form of thanks. I looked at the clock again.

Lisa got it. "I'm sorry we're so late."

"I'm glad to know you're sorry," I said. "That's about all I know. For example, where have you been?"

"We had to go to a bunch of stores before we found the right dress."

"And how was I supposed to know that?" Lisa and Marina had met in Alabama, and Marina had lived in this house for several months when she first moved here. They were close, and they had not been together alone for months. They had a lot of catching up to do. But just then I saw no reason for it. All I could think of was, who has she been with? "I've been here just about all day and I haven't noticed the phone even trying to ring."

Marina moved out of the room. "I better get on home. See you all later."

Lisa looked over at me. She had a look; I'd never seen it before. "I'm going to see Mo off."

Momentarily Lisa was back. I heard her come in the door, then I heard her in the living room.

"I just checked the answering machine," she said. "It's turned off," she said. "I tried to call about one, when it was starting to look desperate, and it didn't pick up. I tried again at five and then again at seven, and it still didn't work."

I hadn't even thought to look at the machine. We usually turned off the ringer at night, and turned the volume off too. It seemed that when I'd hit the buttons this morning, thinking I was turning it back on, I had in reality switched the machine off entirely. Surprised? Lisa was kind enough not to mention it; she knew I knew, and let it go at that. And then, I'd been out every time she'd tried. I pulled on my earlobe. "I had myself convinced that you were with somebody else."

Lisa spun on her heel. Shaking her head, her lips drawn. "Not this again," she said. "Not this jealousy shit again. Not from you, not for me. You can trust me, I've told you before. And what good would I be if I told you such things and knew they were a lie? Take my word. I'm leaving you here alone for a while to stew it out of yourself. I'll be at Mary's." Mary was Lisa's sister, who lived a few blocks away. "Don't follow me. I'll be back before bedtime."

She walked right past me, and left without slamming the door or adding any other melodramatic touches. While she was in Moldova, I'd had a few attacks of fearful jealousy, inspired by one thing or another: I'd call in the early morning, her time, and her phone would ring and ring. Seven a.m. on a Saturday; where could she be? I did not think first of the many times the phone service there was faulty; and I knew that people in Moldova sometimes had to cut down telephone poles for firewood. But such facts did not deter me. All I could think was, she was awakening that morning with somebody else, perhaps this Tim character, like her last lover a Peace Corps veteran, the one she was always trading books and cassettes with.

I know how foolish all this sounds, how we'd just gotten together anyway, and so what if she did spend the night with somebody, she was thousands of miles from home, and maybe she got lonely—I know how unbecoming jealousy is, how downright ugly, small, and mean it makes us. It is as purely human as we get. It reveals too much; when we see it we want to turn our heads. And it would get ahold of me—and I would do things like this: make an ass of myself in front of one of her closest friends, and chase Lisa clean out of the house.

When she came back I apologized yet again; it seemed that half the words out of my mouth that summer were apologies. Now it was time for all my highfalutin ideas about faith and right living to get out of my head and walk in the world, and it wasn't working too well. I'd had to stop seeing Anita because my finances were so tight, so I was trying to figure this one out by the seat of my pants. I had no idea how to act as the faithful person I was trying to become. You can see it, I'm sure: I was afraid. Not to put too fine a point on it, I was scared shitless.

I was being *seen*, and I didn't have myself pulled together yet. I didn't feel *ready* to be seen. I was sure Lisa must think me truly cursed, a loser. But she'd make light of my clumsiness. "You're just being human," she'd say. In general she didn't seem inclined to project my ineptness into every area of my life. "We've got a beautiful garden out there, and you did that," she said to me one evening. "Don't tell me you can't do anything." She put me in my place when it was warranted, and firmly—but she never seemed to waver. She forgave what she saw in me; and she seemed to have some faith in me that I lacked entirely.

Burton, who classified the varieties of melancholia in a rather taxonomic fashion, placed "religious melancholy" as a kind of subspecies

under "love melancholy." That summer I would find my own reasons for conjoining the two.

From watching Lisa I had learned this: the faithful were a different tribe. She had never inquired after my doings, my comings and
goings, when she was in Moldova, not even in response to my ques-
tioning hers. She was not attached to things, not to clothes or jewelry, not even to books or CDs. Even though she loved music, and
from her work could obtain at deep discount—if not free—nearly
any CD she wanted, she wouldn't have a CD player in her house.

I'd been stunned when she told me this. With a perk like that I'd
have to add a room, just to store all the CDs I'd bring home. "Well,"
she said to me, "I like what I have already, and new things come my
way as often as I need them to. So why should I want more? I'm satisfied."

Satisfaction was an emotion I rarely knew. Could faith bring to a
person some fulfillment akin to satisfaction? Lisa had her ear tuned
to something larger, most of the time. She came from a Catholic family, the youngest of seven children, and from what I had seen of
them, faith mattered to the Werners. And it seemed Lisa had paid attention. In her I thought I could see faith informing, undergirding,
and guiding her—but it never seemed terribly obvious; although I
knew better, it sometimes seemed she came to it naturally. She was
patient, and she was calm, and she was observant. She seemed to feel
no compulsion to force things, and risk a false resolution. The faithful, I learned from watching Lisa, don't feel that their every need and
want ought to be met as a matter of course. Mostly, they don't live in
ongoing fear of judgment; they know themselves beloved, and forgiven.

Not like some of us.

In mid-August Lisa and I took an overnight trip to southeastern
Montana. On our way back to Missoula I was driving a back road
through the Big Hole valley. The road was long, straight, and empty,
and I was paying more attention to the landscape than to the highway. My eyes followed a troupe of antelope as they ran across the

prairie. Lisa shouted and bolted upright in her seat. The car was angling toward the shoulder. I hadn't noticed. I mashed the Toyota's brake to the floor and yanked the car onto the shoulder. It sputtered and stalled.

"Goddamnit," I said. I snapped off the radio. Lisa was backed against her door, her eyes wide. "Goddamnit. I just can't do anything right, huh? Not even drive." The sickly smell of gasoline filled the car. Lisa was silent over there, watching.

I looked over at her. "Well?" I asked. She was still silent. I wanted some reaction out of her. "If you won't trust me to drive, then you take over the wheel." I pulled the keys out of the ignition and hung them in front of her face until she reached up and took them.

I got out of the car and walked around to her side. She sat looking out the windshield. I crossed my arms. Finally she lifted herself over the emergency brake lever and sat in the driver's seat. I opened the door, climbed into the passenger seat, crossed my hands in my lap, and looked straight ahead.

Lisa turned the key and got the car started. She looked over at me. I turned my head. Her eyes were brimmed with tears. She blinked them back.

"That was totally uncalled for," she said, steely and firm. She took hold of the wheel at three o'clock and nine o'clock, pushed herself back into her seat, and looked over at me.

I raised my eyebrows. "I hate it when people panic," I said. That's bullshit, I say now. What I hated was that I'd proven myself inept and inattentive for the umpteenth damn time, and Lisa's fear in the car called it to my attention.

Jesus God, what an asshole I could be. That day in the Big Hole I watched Lisa check the mirrors, let out the clutch, and steer the car back onto the highway. I reached into the back and got her a box of raisins. I flipped through the tape case and put one of her favorite tapes into the deck. It even played without crinkling. Someone was close enough to see me. Hence all this destructive chaos, all this ambivalence and jealousy. All these devices for distance and safety. It all came back to fear, be it rational or no.

This was where faith came in. I was still rather surprised by all of this: at thirty-three, I had never committed myself so surely to a relationship, and despite all my ambivalence and defensiveness I was certain that I wanted to make this work. If I waited until I felt ready to be seen, I might wait a good long while. Perhaps my temperament, or my illness, made me ill equipped for intimacy; plainly the fearful, faithless way I was natured was going to be an ongoing handicap here—just as it was in trying to maintain any sort of steadfast faith. But how could I make myself ready anyhow? There is no academic course, no book that will tell you. It is a motion within. Perhaps the only way I would learn to be seen was by the practice of being seen. And only faith would make me ready for that.

Lisa glanced over at me and let a slow smile cross her face. She rested her hand on my forearm for a moment. My mind slows down every time she does that. She looked back to the highway. She was softly, beautifully, singing along with the tape. My whole life I had been a blessed man, given into the hands of good and faithful women—my mother, my grandmother, and now Lisa. Women who lived fully in the concrete everyday world, and who were stable, in place wherever they were.

Here is where the notion of "love melancholy" dovetailed for me with "religious melancholy." For centuries the Catholics have spoken of the "vocation of wedding," the idea being, I think, that one who undertakes an intimacy with another mortal will necessarily confront many of the same struggles and confusions as the priest or nun who takes a vow with God: You will be seen. You will be known, more plainly than you can ever know yourself, and you will be ferried into regions that offer no comfort, no hiding place. The essence of the other will now and always be mystery—but to attend to the relationship faithfully you must become real in it, do your most to surrender the self and its defenses; and you will do this a dozen, two dozen, three dozen, and more times every day as you stand naked and your shortcomings and vulnerabilities are exposed.

Religious melancholy, love melancholy: in both cases the root of my problem was fear, faithlessness. How could I claim trust and faith in a God who shall remain ever unseen if I could not put trust and faith in this woman whom I saw firsthand at all hours, and who appeared eminently trustworthy? So the specific remedy for my love melancholy would be the same as my remedy for religious melancholy: to have faith, and let that move me beyond my initial, defensive impulses and reactiveness. To bear this in mind, even as I forgot it dozens or hundreds of times each day: the self is the least of it.

Lisa turned and looked at me. "You will be fine," she said. "You are learning, I can see it. You don't frighten me, but your frustration comes on so abruptly. Is there any way you can warn me? You're safe, Jeff. Do you hear me? You're safe. You'll learn how. We will be fine. Look out the window." Out there the mountains rose, ponderosa pines steepled up from their slopes, framing a broad valley, the whole panorama right there in our windshield. Lisa lowered her head and slowly moved it from side to side. A vaulted expanse of cloudless azure sky. On the streambanks cottonwoods and aspens trembled in the breeze. In the broad meadows antelope grazed.

Just ahead of us two magpies arose out of the brush. Leisurely they flew across the road and lighted down on the fence posts. I let out a long sigh. Hold On, I said to myself. Keep Your Hand on the Plow.

CHAPTER SEVEN

On a Tuesday in late August, Lisa received a phone call from the Campbell County, Wyoming, School District. The German teacher in one of their schools had resigned, just a week before the school year began. The German Department at the University of Montana had recommended Lisa to them, and they asked her to fax a résumé. Wednesday they called to set up an interview. Thursday we drove to Campbell County, and on Friday afternoon Lisa interviewed with the school board. Monday morning they called our house in Missoula and offered her the job.

She hung up the phone and gave me the details: they needed her to be there as soon as possible, since school had started that very day. Her salary would be more than our present combined incomes. I hugged her, and then I walked to the convenience store to buy the first package of tobacco I'd bought since I'd quit smoking back in May. I was exceedingly nervous. This would be a difficult decision: Lisa had been in Missoula for the better part of the past ten years, and had a wide circle of friends and family there in town and across the state. I'd found plenty there to keep me engaged. And we'd be leaving our garden even before the tomatoes came ripe.

But it seemed an opportunity too good to pass up; Lisa wanted to teach, and high school jobs teaching German weren't all that common. It would be hard to leave our house on Poplar Street and our friends, but neither of us wanted to stay in Missoula permanently. By Wednesday morning we'd settled on it: we would move to Wyoming. Our idea was that Lisa would teach and I would find some sort of part-time job, be a househusband, do some writing. We wanted to find a home out in the country, somewhere on the prairie. The wind-blown and expansive landscapes of Campbell County reminded Lisa of her childhood home in eastern Montana, and I looked forward to acquainting myself with them: the softly rolling sagebrush grasslands all set about with buttes and pinnacles and pronghorn antelope. I also liked Campbell County's proximity to the Black Hills, the Bighorn Mountains, and the Badlands of South Dakota—since moving West I'd made backpacking trips to these places, and now they were all just a couple of hours away.

Too, Campbell County was coal country. It produced nearly half—this one county—of all the nation's coal. My father's family had worked in the underground mines of Appalachia for generations. When in 1989 the Black Thunder mine in Campbell County—the largest surface mine in the Western Hemisphere—broke the world record for monthly coal production, it displaced as record holder the #4 North American mine just over the ridge from Still-house Run. The prominent place coal has had in Appalachian life has come down to us in such mournful but proud songs as "Nine Pound Hammer," "Sixteen Tons," "Dark as a Dungeon," and "Coal Miner's Daughter"; I grew up on that music, and I was curious to see what coal culture in the 1990s looked like, and on the High Plains of Wyoming rather than in the Alleghenies.

On a Sunday in early September, Lisa, Pueblo, and I left Missoula to move to Wyoming. Just as we entered Campbell County, trolling the AM dial I happened onto the great Tennessee guitarist and singer Jimmy Martin—a coon hunter just like my Grandpa Thomas—singing one of my favorite bluegrass gospel songs, the Bill Monroe chestnut "The Old Crossroad."

This was music from home, music scarcely encountered on the radio outside the Appalachians. Martin has a rustic, abandoned, old-time way with a tune, and I couldn't help but feel exhilarated. I rolled down my window and sang along: "The old crossroad now is waiting, which one are you going to take? One road leads to destruction, the other to the pearly gates." I took this as the best of omens: we were moving to the austere, beautiful expanses of the High Plains; we were moving to coal country—which I thought might make the place somewhat familiar to me—and we were moving to a place where, or so it seemed as our moving van pulled into the county seat, Gillette, great hillbilly gospel music came in over AM radio.

Our first week in Gillette we parked ourselves in the Mustang Motel until we could find an apartment, and while Lisa started with her classes, I sat in an overstuffed vinyl chair outside our motel room and studied the classified ads. I watched miles and miles of coal cars pass through the switching yards across the way. I was giddy with high hopes, giddy with our great good fortune, and nothing could dim my glee. Not even our motel's Saudi proprietor, who informed me that the last fellow who'd stayed in his establishment while looking for an apartment had died before he managed to find a place he could afford.

Mbark glanced over at Pueblo. "His dog died too," he said over my disbelieving laughter. I thought he was joking, thought this might be some local version of the Tall Tale designed to cut down immigration, the kind of story people in Oregon tell Californians, about how the rain in Portland never stops. Maybe Gillette was so ideal that nobody ever moved out of town, and that's why it was so hard to find a place to live.

Mbark looked up at me. "I'm sure you people will have better luck, though," he said.

"You bet we will," I said, believing every word of it. Some say the expanse of those plains encourages such unwitting, unfounded exuberance in the newcomer; at any rate, Mbark seemed to have seen it before. He raised his eyebrows a little, and left the room. I turned my fiddle music back up, and I danced a little flatfoot dance.

You can't say I wasn't warned. There were no rentals out on the plains where we'd hoped to settle—rather naively, as it turned out:

all that land was owned by the ranches or the mines. Mostly the mines. Then we tried looking in Wright, the town where Lisa would be teaching. This was an odd place, too: the town did not exist until 1976, when one of the coal companies built it to spare their workers the forty-five-mile drive from Gillette to the mine. Imagine a place where the oldest architecture includes slots built into the kitchen walls expressly for a microwave oven. Permanence isn't the first word that comes to mind; but Wright seemed a nice enough little town, and it would spare Lisa a forty-mile drive twice a day, so we went looking there. No vacancies.

So it would be Gillette. On learning that we had a cat and were unwilling to part with her, the rental agents would snort. "There just aren't many places in this town that will accept animals," one named Angie told us. "But I'll show you what we've got." What's life without a cat or dog in the family, I wanted to ask. If you wanted an animal in this town, evidently you had to own. And to own you had to have a certain income, and it had to be predictably regular, and you had to have collateral and a good credit rating.

And I was a liability in all the above. Apartment living it would be. Rents in Gillette were as high as they'd been in Missoula, but without any of the cultural amenities Missoula offered; and the Gillette apartments we saw were one variety or another of industrial drab, prepackaged rooms and plywood walls, stinking shag carpets in a palette of colors unknown to nature. A fog of condensation on the windowpanes. When the wind blew—which would describe, I was learning, just about every minute of every single day—those windows rattled and rattled and rattled. Who built these places, and where did they think they were building them? Homesteaders hereabouts built their homes from sod: steady in the wind, well insulated against the long, severe winters. Had our kind become so stupid in just one century?

In a noble but finally futile attempt to instill some sense of home and hearth, the apartments were all outfitted with woodstoves. This heartened me some; but in all of Campbell County there was nary a tree. Perhaps they were coal stoves; certainly that fuel was locally abundant. Pretending to be a discerning, practical-minded male I opened the stove door in one of the apartments. I looked inside. I twisted the flue. One load of coal in that stove would burn down the whole apartment complex. So where did the firewood come from? I asked Angie.

One of the living room walls was paneled with mirrored tile, and Angie was standing before that wall, focused like a prizefighter, except on fixing her hair. She was at it with both hands, her clipboard tucked under a bicep.

"Damn that wind!" Angie said. Turning to Lisa: "One thing you'll learn, if you're going to spend any time outside here, even to walk to your car in the morning, you'd better put on a lot of hair spray." Lisa nodded.

I wasn't sure how to respond. I was sick of this town already. Sick of the air of futility and transience about these apartments. I wanted to ask this shovelhead if she had ever entertained changing to a hairstyle that might withstand the wind without any hair spray, something more natural and closer to the head; did she really think anything short of rubber cement was going to make that bowsprit rising from her forehead stay put in the wind?

Angie turned back to the wall, and I bit my tongue. When she finally seemed satisfied with her 'do I asked again about the firewood.

"Well," she said, looking at her watch. "You're welcome to use it, but you'd have to drive a hundred miles to the Black Hills to get any firewood. You could maybe burn coal in it, and we've got plenty of that. But we don't recommend it. In fact we don't allow it. Hardly anybody in town does. Used to, but too many fires got started."

I might have asked why they didn't simply install stoves capable of burning coal to start with. But what difference did it make? She looked away from me and out the window, consulted her watch again, and smiled. "So"—here she looked down at her clipboard, consulting our rental application—"so, Lisa and Jeff, have you seen anything that interests you today?"

We looked at one another, and shook our heads. Lisa turned back to her. "We sure thank you for taking the time, but I don't think we're interested."

Angie raised her eyebrows. "Nice-looking educated young couple like you, too bad you have that cat. What do you want to rent for, anyway? I've got some real nice homes for sale."

In the days to come we heard the same news from lacquer-haired red-nailed realtors all over town. We finally found a place in the classified ads, with a private landlord who allowed us to keep Pueblo in exchange for a fifty-dollar surcharge to our monthly rent. It was a basement apartment—yes, once again—in downtown Gillette, in a vinyl-sided building that had once been an auto-repair garage. Our front yard was gravel; to lend a pastoral effect our property owner had "planted" artificial Christmas trees here and there in the midst of all those limestone pebbles. Railroad ties, stacked three high and bordering the concrete walk that led from the sidewalk down to our door, held in the gravel.

Inside, even the kitchen floor was carpeted; and it carried, as you might expect, a scum of ground-in kitchen soil atop its neon green fibers. I am no sort of fussbudget, but I'd never seen so much filth. One of those mirrored walls in the bedroom here too, with corners cracked off the tile. Nobody who'd ever lived in this place was planning to stay, and they had cared for it accordingly. Which is to say, not at all. There was a grunge about this whole town, I was convinced, and it settled finally even in the corners of all these rooms. Most of our new home never saw a glimmer of natural light, and it smelled like it. We spent two days scrubbing and vacuuming, and we rented one of those carpet-cleaning machines from the grocery store—it sucked out pounds of grime, but the frumpy smell of the place persisted anyhow. There was nothing more to be done about it; we pulled the moving van up to the place and spent a Saturday unloading all our worldly goods into the basement apartment. Well, we told ourselves, it could be worse: at least we're in easy walking distance of a grocery store, an independent bookstore, the post office, and the public library.

We settled in, and I found a twenty-hour-a-week job—two ten-hour days—as a carpet layer's assistant. Gillette, as you might have gathered, is a carpet layer's paradise; it is not a haven for those with a background in literature and community psychiatry. But that was fine; I was happy to be a "hausfrau," as Lisa's students called me;

they didn't seem to know what to make of a grown man who mostly stayed at home. I established a routine for washing our laundry, doing the shopping, cleaning the house. I still had a few hours, nearly every day, to write.

Lisa and I both had spent just about all our adult lives in rather wholesome and oh-so-tony, oh-so-enlightened college towns—Madison, Auburn, Athens, Ann Arbor, Asheville, Missoula. Towns where everybody listened to NPR. Lots of bumper stickers and bicycles. They were not like the place where I had grown up, but I was by now plenty comfortable in such towns. Every Saturday from April through October, Missoula has a large Farmer's Market, with truckloads of fresh local produce, the organic gardeners there to sell their crops. Patchouli-scented jewelry makers, strong coffee, pastries. A community gathering.

So we were excited when, not long after moving to Gillette, we saw a flyer at the public library advertising a Saturday morning Farmer's Market at the Rockpile Community Center. This was just a couple of blocks from our apartment, and the following Saturday we walked over. We saw nothing but a rummage sale. We asked at the cashier's table where we might find the Farmer's Market. The first woman lowered her eyebrows. She didn't know. But in a moment her colleague came to the table and grinned at us indulgently. "It was a busy one today," she told us. "There was a guy here at seven or so. He had a few dozen eggs. He sold them and left. That's the Gillette Farmer's Market."

Well, maybe I could find some righteous cause to get inflamed about, get myself involved and meet some kindred spirits too. At the start of October I went looking for an environmental group to volunteer with. The phone book listed the Abundant Wildlife Society. Its national headquarters was a five-minute walk from our apartment.

So I called up this Abundant Wildlife Society, anxious to vent my spleen in some nominally sanctioned way. And directly learned that this group defined as "wildlife" and wanted to see in "abundance" only those animals humans customarily like to hunt: elk and deer and antelope. Everything else—in other words, all the animals that might compete with the human hunters for this prey—was a "predator," and this Abundant Wildlife Society advocated unlimited and unregulated shooting and trapping of mountain lions, coyotes, and the wolves that recently had been released in the Lamar Valley of Yellowstone National Park. I knew this was a popular local sentiment: on our drives around the county we'd seen any number of coyotes hung from fences, a coat hanger punched through their sinews and wired to the fence. Every summer the Abundant Wildlife Society helped the Gillette Chamber of Commerce put on a coyote hunt, open to the paying public. "It's the town's biggest tourist draw," the society's president told me. "People come to see Devil's Tower and the Badlands and the Black Hills and then they come on over here to shoot 'em a coyote. Puts thousands and thousands of dollars into the local economy. Kills a lot of varmints too." I bid him goodbye then.

I went looking for places where I could go walking. Pretty quickly I learned that while Campbell County and the surrounding area include vast tracts labeled on the map as the Thunder Basin National Grassland, administered by the U.S. Forest Service as public land, much of it was not, in fact, open to the public. Every acre on which a mining company had a lease—and in that area that means a lot of acres—was fenced, posted, and inaccessible. I finally found a tract suitable for daylong walking, forty-five miles from Gillette, too far for the everyday hikes I'd hoped to make.

As the first blowing snow came in mid-October, I was raiding the stacks of the public library—which was one of the finest I'd seen, and no small consolation that—reading whatever I could find about Gillette and Campbell County, trying to discover there what they used to call the "genius of place"—the way a landscape shapes the people who live on it, the rooted and intertwined sense of community and place I'd known back home in Appalachia and in Missoula.

I wasn't looking for West Virginia or southern Ohio, or even Missoula or Asheville; I knew better. I just wanted to find a sense of place here. For most of its history Gillette had no real reason for being: it was one of those western towns that came into being only because one of the railroads happened to route a trunk line across that very portion of the prairie. Before the Energy Crisis of the mid-

1970s, Campbell County's only claim to notoriety was its impor-
tance to dam building in the West: after building some earthen dams
on a ranch near Recluse, Floyd Dominy became so inspired about
them that in time he managed to maneuver his way to the head of
the federal Bureau of Reclamation, where he spent his life trying to
dam every river of consequence in the West; the dam Dominy's
agency built at Glen Canyon on the Colorado River in the mid-
1960s attracted the ire of David Brower, at the time head of the
Sierra Club; their debates about dams and a hundred other things
are recorded in John McPhee's *Encounters with the Archdruid.*

In the early 1990s Wallace Stegner wrote of Gillette: "not too
long ago a sleepy cowtown on the verge of becoming a real place,
now a coal boomtown that will never be a place." In 1975, three
thousand people lived there; it was the trading hub for the region's
ranchers. Then came the energy crisis, and the town's population
quickly doubled, then tripled and quadrupled, as the town struggled
to accommodate an oil boom, a coal boom, and a seemingly imminent uranium boom. Tent towns sprang up close to the oil fields and
the mine sites, and stayed there into the −35° winters, since there
was no other place for all the newcomers to go. They came anyhow,
from all over the West, and from my neck of the woods too—the
Clean Air Act that made Wyoming coal so popular also made ours,
high in sulfur content and more likely to cause acid rain, almost un-
saleable and brought our mining industry to a standstill. In Gillette's
boom years the truly blessed found places in the trailer courts that
mushroomed all over town. All the spouse abuse and incest and al-
coholism and violent crime in the city got a psychiatric complex
named for it: the Gillette Syndrome. The town had its fifteen minutes
of fame then; journalists swarmed into town and filed reports in
shocked tones on television newsmagazines and in *The New York
Times* and *The Wall Street Journal* and *National Geographic.*

But the civic leaders and coal companies had already named
Campbell County the "Energy Frontier," and you know what happens on the frontier: somebody's gonna be brought around to "civilized values." In the old West the Temperance Union and the
Presbyterians and the town sheriff performed these tasks; in Gillette

it was the coal companies. They got federal monies to help them build new housing—as I suppose any coal company deserves, being that they're so strapped for funds—and when that money ran out the coal companies built their own apartment complexes and ranch-styles, and sold them to their workers. Since the miners were well paid, the housing was expensively priced. Consequently few people other than the miners (and carpet layers) could afford to live in Gillette, and by the time we arrived, there were hardly any elderly people left in town. It was nearly impossible to meet a Campbell County native of any age, or anybody who was not in some way connected with the mines. Imagine a western set in contemporary America, where the corporation makes all the rules: old Gillette was tamed and quartered by the suits from ARCO and Kerr-McGee and Kennecott.

From those companies the county got the largest coal mines in the Western Hemisphere, mines that in the mid-1990s were still providing steady and well-paying jobs, a rare commodity on the High Plains—but in exchange local officials had turned over any semblance of autonomy to the mining companies, who were only too happy to control the county, not to mention the state itself. So there was no "coal culture" in Campbell County such as I had known back home; nor was there much of the "ranch culture" that exists elsewhere in Wyoming. Instead, what there was in Gillette and Campbell County was American Corporate Culture. Strip malls, fast-food, disposable buildings. Sometimes it seems this is where we are all headed, every place on the continent; we have now all these major league sports arenas named not after the cities where the home team resides but after the highest-paying corporate sponsor. Anyhow, Stegner was right: as long as it yielded its local culture to the coal companies, Gillette would never be a place.

It was, at any rate, a hard place for us to feel at home. Sometime that fall I found out that the old-time music broadcast I'd heard on AM radio as we pulled our moving van into Gillette had nothing to do with Campbell County: it had come out of Salt Lake City, on a radio network for over-the-road truck drivers. "The Old Cross-road," indeed; and which road had we taken in coming to Gillette?

There was a constant noise vaguely in the air. It was nothing rending or piercing, just a low and chronic sad whine, as if all that disemboweled earth about the town had voice to moan.

SO FOR A WHILE it was a handy thing, this seemingly dreadful place where we'd come: a handy thing to bitch about, a handy scapegoat for any troubles or frustrations, a handy target for any miscellaneous piss and vinegar I might have had floating about, a handy conversation piece with all our friends off in more enlightened places.

And talk I did. I went into full-on full-bitchery, and made a sport of collecting gruesome details about Gillette—just so I could insert them, with great outraged glee, into the hours upon hours of long-distance talk, the dozens of letters I wrote that autumn. The daily mail was a lifeline; if a letter came for me I would put it on the corner of my desk, promising myself that I would not open it until I had this much work done. I checked into getting Internet service so I could write people via e-mail too. But our computer was too outdated to run the software. I kept right on with it anyhow: to friends, to family, to total strangers, to letters-to-the-editor columns, to my journal, and to Lisa I unleashed that voice. I heard it coming strong and sure out of my mouth, like no other voice I could summon. This was what I wanted—to live in the "real world," so-called—and look where we landed: no place. A place far more real than I had bargained for. I pitched headlong into a corrosive, bitter cynicism.

But I wasn't there for long. That sound I heard coming from my throat, I finally realized, was the voice of judgment. "Humble" comes from the Latin *humus*, for "earth"; the word is also close kin to the Greek *chamai*, meaning: "on the ground."

On the ground: that is where I needed to be. Back on the horizontal. Back to nothing. Therefore part of everything. But how? In this place? Absent in Gillette were any of the ways I'd ever known myself as an adult. My life now was entirely different from the one I'd had that August day a year and some months before when I quit the pills; this new development was simply the latest installment of my unraveling.

That's how I see it now, anyhow; at the time, I was none too sanguine about it. The saints and mystics who wrote of the "dark night of the soul" often referred to the "adolescent" feeling it summoned, and I was starting to see their point: it can grow us up. No doubt I would remain a skeptical person; perhaps my first, visceral response would be to curse and moan and sneer, forgetting utterly all the unmerited grace and the human goodwill and generosity that had carried me this far. *Thank you.* I try to remember to repeat those words instead, sotto voce, when I'm falling into this kind of fit. The self is the least of it, and thank you for that. I am still here, and thank you for that. The right response is *Thank you.*

The world, near as I can tell, will always offer me plenty of reasons for cynicism and anger. Every day in Gillette that autumn (and too often still), I asked the world to give me some signs, show me some reasons why I should remain faithful, but faith, as I was coming to understand it, cannot rest on reasons anyhow. I understood now why some denominations maintain an "itineracy" policy for their clergy, regularly shifting them from one town to another: drawing any measure of one's faith from earthly "attachment"—even to a congenial community or landscape—gives it pretty shallow purchase. It seems faith must of necessity root itself in mystery, at some removes from the everyday transient world of human doings and comings and goings. It cannot rest on our politics, our feelings, our talents; nor upon our chosen places. Nor, even, upon the glories of the natural world, the clearest expression of our Creator that we've got.

This was hard for me to learn; I doubt the lesson will be finished when I draw my last breath.

But I think I had learned a few things since the pills failed me fifteen months before: while I kept waiting for that familiar hopelessness and weight to return, it did not, even when the solstice time came and went. I found myself acting as if there were in fact a future for me, that it wasn't just a matter of surviving one day to the next. In November I began helping out at a soup kitchen, and became a kind of community case worker for the men I met there, giving them rides to the doctor, to AA meetings, wherever they needed to go. I helped get a community writing workshop started.

I did not join a church. This is what a professing Christian ought to do at once upon moving to a new place, I've learned since, and I am still not sure why I didn't try it that fall; in no small portion it was cowardice, I suppose, the ongoing fear of letting strangers see me. I did visit several churches around town, made a series of one-Sunday-stands trying to get a feel for the preaching and music and congregation, and I met many kind and gracious people, sat through some spirit-filled services—but I never did go back to any of them. I talked with Tony once a week, and I read my devotions then sat in prayer morning and evening; maybe that was enough for me right then.

Further anodynes: yup, I still sought them. It would appear that the homeopathic remedy had worked quite well—but so many other things had happened; I wasn't sure how much of my progress I could attribute to the remedy. Homeopathy tends to be subtle and slow in its effects (the deeper ones, anyhow), so it's difficult to establish the clear-cut cause and effect relationship our rational minds want. All I can say, to this day, is this: it surely helped to accomplish what Dr. Beans promised during my first visit: my life now did in fact feel more natural to me. But of course I wanted more. I didn't want to be "better than well" again, all hyped-up and Zoloft-happy; but if I could be simply "well," I'd take that; I'd even settle for being "better." So I kept trying: sometime that autumn I read that certain fish oils, taken in capsule form, might lift the very sort of "treatment-resistant" depression I had. I went right out and spent a nice wad of cash on some; within three days I was clogged and leaden, mind and body. I tossed them out.

Shortly thereafter, from a health food store I bought a pound of dried parts of the wild plant St. John's-wort, mixed it with grain alcohol in large brown jugs, and let it work for a couple of weeks.

Then I funneled the tincture into dropper bottles, and dosed myself with the stuff twice a day. I waited for six months—by which time the herb was being touted in the national news media as an "herbal Prozac"—and I felt no different. Perhaps this was as good as I could hope to feel. Perhaps I was, indeed, "well."

And who can say how much music helped? For months it was the only language I could comprehend, a salve beyond any mere words. In this I had been preceded by melancholics the world over, as far back as we can figure; the earliest physicians considered music specific for melancholia—"play them airs on the lute," reads an Italian health manual from the fifteenth century. In the Biblical Book of Kings, David's harp was the only balm for King Saul's melancholia. In the 1880s, a Boston physician provided all his female neurasthenics with a banjo. And who could name all the classical movements that aim to evoke melancholia—it was almost obligatory for the Romantics; and who could name all the composers who were melancholic themselves? Schumann, Berlioz, Elgar, Mahler, Rachmaninoff, Tchaikovsky, Ives. Just for starters. Prominent figures from other musics: Irving Berlin, Noël Coward, Stephen Foster, Cole Porter, and of course the great princes of bebop: Charles Mingus, Bud Powell, Charlie Parker. From rock, too many to mention—the saddest perhaps being the great British songwriter Nick Drake, who committed suicide in 1974 with an overdose of the antidepressant amitriptyline; he was twenty-six years old.

If music was in fact an anodyne for melancholia, why had it failed Drake, and so many others who were so intimately involved with it? But even our pills, miracle workers though they be, will sometimes fail against melancholia; so we can't invalidate it on those grounds. That autumn I was blessed with music. Our apartment, like most in Gillette, came with a free cable hookup, and we signed on for a twenty-four-hour music feed rather than television. I set the remote control to the "Chamber Music" channel, and day and night the house was filled with music new to my ears. That is, when I wasn't listening to clawhammer banjo tunes and fiddle music from home. I've since learned that "modal" music was long thought especially helpful to the melancholic; this was a curious thing. I had long been mesmerized by the slightly atonal sound of some modal scales; that quivering, eerie sound was all over the traditional music of Great Britain and Appalachia, and often heard in modern classical music too, not to mention Miles Davis' jazz masterpiece, *Kind of Blue*.

As for Lisa and me: Our honeymoon on Poplar Street was over; we were there in Gillette virtually alone, too new in town to have any cozy circle of old friends, and it was tough for a while. The flat-out truth was, it was still hard for me to be seen, to let myself be known, and sometimes I swallowed hard and walked through this; other times I retreated from it, gave in to the gnawing fear, and made sure I had some distance.

She had long days to work, an hour's drive just to get to school and back, and she'd come home after a thirteen-hour day of noise and commotion, and I'd been alone in the apartment all day. Some days I didn't adjust so well to her returning, after all that solitude, and so I did not always meet her with the warm welcome she needed. I wondered sometimes if I were just too much a solitary creature to be a partner.

But I was enjoying sharing life with somebody, learning how to honor somebody else's needs and wants, joining together to try to accomplish them. At school there was a lot of pressure on Lisa: for starters, having had no time to develop lesson plans, she'd begun the school year already way behind. Worse, she'd been told that the German program would be eliminated if enrollment didn't increase. So my working as a househusband, doing the cooking and cleaning and laundry and shopping, made it possible for her to devote her time to her teaching, and by November she was all caught up. This gave me great pleasure.

It was a blessed life I had. Maybe I was temperamentally unsuited for what we mean by "happiness." But I had a routine, with tangible work to accomplish, and I had also some disciplines—my morning and evening prayer times, the time I spent writing. I came to know, one day after another, the sort of hope faithful observation of such disciplines can bring. There was time to give to the work of tending to our home and our eating. I had time to myself. Apart from my weekdays, there were also Sundays, when Lisa tried to get done her whole week's preparation work; after a late breakfast she went to work and I drove out to the grassland and spent the day walking.

During the week I made the most of the ingredients available locally and cooked meals that reminded us both of the country-style cooking we'd grown up with: chicken and dumplings, chili, stuffed cabbage rolls. I came to understand, with a vengeance, the concept of "comfort food," and I put on a bit of weight. We ventured out, took weekend trips to Denver and to Sheridan, and on another, a camping trip in the Bighorn Mountains.

When we stayed in town, on Fridays I would buy flowers and wine to celebrate her making it through another week. On Saturday afternoons we cooked together, and spent the evenings reading to one another or on occasion going out to a movie. Ten or fifteen times a week, apropos of absolutely nothing, I would glimpse Lisa looking out a window, or petting Pueblo, or talking on the phone with a troubled student, or she would be in the middle of telling me some detail of her day, and I would know: I wanted to give to this woman, wanted to help her get the things she wanted and needed; I wanted to grow with her, would make myself keep walking through the fear to make that happen.

Okay, so I wasn't actively involved in the community, still led a mostly reclusive and isolated life, didn't hold down a full-time paying job. Maybe I would never return to any of those. Maybe I wasn't "happy," but it sure didn't seem like I was missing anything. For now, this was enough. This life felt to me like health—in the literal sense of the word—it felt like wholeness. I was in love and I wanted to stay there—I was committing myself. I was making myself useful in small ways. I was trying to yield myself to things larger than self; I was trying to occupy some suitable perch in the world without. It was the fullest life had ever been. So within our dismal dark apartment in this drear town, my life was becoming real, engaged and full and visible in the world. And it was, in most every respect, a life well suited to my temperament, such as I hadn't had for years. Even there in Gillette I was taking my place; I was living a life. I was nostalgic no longer. We were making a home.

This was enough. I had taken root.

CHAPTER EIGHT

ON CHRISTMAS EVE, one year since we'd come together, Lisa and I were engaged in her family home in Belt, Montana, under the tree after Mass. The ring I slid onto her finger was the one her father had given her mother fifty-two years before. Christmas Day we flew out of Great Falls to the Ohio Valley to spend the next week with my family. That evening, in an empty bar in the empty Pittsburgh airport, we gave my father the news. He called over the waitress, and he with his Bud Light, Lisa with her scotch and me with my Jack Daniel's, we toasted and toasted and toasted.

We told him our plans: we would marry the coming June, have a small ceremony outdoors in the North Carolina mountains with our immediate families and the wedding party; Tony would pronounce our vows. We'd have a reception there, then we would travel to the Ohio Valley to celebrate with my family. From there we would drive to Montana, where we would gather with our friends in Missoula and with Lisa's family in Belt. We'd return to Wyoming in August.

Dad's eyes misted. His blue eyes shone; he was a striking man, with his full head of white hair and his amiable broad face. He reached out his hands; Lisa took one and I took the other.

"This one's given me some worry," Dad said. He looked me

straight-on. "Sometimes I've wondered whether or not he'd make it." Dad was weeping, and so was I. "But he's a good boy." He looked at me, and laughed. "I mean, a good man." He squeezed my hand and I squeezed back.

Dad was in an expansive mood that week. He had some news of his own: he was planning to retire soon, on his fifty-fifth birthday, and move his fifth-wheel camping trailer onto the lot he owned right on the riverfront. "I'm going to fish and ride my Jet Ski all day," he told us. We stayed in his house for the next three days, sleeping at night in my boyhood bedroom. Days we went riding and visiting: the day after Christmas, we rode from Hannibal to Woodsfield to visit my Grandma Smith. After my Smith grandparents moved out there, we didn't see much of them; now Dad stayed in close touch with his mother, who was seventy-seven and a widow since 1979. Grandma Smith stayed active with the Woodsfield Methodist church, and served as manager of the Methodist Women's Thrift Store. She was the Smith family's sole repository of family history, photographs, recipes, and keepsakes, and I always enjoyed talking with her. On our way there Dad pointed out to Lisa Buckhill Bottom, the broad swath of floodplain land on the river between Hannibal and Clarington where he had grown up. "It was beautiful here then, Lisa," he said. He looked out the windshield and held out his palm toward the river bottom. "It was quiet, not a quarter of the traffic that's on this road today. It being the river bottom, the dirt would grow just about anything. There were two huge poplar trees in our yard. Then the plants came." Out the window the aluminum plants sprawled across the bottom. I had never heard my dad talk like this; usually he had little inclination to reminisce, and now all the way to his mother's house Lisa's questions drew forth from him one story after another of his boyhood in Monroe County.

"This place has been good to us," Dad said to Lisa. "It's sure changed some, but all along it has been good to us. I think you'll like it here."

I hoped he was right. Apart from her visit to the North Carolina mountains, Lisa had spent no time whatever in Appalachia, and I wondered how comfortable she would feel, wondered if she would feel hemmed in by the hills and hollows. She did, a little, but it barely showed. Midweek we drove our rental car across the Ohio and a couple miles back in the hills to the house Mom shared with her husband, Paul Fuchs, up above New Martinsville atop Tarpen Ridge.

Mom and Paul both worked in town, Paul at the same chemical plant where my father and brother and uncle and former stepmother also worked; Mom was a savings officer at a bank. Paul was a refrigeration expert, and an all-around handyman, good with any machine, very much a man of our time. His ancestors had settled on Tarpen Ridge generations before, so he was also very much a person of that place, with a vivid sense of its past; like many an old-time mountain man, he was virtually sufficient unto himself.

Our first evening there Paul harnessed two of their quarter horses to his buggy and took us all on a long ride out the ridge. Back of us was the Ohio; down the steep slope to our left was Doolin Run. All about us old white farmhouses sat nestled into the hillside or stood sentinel on some other ridgetop. When the sun peeked out from the clouds their windows glowed yellow. We would crest the ridge and south from there you could see the Alleghenies ascending downstate toward the Blue Ridge, mile after mile of stair-stepped, thickly forested ridgelines climbing into the far horizon with mist laid in braids over the hollows that ran between the ridges. The buggy bounced on the dirt road. We rounded the curve up onto the ridgetop. Slowly Lisa's head turned from side to side. She squeezed my forearm. Her eyes went a little round and her mouth too.

As we lay in bed that night, Lisa said, "Your mother is beautiful." She always had been, but the beauty of her youth was a given beauty; the beauty she had now was substantial, an earned beauty, the dividend of character and faith and generosity. Mom met a stranger without prejudice; like her father, she seemed to find something likable and singular about every person she came across. Lisa met people in just the same way. They took an immediate liking to one another. After our buggy ride the two of them turned away from the television—Paul's satellite dish was beaming *A River Runs Through It*, set in and around Missoula, to us there in West Virginia—and set in to talking about books and movies and dogs and cats and horses, and about their fathers: Lisa's relationship with Vince was close, similar to my mother's relationship with her father.

Just like that, she was in the family.

On the morning of my thirty-fourth birthday Lisa and I awoke in my Grandma Thomas' house up Stillhouse Hollow. Three inches of snow had fallen overnight, and the world outside was hushed. We folded the quilt—one of Grandma's handmades—replaced it in the rack, and pulled up the white chenille bedspread. From the kitchen below us came the smells of frying cornmeal mush and side meat and potatoes, an old country-style breakfast that was just about my favorite. Grandma had been fixing that same breakfast her whole life; it had been my Grandpa's favorite too. She never made any mention of it, but Grandma made it a practice to fix a person's favorite foods when they visited. By the time we got downstairs and into the kitchen she was cracking eggs onto another skillet.

"Mmmmm," Lisa said, walking over to the stove.

"You're just an old country girl, aren't you?" Grandma asked her, gently sliding her turner under an egg.

"I don't know about that, but this sure smells good," Lisa answered. "Can I help?"

I knew better than to ask. "It's his birthday breakfast and it's just about ready," Grandma said. "You kids just sit down there and I'll have it in front of you shortly."

The whole day stretched out before us. I wanted to spend it showing Lisa the countryside. So after breakfast we went out driving away from the riverfront, onto the skein of back roads out in the county.

That evening as the sun went down behind the ridges to the west we pulled the car onto the Mount Vernon church grounds. Here there was an old country church, groves of old oak and maple trees, a shelter for revival meetings, and a view of the river valley below, looking southeast right into Hannibal.

We bundled ourselves against the ridgetop wind and stepped out into the snow. We had driven miles and miles that day, without ever leaving the county and without coming back to the riverfront. I had shown Lisa the covered bridges, the dozens of old country churches, the dairy farms, the caves, the houses where I'd spent overnights, and the fields where I'd helped bale hay, the homeplaces of the farm girls I'd carried schoolboy crushes for; we'd walked up hollows alongside runs I had fished and swum as a boy.

As we had neared the riverfront again on State Route 536, we passed the Hilltop Community Center, catching the pinks and blues of the late afternoon sky on its broad white side. A hand-lettered sign outside it read: "New Year's Eve Square Dance Here 8:oo." I turned to Lisa and raised my eyebrows. All day on the rental car's tape deck, I had been playing the same sort of music we might dance to there: the exhilarating and soulful old-time rural string-band sound native to these hills, the music I'd danced to with my class-mates in that same building twenty-five years before. We'd made no plans for New Year's Eve, and Lisa responded to my implied question: "I would love to."

A few minutes later, there we were on the church grounds, watch-ing the day go down. We walked through the old graveyard laid into the ridgetop, the feet of the dead facing east toward the Ohio; with the easy slope of the hillside canted right at the river one might imag-ine them watching over it still. There was just enough light left to read the stones. They dated back into the 1820s; from the dates one could see the various epidemics that had moved through the commu-nity. Whole families lay dead and buried within the same week; many of the markers were the small headstones used to mark the graves of children. For years, and until fairly recently, Monroe County had little in the way of nearby medical services, and people relied on midwives and herbalists like my Great-grandmother Olive. Those days, and the even harder times that preceded them, are still very much a part of local memory.

We walked out the ridgetop, away from the graveyard, and I leaned my back against a large maple tree. Lisa leaned back against my chest and gathered my arms around her belly. We were overlook-ing the river. "It must have been magnificent here at one time," she said. "All the trees, all the water, all the good farmland. I could still see it out in the county today. And what it must have been like here on the river! All the boats passing through in their own sweet time, the river slow and wide. When your dad was talking the other day about what that bottom was like before the plants came, in my mind's eye I could see what it must have looked like. It must have been a sweet, fertile place. Even now you can smell the water in the air."

She paused and sank back into my arms. On Buckhill Bottom now the smokestacks from the aluminum plants belched their exhaust, gray and orange and green, into the darkening sky and their warning lights blinked and blinked. Further south there was the dam.

"You are lucky," Lisa said after a few moments. "Your family belongs to this place as it is and as it was, and there's a lot to be said for that." The dark gathered all around us. At its peak the church steeple still glowed a little. The night was coming on cold and clear, making for a clear view of the stars. In the southwest sky I saw Saturn glowing. I pointed it out to Lisa.

She leaned back and looked up at the stars. I lived in Saturn's landscape still, in its shadow and in its light; I was a child of Saturn, just as I was a child of this place, these hills, these hollows, that river. Born lucky, and lucky still. Here I stood, a man in love, a man restored to his family, a man in his place. In his place thanks to friends and teachers and lizards and sycamores and physicians and books and landscapes and families and love; I did not know, and still do not, what I had done to deserve such great good fortune. I breathed deep, feeling Lisa's spine nestled into my sternum, taking the smell of this place into me deep. Her hands held mine before her. She leaned back her head. "Happy birthday, Jeffery," she said. She clasped my hands to her. "You are home now."

After church on New Year's Eve, Lisa and I went out walking up Stillhouse Hollow. When we came back to the homeplace we ate our supper, ham and scalloped potatoes and beets and green beans and applesauce, and after we'd done the dishes we went into the living room. Grandma sat on the couch. There was a large box beside her and a smaller, gift-wrapped one next to her. We sat on the floor. She handed Lisa the wrapped box. Lisa opened it; inside was a mixer and a set of bowls. "That's for the home the two of you are making together." Then she handed to me a pair of gold rings. "These are for your wedding band," she said. "One was your granddad's and one was mine." We had decided to ask a jeweler friend of mine to melt down jewelry given to us by my various family members, and to fashion my wedding band from the mix. Next Grandma reached to the end table beside her and handed me a large clothbound book. It was a history of Monroe County. "To help you remember where you come from," she said to me.

Then she handed me a small, old black box, thin as my finger and nearly as long as my hand, held shut with a rubber band. Lisa looked up at her, and Grandma raised her eyebrows and grinned slightly. They were giving nothing away, but it looked as if the two of them had already discussed this one.

I slowly undid the rubber bands. Lisa squirmed. "Jeffery, get on with it," she said. I wrapped the rubber bands around my wrist and slowly lifted the lid off the box. Inside was a rust-colored Parker Duofold fountain pen. I heard myself gasp. "That's for your work, Jeff," Grandma said. "And maybe once in a while use it to write a letter home." This was its original box, Grandma explained to me. "Your granddad gave me that pen on our first wedding anniversary, which would have been—what?—oh, about sixty years ago. I used it for years and years, even after the ballpoints came out. That was my letter-writing pen. I'm sure I wrote just about all my notes and cards with it. When your Aunt Jo was born, and your mother, I'd have used it to write the notes telling people. It'll only fill from an ink bottle and time came when you couldn't get those around here anywhere. So I had to put it away, and I'd bet the bladder needs to be replaced before you can use it. But that's the original gold nib, and I'm pretty sure it's still good."

Then she turned to the big box beside her and worked loose its flaps. Inside were envelopes and envelopes full of photographs, dating back to the mid-nineteenth-century, of my Dally and Thomas ancestors, and then forward through the years of my grandparents' marriage. We sat on the floor and went through those boxes one picture at a time. There was my grandpa with his coonhounds; there was the young Martha, blond-haired and eighteen, standing beside her sister Ruth at their sister Elizabeth's wedding, the both of them resplendent in their bridesmaid dresses; there was my Great-grandma Bertha beside her kitchen garden when she lived across the Run. Here was my mother, at eight weeks and six months and at seventeen and twenty-three. At seven-thirty Lisa and I looked at one another; if we were going to get to the square dance we'd have to leave soon. We both shook our heads; the dance could wait for another visit.

Three hours later Grandma closed the box. Then she lifted from under the pillow beside her a small, square color photo and laid it on top of the box. "I want you to take this picture with you," she said. I looked over at it. My Great-aunt Ruth standing out in the yard, leaning against one of the sycamore trees down by Stillhouse Run. Leaning up against her legs was a small blond boy. Aunt Ruth had her head bent down toward the boy and her hands rested gently on his shoulders. The boy's arms were bent back, the elbows pointing right at the camera, and his small hands were holding hers. My face was turned up toward hers and hers down to mine and both were smiling, broad and easy. "My goodness," Grandma said softly. "I'd almost forgot how much Ruth loved those old sycamores. Down on our homeplace in Sardis and here too."

Next day Grandma fixed her traditional New Year's Day meal: sauerkraut, spare ribs, kielbasa, and mashed potatoes, and the family gathered. Before the meal was served I joined the women in the kitchen; the men were in the living room watching football games, and as I always had, I preferred to be with the women. There was nothing for me to do, they told me; so I sat down at the window and I watched my grandma and my Aunt Jo and my mother and my cousin Melanie as they set the table, talked and joked and told stories. Lisa was working alongside them, almost as if she'd been there for years, listening and laughing and from time to time joining in.

After dinner, with our rental car loaded across the Run, these women walked out onto the front stoop with us. In a couple of hours we would fly out of Pittsburgh, back to Wyoming. My father would walk us to our gate, and stand in line with us as we waited to board our flight; he would hold us both to him and weep freely as we stood by the gate. "Welcome to the family," he'd say to Lisa before we turned to walk onto the plane. He'd turn then and embrace me: "And welcome back, son."

But now we stood in a circle with these family women, Stillhouse Run behind us warbling its way to the Ohio. All around that circle went embraces and kisses. They walked us down to the footbridge, where I took Lisa's hand and touched it to the sycamore tree. We turned for a last round of embraces, and told everybody we'd see them in June. Then we turned again and walked across that footbridge, silent, the Run flowing cool and clear beneath us. On its banks I thought I saw some boy lying out imagining himself into all the shapes and shades of creation. I hadn't been near that boy in many a year but now I could just about see him there, this boy who knew where he belonged and inhabited his skin accordingly; salamander he might yet become, adapted to the cold, adapted to the warm; like any amphibian he might yet make himself at home in the water, at home on the dry, dry land; like any pilgrim, carrying his home within his own skin wherever he might walk.

ON A MID-FEBRUARY SUNDAY a gentle chinook wind melted away the snow, and in that brief interlude of springlike weather I went walking on the Wyoming prairie. Near sundown I was sitting atop a butte looking east over the plain. A gibbous moon hung in the sky; all across that expanse the breeze trembled the tall grass. There was nothing to stop my eye; in all directions it seemed I could see clear to the vanishing point. They say it was on the grassland savannas of East Africa—a landscape rather similar to this one—where our kind first evolved into an upright primate, and perhaps genetic memory would account for the eerie, limbic feeling of familiarity this lifelong mountain dweller felt there.

But there wasn't a tree in sight. "The Great American Desert," Stephen Long called this region after his 1819 exploratory expedition into the High Plains. In the 1840s and 1850s thousands of whites passed through en route to California or Oregon or Washington; they were inclined to say that the plains resembled "hell, with the fires put out."

Then California's gold played out and the forested coasts of Oregon and Washington got crowded; and perhaps most significant, the railroad bought up vast acreages on the plains, for a pittance, from the government, and as the railroads tried to sell off the land, the speculators and realtors moved in to pitch the High Plains. They advertised this region as a land of agricultural potential aplenty, and perhaps they believed it, just as they believed that "rain would follow the plow." So in that harsh climate many homesteaders put land under cultivation that even in a good year would support little more than the grasses it produced so well on its own. But we kept trying to make this arid plain into a pastoral paradise, one that would support vegetables and orchards and water-hungry European cows. We would make this desert green, or die in the doing so. Mari Sandoz's *Old Jules*, an elegiac and blunt memoir of early European efforts to make the High Plains amenable to our schemes, records in a matter-of-fact way an astonishing number of suicides.

Nothing about this place seems to welcome us. In winter the winds howl and the snow blows slantwise in the sky as if it would abrade us to the nubbins; spring is mostly more wind, only with the air slightly warmer; summer is a direct unceasing blare of sun and wind. Without trees, none notice the autumn, a project the weather cooperates with, since on the plains it typically starts snowing before the end of September. In the century or so since the time described in *Old Jules*, our technological advances have availed little here: Frank and Deborah Popper, a pair of sociologists from Rutgers University, have recently proposed that the region be emptied of people and made into a large "Buffalo Commons," given back over to the bison who have been the region's most successful inhabitants. Of course, plains natives dislike this idea, but it seems the region is doing a slow emptying-out all on its own: the region has the lowest birth rate in the nation, and rates of out-migration are high. The dearth of rain, the blaring light, the ceaseless wind, the long blizzard-blown winters: this place tends to make a mockery of our every endeavor. The High Plains remains a landscape that we cannot fit to our schemes.

Behind me the sun drifted down another notch in the sky. It was time to start for home, and I sidestepped my way off the butte. Perhaps melancholia, I was thinking, in its seemingly vacant aridity and its apparently lifeless monotony, resembles this High Plains landscape. In the narrow squint of our contemporary desires, this place does not reveal its virtues so readily; we might say the same of melancholia. But every landscape encompasses more than we can see.

I was walking east, stepping into my long shadow. Some say that "chaos theory," the New Physics notion that all of creation invariably resolves itself into some hidden order, may usefully be likened to melancholia. I am hesitant to apply such a sweeping idea to this poorly understood illness, but on that February day it was eighteen months since I had left off the antidepressants, and a full year since I had lost my work at the mental health center. As I walked that parched and unpeopled prairie I knew: I had conquered nothing, mastered nothing, transcended nothing. I had simply settled into something that had been waiting for me—who knows how long?—and made the descent it seemed to require.

In that descent I had lost all sense of myself; but as that alienation persisted, I'd felt replacing my small self a sustaining kinship with something larger: with animals, and plants, and landscapes, and with other people alive and long dead. And I'd been given a life unimaginable to that former self: now I was in love, and I was trying to live with faith in something unseen, and I was restored to my family. Perhaps there is no unity without mystery; perhaps I had to become utterly disoriented before I could find and inhabit the landscapes that claimed me, my native places.

I knew that I would never fit the shape of an "upbeat" and "outgoing" modern person, and still I was content. "Be not conformed to the world," wrote the apostle Paul in the Book of Romans, "but be ye transformed by the renewing of your mind." And there was some renewal: I wasn't lapsing into any familiar despair or frustration. But make no mistake, there was plenty yet to transform: I still carried my yen for complication, my inclination to founder in confusion and indecision. And the challenges of committed love and living in faith were undiminished: too often I wavered, grew anxious and lost sight of the selfless and timeless—that is to say, the faithful and deeply rooted perspective I aimed to hold uppermost. I knew this new life would yield its riches only to the extent that I learned to welcome the work it entailed. If I wanted to unfurl and come ripe I must learn to embrace the given, day after day; and I must learn to keep my hands gritty and dirty, working the soil of everyday mindful living.

But my mind was renewed: now I knew my way into that soil. This is what melancholia taught me: in some landscapes we see unity more plainly from beneath the earth. Take the one I was walking that February dusk: on the High Plains the largest part of the biomass—that is, the sum of life-forms that make a place home—is underground, beyond our everyday purview. We think it a vacant and sterile place, but beneath that apparently empty plain, life flourishes: in their subterranean homes hunker prairie dogs and burrowing owls and rattlesnakes. And the plant life—mostly grasses, since the subsoil isn't moist enough to seat the roots of a tree—has evolved the most elaborate root systems we know: twenty-five miles of knotted and branching roots can dwell within a single square yard of High Plains sod. Tallgrass taproots reach fifteen feet down into the earth, while the shoots we see above are only a third so high.

I let my arm trail behind me in those grasses as they swayed in the wind. From their entangled contraction in the dark earth those long roots spired upward and joined into stalks, and then rose into the air to form this graceful and muted expanse of browns: siennas and ochers and russets and umbers and tans, some diaphanous, some bladed and ribboned, some beswirled, all waiting for the wind to ferry their seedpods to some spot of congenial soil. There they would sink into the earth and send down roots. To this melancholic the plant life on the High Plains seemed instructive: in any arid and barren place you must splay the roots broad and deep and let them undertake some saturnine burrowing; you must trust them to trawl through the hardpan and clay that will scarcely nourish them, and find their way to water. Then they will learn their way into the light, and take their place in the oneness that prevails in every portion, from the deepest reach of the taproot up into the landscape and outward to the ends of the firmament above.

In every portion this oneness prevails. This is what melancholia taught me: wherever this body takes root—in whatever soil would feed it, in whatever water will wash it, in whatever wind scours it, in whatever light would dance its leaves: if faith be intact it is a oneness, inseparable from the oneness all about it. So now you see this pilgrim walking across the plain, and his striding body, with the legs branched out from the trunk, takes the shape of the root. Takes the shape of the root and draws up water from the earth and into him unseen. And there beneath him you see the roots that join this human animal to earth and sky and water; you see the roots that hold him, and each of us, afoot; you see the roots that hold this landscape, and every landscape, together as one.

This is what melancholia taught me: all this oneness begins in those roots, and those roots take shape from their grasp; and that grasp is the shape of faith, the root tunneling blind through the closed dark earth in its ever uncertain—but still unceasing—reach: for water.

EPILOGUE & ACKNOWLEDGMENTS

FOUR MONTHS after that February walk, Lisa and I were married in the mountains of western North Carolina. We made our cross-country drive, and on our return to Wyoming that August we moved into an apartment in Wright, where Lisa returned to her teaching and I began working on this book. For the splendid dinners and talk we thank Richard Ward and Rachel Nava, John Flocchini, and Rick Dare. For friendship and long walks my thanks to Derek Dunsmoor. For their endlessly patient assistance with my research needs, I thank the staff at the Campbell County Public Library.

At the finish of that school year we moved to the mountains of northern New Mexico, where we were fortunate enough to live in a quiet and unspoiled place with thousands of acres of wild country about us. There Lisa took a break from teaching while I finished an early draft of this book. Our thanks to Tom and Carolyn Golden for the house and the writing space; to Jane and Randy Lumsden-Nakasone, Amy and Mike McFall, and all their children for their generosity and their wonderful company. My thanks also to Reverend Mike Stahl of the Las Vegas United Methodist church for his support and counsel, and to Carolyn Rakeley and the staff of the Samaritan House Homeless Shelter for giving me something useful to do. And from the both of us, a very special thanks to Willie Groffman, true and fearless traveler on the great divide, for friendship, impromptu barbecues, road trips, music, terrific book talk, and wonderful gardens.

After a year in northern New Mexico, Lisa wanted to return to teaching, and we both wanted to live nearer to one or the other of our families. So Lisa went looking for a position teaching German in the northern Rockies, or in the central and southern Appalachians. Nothing came open in the West, but there was a job available in Coshocton, Ohio—in the Allegheny foothills two counties away from Monroe, a two-hour drive to Stillhouse Run. Just about perfect. She got the job, and in July 1998 we moved to Coshocton. We've been here a little more than eight months as I write this, and we've been blessed in many ways; it feels like home already to the both of us. Our thanks to the members of the West Lafayette Mennonite Fellowship for making us feel so welcome. My thanks to the staff of the Coshocton Public Library, particularly Cathy Haynes, Ann Miller, and Linda Yoder, for helping with my finishing-the-manuscript research needs; and my thanks also to the Friends of the Library and the Reference Staff at the Ohio State University Library in Columbus.

My thanks to those whose professional knowledge, compassion, and wisdom helped me learn to see melancholia differently, and helped me to heal: Anita Doyle of Missoula and Dr. Donald Beans of Bigfork, Montana. For their good work and the great pleasure it was to work with them I thank my former case management colleagues at Stepping Stones in Missoula, the Blue Ridge Mental Health Center in Asheville, and the ABCCM Homeless Shelter in Asheville.

I owe particular thanks to the clients I worked with in those places. Their names are too many to list here even would the laws of confidentiality allow it, but for their examples of courage and forbearance I am forever grateful.

Back in Missoula from 1992 to 1995 I was blessed with some of the finest and most generous teachers around. For their encouragement and counsel, I thank Terry Tempest Williams, Gretel Ehrlich, and Chris Offutt. While I was yet in North Carolina, I cold-called William Kittredge in Missoula to ask if he would let me sit in on one of his Nonfiction workshops; he graciously promised to do so, remembered that promise when I showed up in his office two months later, and in the years since has been an unfailing source of good straightforward advice, selfless generosity, and encouragement. It is hard to imagine a better mentor or a finer human being. I cannot thank him enough.

Bill helped my work find its way to Lizzie Grossman, late of Sterling Lord Literistic, who was my agent for five months before leaving that line of work to devote herself to environmental activism and her own writing. When Lizzie left Sterling Lord, she matched me up with a colleague there, Chris Calhoun, and I am grateful to Chris for his ongoing patience, encouragement, and support for my work—not to mention his ability to make me laugh out loud three or four times in every conversation we have.

I am also grateful to Lizzie for delivering the proposal for this book to Ethan Nosowsky of the editorial staff at North Point Press/Farrar, Straus and Giroux. To Ethan I owe a particular debt of thanks: for his unceasing enthusiasm for this project; for his long patience as the manuscript found its slow way onto paper; for his faith in this work at times when my own was failing me; and for his exemplary vision and tireless work in helping to shape it into its final form.

It also has been a blessing and a privilege to work with other members of the staff at Farrar, Straus and Giroux. My thanks to editorial assistant Frieda Duggan for answering all my trivial questions, attending to a myriad of details, and for her hard work at making the manuscript ready for the printer; to Lynn Buckley of the Art Department, who supplied the book with its surpassing beautiful cover; to Jonathan Lippincott for the gorgeous design; and to Jeff Seroy of the Publicity Department for his enthusiasm and kindness.

Over the years, in the many places where I've lived, a number of friends have been generous with advice, reading suggestions, camping trips, walks in the woods, conversation and inspiration, and dozens of other things, and I am deeply grateful to them all. For these, my thanks to Elizabeth Dodd and Chris Cokinos, Bo Clary and Patricia Peknik, all of them friends since our college days in Athens. In Missoula, my thanks to Mark Coleman, Tom Dailey, Debra Earling, Joy Mae Gouker, Jennifer Mandel, Rick Stern, Robert Stubblefield, and Tommy and Beth Youngblood-Petersen. To Don Hamilton in New Mexico, and before that in North Carolina, I owe many thanks for introducing me to homeopathic medicine, for explaining to me its subtleties and objectives, and for looking over the relevant passages of this book to make certain I'd got it right. My thanks to others in the North Carolina mountains: Wendy Barnes, Holly Moore, Brownie Newman, Jackie Taylor (with a special thanks for fashioning my wedding band), and Rodney Webb; to Phil Verthomme for the inspiration, the divining rod, and the banjo; and I owe many thanks to Greg Ford for the late-night phone conversations, the music, the encouragement, and his hospitality on the too-rare occasions when we get to visit.

Thanks to Robert Clark of Seattle for the books—the ones he's written himself as well as the ones he's given us—for his friendship, his generosity, and for the wisdom of his counsel. To Reverend Tony Sayer of Asheville for the courage of his insights, for the encyclopedic reach of his knowledge, for his depthless enthusiasm about books, for the wonderful long phone talks, and for his unceasing generosity of spirit. My thanks to Robert and Tony also for their willingness to read this book while in manuscript, and for their suggestions and comments, which I think improved the book considerably; of course, neither they nor anyone else mentioned here is responsible for any of the oversights or errors that may yet obtain in the book.

My thanks to Vince and June Werner of Great Falls, Montana, for welcoming me into their family, and for their endless support, encouragement, newspaper clippings, and reading suggestions. My gratitude to other members of the Werner family: Joanne Werner and

Catherine O'Connor for reading suggestions, openhearted conversation, and their support; Jeanne Werner for insightful book talk; Susan Werner for her good cheer and medical advice; Paula Butler for the jokes and support; Greg Werner for his help with keeping the antique Mac up and running; and Mary Werner, Ron Brown, and son, Sam, for their hospitality and the great pleasure of their company.

I thank my own family for the abiding sense of place—something rare and precious in modern America—that they instilled in me, and for their own courage and commitment in staying home in West Virginia and southern Ohio. I thank them for trusting me to head off in a variety of directions unfamiliar to them, and for taking me back in when I returned with tail tucked between my legs. For all of these, for their endless encouragement and support, and for many other things I thank them, with love.

On my father's side of the family, thanks to my grandmother Joanna Smith, for keeping the family stories, recipes, and traditions, and passing them along to us. I thank my uncle Joe Smith for a lifetime of sharing passions and stories and music and books. My deep gratitude to my father, Bob Smith, for his generosity and kindness; for the example of his determination and hard work in every endeavor. I thank my stepmother Patty Smith for helping to make Dad's retirement so peaceful and rewarding, and also for making us feel so welcome in their home and at their riverfront retreat. I thank my brother, Jim Smith, for the long walks in the woods, his advice and help with matters mechanical, and for his friendship; my thanks also to Jim's longtime partner Amy Brown, and her daughter Kaelee, for their warmth and kindness and support.

I am deeply grateful to my maternal grandmother, Martha Dally Thomas, and for many things: her faith and spirit; her generosity; her wonderfully told stories of past times in Monroe County; her cooking; the welcoming refuge that her home up Stillhouse Run has always been for me; and of course for the Parker Duofold. Thanks to my aunt Betty Jo Isaly for being so interested, for her medical advice, and for her kindness; to Aunt Jo's longtime partner Al Greenwood for his matchless curiosity and the delightfully singular way he follows it; and to my cousin Melanie and her husband Ron Beitzel, our thanks for welcoming us to Ohio so warmly, and for their thought-fulness. Thanks to my stepfather Paul Fuchs for making us welcome on Tarpen Ridge, for the horseback and buggy rides, and for his knowledge of so many things old. And I can't begin to communicate the depth of my gratitude to my mother, Jane Thomas Smith Fuchs: for nurturing in me a love of books, music, animals, the outdoors, and learning; for finding, through the years, the means for me to pursue these; for her good sense and her calm—for all of these I thank her.

The dedication of this book does not begin to express my grati-tude to Lisa Werner. Without her it simply could never have been. Spiritually, emotionally, materially she has given and given to this book and its author. I will, I hope, spend the rest of my life trying to repay her.

And my thanks to our Almighty Creator. For everything, even melancholia.

Jeffery Smith
Coshocton County, Ohio
Easter Sunday 1999

SELECTED BIBLIOGRAPHY

Since my childhood, books have had everything to do with the turns my story has taken; perhaps never more so than in the months narrated in this memoir. And of course, as with any book, other books had a lot to do with the way this one was thought about and made. So here is a list of the books I found particularly inspired, thought provoking, and useful as I conceived, researched, and wrote my own.

A few were nothing less than essential, and warrant separate mention:

Robert Burton. *The Anatomy of Melancholy*. Edited by Floyd Dell and Paul Jordan-Smith. New York: Farrar and Rinehart, 1927.

Stanley Jackson. *Melancholia and Depression: From Hippocratic Times to Modern Times*. New Haven: Yale University Press, 1986.

Arthur Kleinman and Byron Good. *Culture and Depression: Studies in the Anthropology and Cross-Cultural Psychiatry of Affect and Disorder*. Berkeley: University of California Press, 1985.

Raymond Klibansky, Erwin Panofsky, and Fritz Saxl. *Saturn and Melancholy: Studies in the History of Natural Philosophy, Religion, and Art*. Translated by Frances Lobb. New York: Basic Books, 1964.

Kay Redfield Jamison. *Touched with Fire: Manic-Depressive Illness and the Artistic Temperament*. New York: Free Press, 1993.

David Karp. *Speaking of Sadness: Depression, Disconnection, and the Meanings of Illness*. New York: Oxford University Press, 1996.

•   •   •

Other books that informed my approach directly or indirectly:

BOOK II: STILL LIFE

Diane Ackerman. *A Natural History of the Senses*. New York: Random House, 1990.

Henry Adams. *The Education of Henry Adams*. New York: Literary Classics of America, 1983.

Dante Alighieri. *The Divine Comedy*. Translated by John Aitken Carlyle, Thomas Okey, and P. H. Wicksteed. New York: Modern Library, 1932.

A. Alvarez. *The Savage God: A Study of Suicide*. New York: Random House, 1972.

Stephen E. Ambrose. *Undaunted Courage: Meriwether Lewis, Thomas Jefferson, and the Opening of the American West*. New York: Simon and Schuster, 1996.

American Psychiatric Association. *Diagnostic and Statistical Manual of Mental Disorders: DSM-IV*. Washington, D.C.: American Psychiatric Association, 1994.

E. James Anthony and Therese Benedek, eds. *Depression and Human Existence*. New York: Little, Brown and Company, 1975.

Lawrence Babb. *The Elizabethan Malady: A Study of Melancholia in English Literature from 1580 to 1642*. East Lansing: Michigan State College Press, 1951.

Jerome Barkow, Leda Cosmides, and John Tooby. *The Adapted Mind: Evolutionary Psychology and the Generation of Culture*. New York: Oxford University Press, 1992.

Samuel H. Barondes. *Molecules and Mental Illness*. New York: Scientific American Library, 1993.

George M. Beard. *American Nervousness: Its Causes and Consequences*. New York: Putnam, 1881.

Joseph Becker and Arthur Kleinman, eds. *Psychosocial Aspects of Depression*. Hillsdale, N.J.: L. Erlbaum and Associates, 1991.

Robert N. Bellah, Richard Marsden, William M. Sullivan, Ann Swidler, and Steven M. Tipton. *Habits of the Heart: Individualism and Commitment in American Life*. Berkeley: University of California Press, 1985.

William Boericke. *Materia Medica with Repertory*. St. Louis, Mo.: Formur International, 1988.

Peter Breggin. *Talking Back to Prozac: What Doctors Won't Tell You About Today's Most Controversial Drug*. New York: St. Martin's Press, 1994.

Bill Bryson. *A Walk in the Woods: Rediscovering America on the Appalachian Trail*. New York: Broadway Books, 1998.

Guido Ceronetti. *The Silence of the Body: Materials for the Study of Medicine*.

Translated by Michael Moore. New York: Farrar, Straus and Giroux, 1993.

Massimo Ciavolella and Amilcare A. Iannucci, eds. *Saturn from Antiquity to the Renaissance*. Toronto: University of Toronto Italian Studies, 1992.

David B. Cohen. *Out of the Blue: Depression and Human Nature*. New York: W.W. Norton and Company, 1994.

Ralph Colp Jr., M.D. *To Be an Invalid: The Illness of Charles Darwin*. Chicago: University of Chicago Press, 1977.

Kathy Cronkite. *At the Edge of Darkness: Conversations about Conquering Depression*. New York: Doubleday, 1994.

Mihaly Csikszentmihalyi. *The Evolving Self: A Psychology for the Third Milennium*. New York: HarperCollins, 1993.

Richard Dawkins. *River out of Eden: A Darwinian View of Life*. New York: Basic Books, 1995.

Eric Cunningham Dax. *The Pictorial Representation of Depression*. Basel, N.Y.: Karger Press, 1965.

Alfred Dean, ed. *Depression in Multidisciplinary Perspective*. New York: Brunner/Mazel, 1985.

Jared Diamond. *The Third Chimpanzee: The Evolution and Future of the Human Animal*. New York: HarperCollins, 1992.

Emily Dickinson. *The Complete Poems*. Edited by Thomas H. Johnson. Boston: Little, Brown and Company, 1960.

Richard Dillon. *Meriwether Lewis*. New York: Coward-McCann, 1965.

Michael W. Dols. *Mājnun: The Madman in Medieval Islamic Society*. Oxford: Clarendon Press, 1992.

Rene Dubos. *So Human an Animal*. New York: Charles Scribner's Sons, 1968.

Kat Duff. *The Alchemy of Illness*. New York: Pantheon Books, 1993.

Gretel Ehrlich. *A Match to the Heart: One Woman's Story of Being Struck by Lightning*. New York: Pantheon Books, 1994.

Debra Elfenbein. *Living with Prozac*. San Francisco: Harper San Francisco, 1995.

Heiner Ellgring. *Nonverbal Communication in Depression*. New York: Cambridge University Press, 1989.

"The Ethology of Psychiatric Populations." *Ethology and Sociobiology*, vol. 8, no. 35 (1987), special supplement.

Johannes Fabricus. *Alchemy: The Medieval Alchemists and Their Royal Art*. London: Diamond Books, 1994.

Harvie Ferguson. *Melancholy and the Critique of Modernity*. New York: Routledge, 1994.

Marsilio Ficino. *Three Books on Life*. Translation by Carol V. Kaske and John R. Clark of *De vita triplica*. Binghamton, N.Y.: Medieval and Renaissance Texts and Studies, 1989.

F. Scott Fitzgerald. *The Crack-Up*. New York: New Directions, 1993.

Michel Foucault. *Madness and Civilization: A History of Insanity in the Age of Reason*. Translated by Richard Howard. New York: Pantheon Books, 1965.

Marie Louise von Franz. *Alchemy: An Introduction to the Symbolism and the Psychology*. Toronto: Inner City Books, 1980.

James George Fraser. *The Golden Bough*. New York: Macmillan, 1922.

Sigmund Freud. "Mourning and Melancholia." *The Standard Edition of the Complete Psychological Works of Sigmund Freud*. Vol. 14. Translated by James Strachey. London: Hogarth Press, 1967.

Winifred Gallagher. *The Power of Place*. New York: Poseidon Press, 1993.

Paul Gilbert. *Depression: The Evolution of Powerlessness*. 2d ed. New York: Guilford Publications, 1992.

Timothy H. Goldsmith. *The Biological Roots of Human Nature: Forging Links Between Evolution and Behavior*. New York: Oxford University Press, 1994.

Gerald Grob. *The Mad among Us: A History of the Care of America's Mentally Ill*. New York: Free Press, 1994.

H. H. Hardesty. *History of Monroe County, Ohio*. Chicago and Toledo, Ohio: H. H. Hardesty and Company, 1882.

Hesoid. *Theogony* and *Works and Days*. New York: Oxford University Press, 1988.

James Hillman. *Revisioning Psychiatry*. New York: Harper and Row, 1975.

———. *Suicide and the Soul*. 2d ed. Woodstock, Conn.: Spring Publications, 1997.

Dana Jack. *Silencing the Self: Women and Depression*. Cambridge: Harvard University Press, 1991.

John Brinckerhoff Jackson. *A Sense of Place, a Sense of Time*. New Haven: Yale University Press, 1994.

Jerome Kagan. *Galen's Prophecy: Temperament in Human Nature*. New York: Basic Books, 1994.

———. *The Nature of the Child*. New York: Basic Books, 1984.

Leon R. Kass. *Toward a More Natural Medicine: Biology and Human Affairs*. New York: Free Press, 1985.

Susanna Kaysen. *Girl, Interrupted*. New York: Random House, 1994.

Stephen R. Kellert and Edward O. Wilson, eds. *The Biophilia Hypothesis*. Washington, D.C.: Island Press, 1993.

Horace Kephart. *Camping and Woodcraft*. Knoxville: University of Tennessee Press, 1988. Reprint of 1917 edition, New York: Macmillan. With an introduction by Jim Casada.

———. *Our Southern Highlanders: A Narrative of Adventure in the Southern Appalachians and a Study of Life among the Mountaineers*. Knoxville: University of Tennessee Press, 1976. Reprint of 1922 edition, New York: Macmillan. With an introduction by George Ellison.

Donald Klein: *Understanding Depression*. New York: Oxford University Press, 1993.

Marjorie H. Klein, David J. Kupfer, and M. Tracie Shaw, editors. *Personality and Depression*. New York: Guilford, 1993.

Arthur Kleinman. *Social Origin of Distress and Disease: Depression, Neurasthenia and Pain in Modern China*. New Haven: Yale University Press, 1986.

———. *The Illness Narratives: Suffering, Healing, and the Human Condition*. New York: Basic Books, 1988.

Nathan S. Kline. *From Sad to Glad*. New York: G.P. Putnam's Sons, 1974.

Arthur Koestler. *The Sleepwalkers: A History of Man's Changing Vision of the Universe*. New York: Viking Penguin, 1990.

George F. Koob, Cindy L. Ehlers, and David J. Kupfer, eds. *Animal Models of Depression*. Boston: Birkhäuser, 1989.

Peter D. Kramer. *Listening to Prozac: A Psychiatrist Explores Antidepressant Drugs and the Remaking of the Self*. New York: Viking Penguin, 1993.

Julia Kristeva. *Black Sun: Depression and Melancholia*. Translated by Leon S. Rondiez. New York: Columbia University Press, 1989.

David J. Kupfer, Timothy H. Mark, Jack D. Barcher. *Biological Rhythms and Mental Disorders*. New York: Guilford, 1988.

Howard J. Kushner. *American Suicide: A Psychocultural Exploration*. New Brunswick, N.J.: Rutgers University Press, 1991.

R. D. Laing. *The Politics of Experience*. New York: Ballantine Books, 1967.

Christopher Lasch. *The Culture of Narcissism*. New York: W.W. Norton and Company, 1978.

Robert Jay Lifton. *The Protean Self: Human Resilience in an Age of Fragmentation*. New York: Basic Books, 1993.

Charles J. Lumsden and Edward O. Wilson. *Genes, Mind, and Culture: The Coevolutionary Perspective*. Cambridge: Harvard University Press, 1981.

Tom Lutz. *American Nervousness, 1903: An Anecdotal History*. Ithaca: Cornell University Press, 1991.

Bridget Gellert Lyons. *Voices of Melancholy: Studies in Literary Treatments of Melancholia in Renaissance England*. London: Routledge and Paul, 1971.

Theresa A. Maienknecht and Stanley B. Maienknecht. *Monroe County, Ohio: A History*. Sardis, Ohio: Theresa A. Maienknecht and Stanley B. Maienknecht, 1989.

J. John Mann. *Models of Depressive Disorders: Psychiatric, Biological, and Genetic Perspectives*. New York: Plenum, 1989.

J. John Mann and David J. Kupfer. *Biology of Depressive Disorders*. New York: Plenum, 1993.

Michael MacDonald. *Mystical Bedlam: Madness, Anxiety and Healing in Seventeenth-Century England*. Cambridge: Cambridge University Press, 1981.

Michael McGuire and Alfonso Troisi. *Darwinian Psychiatry*. New York: Oxford University Press, 1998.

Herman Melville. *Moby-Dick; or, the Whale*. Berkeley: University of California Press, 1981. Reprint of 1979 edition, San Francisco: Arion Press.

Mark P. O. Morford and Robert J. Lenardon. *Classical Mythology*. New York: Longman Press, 1985.

Lewis Mumford. *Technics and Civilization*. New York: Harcourt, Brace and Co., 1934.

Michael T. Murray. *Natural Alternatives to Prozac*. New York: Morrow, 1996.

Michael J. Norden, M.D. *Beyond Prozac*. New York: HarperCollins, 1995.

Janet Oppenheim. *Shattered Nerves: Doctors, Patients, and Depression in Victorian England*. New York: Oxford University Press, 1991.

Mortimer Ostow, M.D. *The Psychology of Melancholy*. New York: Harper and Row, 1970.

Nina Paley. *Depression Is Fun!: A Nina's Adventures Cartoon Collection*. Capitola, Calif.: T.H.C. Press, 1992.

Donald Culross Peattie. *Green Laurels: The Lives and Achievements of the Great Naturalists*. New York: Simon and Schuster, 1936.

———. *A Natural History of the Trees of Eastern and Central North America*. Boston: Houghton Mifflin Co., 1950.

Sylvia Perera. *Descent to the Goddess: A Way of Initiation for Women*. Toronto: Inner City Books, 1983.

Sylvia Plath. *The Bell Jar*. New York: Alfred A. Knopf, 1998.

Roy Porter. *A Social History of Madness: The World through the Eyes of the Insane*. New York: E.P. Dutton, 1989.

Michael I. Posner and Marcus E. Raichle. *Images of Mind*. New York: Scientific American Library, 1994.

Phillip Rieff. *Triumph of the Therapeutic: Uses of Faith after Freud*. New York: Harper and Row, 1966.

Vicky Rippere and Ruth Williams, eds. *Wounded Healers: Mental Health Workers and Depression*. New York: Wiley, 1985.

Roberta Roesch. *The Encyclopedia of Depression*. New York: Facts on File, 1991.

Charles E. Rosenberg and Janet Golden, eds. *Framing Disease: Studies in Cultural History*. New Brunswick, N.J.: Rutgers University Press, 1992.

Theodore Roszak, Mary E. Gomes, and Allen D. Kramer, eds. *Ecopsychology: Restoring the Earth, Healing the Mind*. San Francisco: Sierra Club Books, 1995.

Simon Schama. *Dead Certainties (Unwarranted Speculations)*. New York: Alfred A. Knopf, 1991.

———. *Landscape and Memory*. New York: Alfred A. Knopf, 1995.

Arthur Schwatz, *Depression: Theories and Treatments: Psychological, Biological, and Social Perspectives*. New York: Columbia University Press, 1993.

Martin Seligman. *Helplessness: On Depression, Development, and Death*. New York: W. H. Freeman, 1992.

Henry D. Shapiro. *Appalachia on Our Mind: The Southern Mountains and Mountaineers in the American Consciousness, 1870–1920*. Chapel Hill: University of North Carolina Press, 1986.

Paul Shepard. *Nature and Madness*. Athens, Ga.: University of Georgia Press, 1998.

Lauren Slater. *Prozac Diary*. New York: Random House, 1998.

Christopher J. Smith. *Geography and Mental Health*. Washington, D.C.: Association of American Geographers, 1977.

Susan Sontag. *Illness as Metaphor*. New York: Farrar, Straus and Giroux, 1978.

Paul Starr. *The Social Transformation of American Medicine*. New York: Basic Books, 1982.

William Styron. *Darkness Visible: A Memoir of Madness*. New York: Random House, 1990.

Thomas Szasz. *Ideology and Insanity: Essays on the Psychiatric Dehumanization of Man*. Garden City, N.Y.: Anchor Books, 1970.

Hubertus Tellenbach. *Melancholy: History of the Problem, Endogeneity, Typology, Pathogenesis, Chemical Considerations*. Pittsburgh: Duquesne University Press, 1980.

Lewis Thomas. *The Fragile Species*. New York: Macmillan, 1993.

Henry David Thoreau. *The Portable Thoreau*. Edited by Carl Bode. New York: Viking Press, 1947.

Yi-Fu Tuan. *Landscapes of Fear*. New York: Pantheon Books, 1979.

D. Hack Tuke, ed. *A Dictionary of Psychological Medicine*. 2 vols. Philadelphia: P. Blakiston, Son, 1892.

Terry Tempest Williams. *Refuge: An Unnatural History of Family and Place*. New York: Pantheon Books, 1991.

Edward O. Wilson. *The Diversity of Life*. Cambridge: Harvard University Press, 1992.

Arthur T. Winfree. *The Timing of Biological Clocks*. New York: W. H. Freeman, 1986.

George Winokur, M.D. *Depression: The Facts*. Oxford: Oxford University Press, 1981.

George Winokur, M.D. and Ming T. Tsuang, M.D., Ph.D. *The Natural History of Mania, Depression, and Schizophrenia*. Washington, D.C.: American Psychiatric Press, 1996.

James Wright. *Collected Poems*. Middletown, Conn.: Wesleyan University Press, 1971.

Robert Wright. *The Moral Animal: Why We Are the Way We Are: The New Science of Evolutionary Psychology*. New York: Pantheon Books, 1994.

William Wright. *Born That Way: Genes, Behavior, Personality*. New York: Alfred A. Knopf, 1998.

Elizabeth Wurtzel. *Prozac Nation*. Boston: Houghton Mifflin Co., 1994.

BOOK III: WAYFARING STRANGER

Anonymous. *The Cloud of Unknowing*. New York: Paulist Press, 1981.

Anonymous. *The Way of a Pilgrim*. Translated by Olga Savin. Boston: Shambhala Publications, 1991.

Roland H. Bainton. *Here I Stand: A Life of Martin Luther*. Nashville: Abingdon Press, 1950.

Matsuo Bashō. *The Narrow Road to the Deep North and Other Travel Sketches*. Translated by Nubuyuki Yuasa. New York: Penguin Books, 1966.

Sacvan Bercovitch. *The Puritan Origins of the American Self*. New Haven: Yale University Press, 1975.

Morris Berman. *Coming to Our Senses: Body and Spirit in the Hidden History of the West*. New York: Simon and Schuster, 1989.

———. *The Reenchantment of the World*. Ithaca: Cornell University Press, 1981.

Wendell Berry. *Sex, Economy, Freedom and Community*. New York: Pantheon Books, 1993.

John Bunyan. *Grace Abounding to the Chief of Sinners*. New York: Viking Penguin, 1987.

———. *The Pilgrim's Progress*. New York: Penguin Books, 1965.

Donald Capps. *Men, Religion, and Melancholia: James, Otto, Jung, and Erickson*. New Haven: Yale University Press, 1997.

Louis Charbonneau-Lassay. *Bestiary of Christ*. Translated by D. M. Dowling. New York: Arkana Press, 1992.

Bruce Chatwin. *The Songlines*. New York: Viking Penguin, 1987.

Geoffrey Chaucer. *The Canterbury Tales*. New York: Penguin Classics, 1951.

E. M. Cioran. *Tears and Saints*. Translated by Ilinca Zarifopol-Johnston. Chicago: University of Chicago Press, 1995.

Jonathan Edwards. *A Faithful Narrative, in the Great Awakening*. Edited by C. C. Goen. New Haven: Yale University Press, 1972.

Erik H. Erickson. *Young Man Luther: A Study in Psychoanalysis and History*. New York: W. W. Norton and Company, 1958.

Ann Fremantle. *The Protestant Mystic*. Boston: Little, Brown and Company, 1964.

Robert W. Funk. *Jesus as Precursor*. Philadelphia: Fortress Press, 1975.

Kenneth Gergen. *The Saturated Self: Dilemmas of Identity in Modern Life*. New York: Basic Books, 1991.

Erving Goffman. *The Presentation of Self in Everyday Life*. Garden City, N.Y.: Doubleday Anchor Books, 1958.

Philip Greven. *The Protestant Temperament: Patterns of Child-Rearing, Religious Experience, and the Self in Early America*. New York: Alfred A. Knopf, 1978.

Romano Guardini. *The Life of Faith*. Translated by John Chapin. Westminster, Md.: Newman Press, 1961.

John Hollander, ed. *American Poetry: The Nineteenth Century*. Vol. 2. New York: Literary Classics of America, 1993.

William Edward Hulme. *Depression: A Spiritual Guide*. Minneapolis: Augsburg, 1995.

William James. *The Varieties of Religious Experience: A Study in Human Nature*. New York: Modern Library, 1994.

Julian of Norwich. *Showings*. New York: Paulist Press, 1978.

Jack H. Kahn. *Job's Illness: A Psychological Interpretation*. New York: Pergamon Press, 1975.

John Owen King. *The Iron of Melancholy: Structures of Spiritual Conversion in America from the Puritan Conscience to Victorian Neurosis*. Middletown, Conn.: Wesleyan University Press, 1983.

Janet Landman. *Regret: The Persistence of the Possible*. New York: Oxford University Press, 1993.

C. S. Lewis. *Mere Christianity*. New York: Macmillan, 1952.

Martin E. Marty. *Pilgrims in their Own Land: 500 Years of Religion in America*. New York: Little, Brown and Company, 1984.

Peter Matthiessen. *The Snow Leopard*. New York: Viking Press, 1978.

Thomas Merton. *The Ascent to Truth*. New York: Harcourt, Brace, and Co., 1951.

———. *Contemplative Prayer*. Garden City, N.Y.: Image Books, 1971.

———. *Life and Holiness*. Garden City, N.Y.: Image Books, 1964.

———. *Mystics and Zen Masters*. New York: Farrar, Straus and Giroux, 1986.

———. *Thoughts in Solitude*. New York: Farrar, Straus and Cudahy, 1958.

———. *What Is Contemplation?* Springfield, Ill.: Templegate Publishers, 1981.

James A. Nash. *Loving Nature: Ecological Integrity and Christian Responsibility*. Nashville: Abingdon Press, 1991.

Flannery O'Connor. *The Habit of Being: Selected Letters*. Edited by Sally Fitzgerald. New York: Farrar, Straus and Giroux, 1979.

G. E. H. Palmer, Philip Sherrard, and Kallistos Ware. *Prayer of the Heart: Writings from the* Philokalia. Boston: Shambhala Publications, 1993.

Walker Percy. *Lost in the Cosmos: The Last Self-Help Book*. New York: Farrar, Straus and Giroux, 1983.

Plato. *The Republic*. Translated by Benjamin E. Jewett. New York: Modern Library, 1983.

Julius H. Rubin. *Religious Melancholy and Protestant Experience in America*. New York: Oxford University Press, 1994.

Jean-Paul Sartre. *No Exit and Three Other Plays*. New York: Vintage International, 1989.

Francis A. Schaeffer. *Genesis in Space and Time: The Flow of Biblical History*. Downers Grove, Ill.: InterVarsity Press, 1972.

Daniel B. Shea. *Spiritual Autobiography in America*. Princeton: Princeton University Press, 1968.

Susan Sontag. *Under the Sign of Saturn*. New York: Farrar, Straus and Giroux, 1974.

Teresa of Avila. *The Interior Castle*. Translated by Kieran Kavanaugh, O.C.D., and Otilio Rodriguez, O.C.D. New York: Paulist Press, 1979.

Leo Tolstoy. *A Confession and Other Religious Writings*. Translated by Jane Ketish. New York: Penguin Classics, 1988.

Evelyn Underhill. *Mysticism: The Nature and Development of Spiritual Consciousness*. New York: Doubleday, 1990.

Siegfried Wenzel. *The Sin of Sloth: Acedia in Medieval Thought and Literature*. Chapel Hill: University of North Carolina Press, 1960.

Charles Wright. *Country Music: Selected Early Poems*. Middletown, Conn.: Wesleyan University Press, 1982.

BOOK IV: HOME

Diane Ackerman. *A Natural History of Love*. New York: Random House, 1995.

Steven R. H. Beach. *Depression in Marriage: A Model for Etiology and Treatment*. New York: Guilford, 1990.

Lauren Brown. *Grasslands*. New York: Alfred A. Knopf, 1985.

Campbell County High School Class of 1954. *History of Campbell County*. Gillette, Wyo.: Campbell County High School, 1954.

Paul Davies. *The Mind of God: The Scientific Basis for a Rational World*. New York: Simon and Schuster, 1992.

Gretel Ehrlich. *The Solace of Open Spaces*. New York: Viking Penguin, 1986.

Federal Writers' Project and Writer's Program, WPA Staff. *Wyoming: A Guide to its History, Highways, and People*. Lincoln: University of Nebraska Press, 1981.

Helen E. Fisher. *Anatomy of Love: The Natural History of Monogamy, Adultery and Divorce*. New York: W.W. Norton and Company, 1992.

Ian Frazier. *Great Plains*. New York: Farrar, Straus and Giroux, 1989.

James Galvin. *The Meadow*. New York: Henry Holt, 1992.

Steve Gardiner. *Rumblings from Razor City: The Oral History of Gillette, Wyoming, An Energy Boom Town*. Gillette, Wyo.: Steve Gardiner, 1984.

A. Dudley Gardner and Verla R. Flores. *Forgotten Frontier: A History of Wyoming Coal Mining*. Boulder, Colo.: Westview Press, 1989.

Mary K. Hincliffe. *The Melancholy Marriage*. New York: Wiley, 1978.

Leora M. Hubbard. *Campbell County Profiles*. Gillette, Wyo.: Leora M. Hubbard, 1985.

Teresa Jordan. *Riding the White Horse Home: A Western Family Album*. New York: Pantheon Books, 1994.

William Kittredge. *Hole in the Sky*. New York: Alfred A. Knopf, 1992.

———. *Who Owns the West?* San Francisco: Mercury House, 1996.

Dennis H. Knight. *Mountains and Plains: The Ecology of Wyoming Landscapes*. New Haven: Yale University Press, 1994.

Stanley Kunitz. *Passing Through: The Later Poems, New and Selected*. New York: W.W. Norton and Company, 1995.

Taft A. Larson. *Wyoming: A History*. New York: W.W. Norton and Company, 1984.

Richard Manning. *Grassland: The History, Biology, Politics, and Promise of the American Prairie*. New York: Viking Penguin, 1995.

Anne Matthews. *Where the Buffalo Roam*. New York: Grove Press, 1992.

John McPhee. *Encounters with the Archdruid*. New York: Farrar, Straus and Giroux, 1971.

———. *Rising from the Plains*. New York: Farrar, Straus and Giroux, 1986.

Clyde A. Milner II, Carol A. O'Connor, and Martha A. Sadweiss, eds. *The Oxford History of the American West*. New York: Oxford University Press, 1991.

Francis Mark Mondimore. *A Natural History of Homosexuality*. Baltimore: Johns Hopkins University Press, 1996.

John E. and Andrea Nelson, eds. *Sacred Sorrows: Enhancing and Transforming Depression*. New York: Tarcher Putnam, 1996.

Samuel O. Okpaku. *Sex, Orgasm, and Depression*. Bala Cynwyd, Pa.: Chrisolith Books, 1984.

Robert W. Righter. *The Making of a Town: Wright, Wyoming*. Boulder, Colo.: Roberts Rinehart Publishers, 1985.

Mari Sandoz. *Old Jules*. Lincoln: University of Nebraska Press, 1985.

Wallace Stegner. *Where the Bluebird Sings to the Lemonade Springs: Living and Writing in the West*. New York: Viking Penguin, 1993.

Frank J. Tipler. *The Physics of Immortality: Modern Cosmology, God, and the Resurrection of the Dead*. New York: Doubleday, 1996.

K. Ross Toole. *The Rape of the Great Plains*. Boston: Little, Brown and Company, 1976.

Walter Prescott Webb. *The Great Plains*. Lincoln, Nebr.: Bison Books, 1981.

Richard White. *It's Your Misfortune and None of My Own: A New History of the American West*. Norman: University of Oklahoma Press, 1991.